Women AND THEIR *Gardens*

THE BRITISH CHARACTER
Enthusiasm for Gardening,
Pont (1938)

Women AND THEIR Gardens

A HISTORY FROM THE ELIZABETHAN ERA TO TODAY

Catherine Horwood

Ball Publishing

CHICAGO

Library of Congress Cataloging-in-Publication Data
Horwood, Catherine.
 Women and their gardens : a history from the Elizabethan era to today / Catherine Horwood.
    p. cm.
 Includes bibliographical references and index.
 ISBN 978-1-61374-337-9 (hardcover)
 1. Women in agriculture. 2. Women gardeners. 3. Gardening—History. I. Title.
 HD6077.H67 2012
 635.082—dc23
                        2011046472

All rights reserved
Published by Ball Publishing
An imprint of Chicago Review Press, Incorporated
814 North Franklin Street
Chicago, Illinois 60610
ISBN 978-1-61374-337-9

First published in the United Kingdon by Little, Brown Book Group

Interior design: M Rules

Printed in the United States of America
5 4 3 2 1

This book is dedicated to the memory of my stepfather, Vivian Milroy, who died just before its completion. He was delighted to know that it combines two things that had given him such pleasure during his long life – gardening and, especially, women.

PLANT NAMES AND SPELLINGS

In direct quotations apparent misspellings have been used
as they appear in the original texts.

CONTENTS

INTRODUCTION

As a child, I thought I hated gardening. I grew up listening to my mother and my aunt comparing the relative merits of *Clematis* 'Marie Boisselot' and *Clematis* Henryi, or endlessly agonising over blackspot on roses with unpronounceable names such as 'Cuisse de Nymphe' and 'Gruss an Aachen'. In those days it was all Greek to me, but once I had a garden of my own everything changed. Gardening became a shared passion, so that a walk with my mother around either of our gardens inspecting new treasures became almost as important to us as an update on her grandchildren. Now the first of those grandchildren, my eldest daughter, has a patch of her own and e-mails her pride in a new plant grouping while vowing never to eat a supermarket tomato again. The bug has bitten once more and the legacy continues.

We are far from unique in being a family of gardening women. Why then are women so rarely celebrated in the history of gardening? 'Ah, Gertrude Jekyll,' said friends knowingly when they heard what I was researching, as though she had been the only woman ever to have made a contribution to gardening worthy of note. People who know a bit about the subject may mention a few more recent names such as

I

Vita Sackville-West or Beth Chatto, but the overriding assumption is that women contributed nothing to the garden before Jekyll and very little since. This is an attempt to correct these misconceptions, telling the stories of those who have been most involved, and putting on record that for centuries gardens have been important to women and women have been important to gardens.

Arguably, women were actually the first gardeners. Evidence from the earliest human settlements suggests that, while men went away to hunt, women harvested and, eventually, cultivated the nearby land, which became a kind of kitchen garden. Once more stable societies with larger-scale agriculture developed, men no longer had to leave their homes for days or weeks on end to find food and women lost most of their influence over plant cultivation. Nevertheless, in

Throughout the medieval period, all classes of women were involved in horticulture, growing flowers and vegetables for food and medicines.

mythology, the Roman deity of plants was the goddess Flora, whose Latin name is the root of 'flower'. Christianity has associated women with gardens since the story of Eve in the Garden of Eden, and during the Middle Ages the *hortus conclusus*, or enclosed garden, was strongly linked with the Virgin Mary and the garden of Paradise.

In reality, women have had a long involvement with plants and gardening although their contribution has evolved over the centuries. In medieval art, women are sometimes depicted tending plants, perhaps sowing or weeding, but there are scant references to them in the written records, and when they do appear they are usually anonymous. The reason for this lack of written evidence in earlier centuries is in part due to individual women being deemed unworthy of mention unless they were of high rank, but it is also because the gardening work they did was menial and either unpaid or rewarded only with a pittance. However, what they undertook was vital, since they were responsible for many of the traditional tasks which put food on the table: indeed, they were judged on their ability to do so.

As with those who used their skills and labour to supply their kitchens, there are few direct records of women gardening for pleasure before the sixteenth century and those who do appear are in the upper strata of society. In the early twelfth century there is an abbess, aunt to Henry I's wife Matilda, who grew roses and 'other flowering herbs' in the convent garden. Three medieval Queen Eleanors were recorded as keen gardeners: the garden of Eleanor of Aquitaine, wife of Henry II, has been recently recreated behind the thirteenth-century Great Hall in Winchester; Eleanor of Provence encouraged her husband, Henry III, to develop the gardens at all his royal residences; and in 1279 Edward I's wife, Eleanor of Castile, brought her own gardeners from Aragon to create a garden for her at King's Langley in Hertfordshire.

By the sixteenth century women become more visible in the records, still mainly as growers of fruit, vegetables and herbs, although there are hints of them having an interest beyond the practical. Sabine Johnson, the wife of a merchant in Northamptonshire, wrote to her brother-in-law in London entreating him to send her a variety of seeds. She knew that, living in the capital, he would have better access to nurserymen coming to the city's markets to sell their crops. He responded willingly and every spring sent her a fresh selection of 'seeds for my sister's new gardens'.[1]

There are no other details of Sabine's gardens, but from this point on we start to learn more about other women's involvement in horticulture, and it is here that I begin the story of women and gardening. It was a time of political unrest, but also of discovery and exploration, with exciting new plants arriving from the Americas and the Orient. Scientific curiosity, technical advances in printing and improved techniques helped to quench the thirst for horticultural knowledge, for the first time accessible to both sexes, and this era can fairly be said to mark the start of women being able to fulfil their desires to create their own gardening worlds.

All the women gardeners who feature in these pages have left a rich and rewarding legacy, from the collectors of once-rare plants that are now available in every garden centre to the pioneers of design whose individual genius can be traced in landed estates, city parks and suburban patios.

Why do women garden? Gertrude Jekyll, or the 'Queen of Spades' as she was called when receiving her RHS Victoria Medal of Honour in 1897, believed that the appeal of gardening lay in giving 'happiness and repose of mind, firstly and above all other considerations, and to give it through the presentation of the best kind of pictorial beauty of flower and foliage that can be combined or invented'.[2] Helen Dillon, another inspirational gardener, adds that one should never think of oneself just as a curator, 'looking after areas of the garden made years ago; I want to be a creator, and reinvent all the time. I believe that neither gardens nor people can stand still. Change is everything.'[3] And Beth Chatto, horticultural doyenne of the late twentieth century, summed up the eternal appeal of gardening to women: 'You can't go on having babies but you can nurture life.'[4]

Catherine Horwood

A PASSION FOR PLANTS

One can never know too much about a plant;
one never can know all there is to be learnt.[1]

Frances Jane Hope,
Wardie Lodge, near Edinburgh (1875)

'WHAT PROGRESS SHE MADE . . .'

In Lancashire some time in the late 1620s, Mistress Thomasin Tunstall, who lived not far from the village which bore her family name near Hornby Castle, carefully wrapped up some roots of one of her favourite hellebores. She had dug them up from a clump growing on the land surrounding her home, Bull-banke, close to the wooded edge of the river Greta which wound its way between the wild fells of Lancashire and North Yorkshire. Painstakingly, she prepared to send them to London to her friend, the famed apothecary and herbalist John Parkinson. Sending plants such a distance was a fraught business and she would have wanted the dormant roots to have a good chance of survival. She may have used damp rags so that they did not dry out on the long journey. Mistress Tunstall knew that Parkinson was developing his garden in Long Acre in Covent Garden and was always pleased to accept new discoveries. Into the package, she tucked a note describing their blooms as small and white 'with blush flowers'.

Parkinson, for his part, was no doubt excited to receive this new variety from his enthusiastic friend and gardening correspondent. Although he was one of London's leading apothecaries, his great passion lay in his garden and the study of plants. He was also gathering information for his first and most successful book on horticulture, *Paradisi in Sole Paradisus Terrestris*, which he published in 1629. In it, he listed the many varieties of plants that he grew in his beloved garden in Long Acre, many of which had been supplied to him by horticultural contacts across the country. He mentions Mistress Tunstall in particular, describing her in his book as 'a courteous Gentlewoman'. Within a year or so, he was delighted to report that her hellebores had 'born faire flowers', and to conclude that she was indeed a 'great lover' of rare plants.[1] But Thomasin Tunstall was more than that; she was a fanatical plant collector.

Writing at the beginning of the twentieth century, Reginald Farrer, an eminent plant collector, blamed Thomasin for the disappearance of the Lady's Slipper Orchid from Britain. 'If only you had loved these delights a little less ruinously for future generations!' he wrote. 'Do you sleep quiet, you worthy Gentlewoman, in Tunstall Church or does your uneasy sprite still haunt the Helks Wood in vain longing to undo the wrong you did?' It feels unjust for Farrer, who knew a thing or two about the passions of plant collectors himself, to accuse Thomasin so harshly, for he would not have known her circumstances. In the very year John Parkinson's book came out, Tunstall and Alice Clopton (who was most probably her sister) defaulted on some loans and incurred even more debt when they had to move out of their home because of their father and brother's mismanagement, so it was understandable that Tunstall turned to her passion for plants to earn some money.

At much the same time, in the south of England, a child was growing up without any such financial worries. She was to spend over twenty-five years filling her homes with more than two thousand exotic plants and her garden beds with countless more. Who cannot warm to a woman who wrote of her obsession for her collection, confessing, 'When I get into storys of plants I know not how to get out.'[2]

Mary, Duchess of Beaufort, was the daughter of Arthur Capel, Baron Hadham, and her childhood during the 1630s was spent at Little Hadham in Hertfordshire. The Capel family have been immortalised in a famous painting by Cornelius Johnson, which, in the style of portraits at the time, features a tantalising glimpse of their Italianate garden in the background. Mary grew up surrounded by garden lovers; her eldest brother, Arthur, later Earl of Essex, had a passion for trees and, in consultation with John Evelyn, created what was probably the first 'wooded' garden in the country at Cassiobury in Hertfordshire. Although this no longer exists it remains the largest open space in Watford. Another brother, Sir Henry Capel, built what may have been the first conservatory in Britain in the late 1670s at his gardens in Kew, on the site that was to become the Royal Botanic Gardens, and he was certainly a source of seeds for his sister.

At eighteen Mary married Henry Seymour, Lord Beauchamp, which was to prove a happy union though a short one, as she was left widowed six years later when her husband died in the Civil War, leaving her with two children. Three years later, however, Mary married again, and again for love. Her second husband was Henry Somerset, later created Duke of Beaufort and inheriting the estate at Badminton in 1683. It was Mary who took on the, for her, pleasurable task of developing the gardens there, despite being kept occupied with the births of more children. It proved to be a major turning point in her life, as for several years before this it is possible that Mary had been suffering from what we would now recognise as depression. As one of her friends wrote, '[Mary] is gone almost into a mopishness with melancholy.'[3] Whether it was her search for a cure through growing herbs in her garden or some other less horticultural road to Damascus that revived her will never be known, but there is no doubt that Mary developed the zeal of a convert and devoted the rest of her life to the cultivation of plants.

Mary was blessed with a generous income from her second marriage and this enabled her to cultivate the gardens at Badminton, just fifteen miles north of Bath, and at Beaufort House in London, adjacent to the Chelsea Physic Garden, which had opened in 1673. By 1701, William Sherard, the botanist and compulsive cataloguer of gardens, suggested that hers were close to the best in Europe, 'being furnish'd with all conveniences imaginable, and a good stock of plants'.[4]

Her good stock of plants was a collection which ran into thousands,

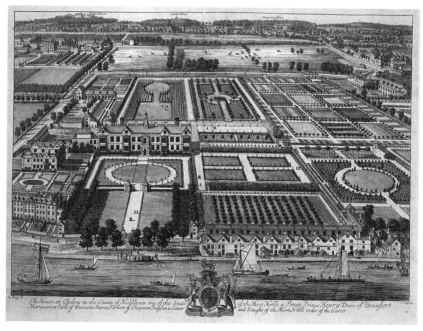

A view of the extensive grounds of Beaufort House, the London residence of Mary, Duchess of Beaufort (1630–1715), and home to a small part of her vast collection of plants. Johannes Kip (early eighteenth century)

and she kept detailed records of them all. Her great passion was for non-native species and her meticulous care for seeds encouraged some of the greatest botanists in Europe to entrust her with their new finds. She grew many in the conservatory she had had built in the 1690s at Badminton, which she called her 'infirmary'. Stephen Switzer, the landscape designer and author of *The Nobleman, Gentleman, and Gardener's Recreation*, wrote in 1715, 'what progress she made . . . the Thousands of those foreign Plants (by her as it were made familiar to this Clime) there regimented together, and kept in a wonderful deal of Health, Order and Decency'.[5]

While she was privileged because of her wealth, there is no doubt that Mary's contribution to late-seventeenth-century British horticulture was inestimable. Her determination to identify and catalogue every plant that came into her possession lasted for a quarter of a century, an enterprise which the garden historian Douglas Chambers believes 'puts her on an equal footing with some of the greatest botanists and horticulturists of her age, many of whom were her friends and correspondents'.[6]

The ambitious development at Badminton included areas of fashionable wilderness 'cobwebbed with stars and radial avenues',[7] but it was the facilities for raising the new 'exotick' plants that were arriving as seeds from the new world which caused the greatest excitement among Mary's horticultural friends. William Sherard, when he became tutor to Mary's grandson at Badminton, thought that 'no place raises or preserves plants better'.[8]

The duchess kept meticulous notes about the new arrivals in a record book, including a 'Catalogue of seeds from the East Indies sent by my brother Harry April 1 1693',[9] and would label them with numbered white sticks. She corresponded regularly with the distinguished physician and collector Sir Hans Sloane, and was later to bequeath to him the twelve albums of her herbarium — dried and preserved specimens. These volumes are now an important part of the British Museum's natural history collection.

It was not just rarities that gave the duchess pleasure. At Beaufort House she created a sumptuous formal garden packed with scented and evergreen plants, and an engraving by Kip made in 1708 shows the formality that one would expect of a late-seventeenth-century garden: the rectangular 'courts', grass walks, fountains and gravel pathways. Being the horticultural perfectionist that she was, Mary also had lists of plantings sent to her at Badminton. Several of these from the 1690s have survived and give a rare taste of what one would have found when wandering those pathways through the evergreen arches and past the pillars of yew. This was a garden of scents and sensibility, as this short extract shows:

> In the great Garden on the East Aspect Border under the Wall is planted with Polianthus. On the Boarder on the other Syde the Walk is an Edging of double Pinks on the other side an edging with Lavender Cotton and Abrotanum. The inside the Border is Virga aura, Double ffetherfew with Double Pinks, painted Sage, Scarlett Lichnell, Collumbine, Italian Starwort with Standards of flowering Shrubs, as Mizerian, Honeysuckles, Althea, Scorpion Senna, yellow Jasmine, Hypericon frutex.

Plant historian Ruth Duthie gives the following modernised spellings:

> Polyanthus, *Primula* × *variabilis*; Pink, *Dianthus plumarius*; Lavender Cotton, *Santolina chamaecyparissus*; Abrotanum (southernwood), *Artemisia abrotanum*; Virga aura, *Solidago virgaurea*; Fetherfew, *Tanacetum parthenium* (aureum); Painted Sage, *Salvia officinalis* 'Tricolor'; 'Lichnell', *Lychnis chalcedonica*; Columbine, *Aquilegia vulgaris*; Italian Starwort, *Aster amellus*;

Mezeron, *Daphne mezereum*; Honeysuckle, *Lonicera periclymenum*; Althaea, *Hibiscus syriacus*; Scorpion Senna, *Coronilla emerus*; Yellow Jasmine, *Jasminum fruticans*; Hypericon frutex, *Spiraea hypericifolia*.[10]

Stephen Switzer, an enthusiastic fan of the duchess, shared with his readers the fact that 'her Servants assured us, that excepting the times of her Devotions . . . Gard'ning took up two Thirds of her time',[11] and this to some degree explains why her children thought she spent too much time and money on her horticultural interests. They filed a lawsuit against her claiming she had not distributed the late duke's estate. She won on appeal but it must have left a bitter taste. The duchess's horticultural legacy is now restricted to archives and libraries; her gardens and greenhouses at Badminton and Beaufort House are gone, the former swept away by Capability Brown and the latter by London development. The herbaria at the Natural History Museum and the illustrations she commissioned for her 'albums' have survived, and she is still commemorated by *Beaufortia decussata*, a suitably exotic variety of Australian myrtle with flame-coloured 'bottlebrush' flowers and spiky stems, named for her in 1812 by Robert Brown, plant explorer and botanist-librarian to Sir Joseph Banks. *Curtis's Botanical Magazine* of 1815 described her as 'an early encourager of the science of Botany' with a 'flourishing botanic garden . . . rich . . . in rare exotics', adding 'the herbarium of that celebrated naturalist . . . bears frequent testimony'.[12]

A generation after Mary another titled woman, Margaret, Duchess of Portland, was gripped by a similar passion for plant collecting, a passion that she was able to indulge for most of her life. The duchess was wealthy in her own right, having inherited a fortune from her mother, Lady Henrietta Cavendish Holles, only daughter of the Duke of Newcastle, and on the death of her husband in 1762, when she was forty-seven, she assumed control of the Cavendish estates. However, it was from her father, Edward Harley, 2nd Duke of Oxford and the man who established the Harleian Library, that Margaret acquired a passion for collecting, though in Margaret it was to become almost an obsession. She filled special 'museum' rooms in her homes in London and at Bulstrode Park, near Gerrards Cross in Buckinghamshire, with minerals, fossils and stuffed animals in addition to works of art and *objets de vertu*. This was far more than a rich woman's indulgence; her collections eventually became the largest in Britain, greater than Sir Hans Sloane's, which formed the basis of the British Museum, but Margaret's were not destined to survive. After her death, a series of family disputes forced their sale and, after auctions lasting thirty-eight days, the collections were dispersed.

Her passion for native and exotic plants matched her obsession for collecting. She knew most of the leading lights in the predominantly male world of botany and plant exploration, being a friend of Philip Miller, chief gardener of the Chelsea Physic Garden from 1722 and author of *The Gardeners Dictionary*; the great Joseph Banks, later head of the Royal Botanic Gardens at Kew; and Daniel Solander, the Swedish botanist and student of Linnaeus. Solander and Banks visited her after their famed first voyage with James Cook in the *Endeavour* in 1768. She gave many commissions to the highly talented German-born botanical artist Georg Ehret, who had settled in England in the mid-1700s and produced some of his best botanical illustrations for her. Jean-Jacques Rousseau was her companion on a plant-collecting expedition to the Peak District, calling himself in later letters '*L'Herboriste de Madame la Duchess de Portland*'.[13] In something of an understatement, the duchess's acquaintance Mrs Lybbe Powys wrote in 1769, 'Her Grace is exceedingly fond of gardening,' adding that she was 'a very learned botanist, and has every English plant in a separate garden by themselves'.[14]

Among the duchess's retinue of staff was the knowledgeable John Lightfoot. In addition to being her chaplain, Lightfoot was a noted botanist and a founder member of the Linnean Society, and he worked with the duchess to catalogue her vast collection of natural history specimens. His letters to her record the delight the two obviously shared in the minutiae of botanical discoveries and their recording.

Mr Lightfoot presents his most dutiful Respect to the D[uche]ss Dow[age]r of Portland, & has the Pleasure to inform her that he has just receiv'd a Letter out of Yorkshire from his Correspondent Mr Teesdale, acquainting him on the 18th of the Ins[tan]t he sent by the Stage Coach from York, directed for the Dss. Dowr. of Portland Whitehall London, to be forwarded to Bullstrode with Speed, a little Box containing three flowering Plants of the Satyrium albidum, & one of the Cornus heracea. Mr Lightfoot would beg Leave to recommend in the Drawing of the Satyrium that one of the Flowers be figur'd separate from the Plant, of its natural Size, & another a little magnified, otherwise they are so small & crowded, that it will be impossible to give a proper or distinct Representation of the Plant. After the Drawing is complete, Mr L: would beg Leave (if it be not too much Trouble) that her Grace would send a Specimen of it in Flower to Uxbridge, as Mr Lightfoot has never seen it in that State. The Roots of all may be kept in Pots to flower another Year.[15]

While the tone of his letters brings to mind Jane Austen's Mr Collins and his obsequious devotion to Lady Catherine de Bourgh, they do serve as a reminder of the problems of transporting live plants across the British Isles, never mind from abroad. In another letter sent after 'two months in gathering and preserving', Lightfoot is convinced that they 'will all certainly be dead & rotten, before they reach Bullstrode . . .'

Trying to reassure both himself and the duchess, he wrote, 'I place all my Confidences in the seed I have collected; these are very good & I hope will in some Measure supply the Loss of their Roots.'[16]

Lightfoot had an even more illustrious 'pupil' in Queen Charlotte. 'Pupil' is not too strong a word, since Lightfoot's role on his visits to Frogmore took the form of regular 'conversations' on botany and zoology with the Queen and two of her daughters, the Princesses Augusta and Elizabeth. The Queen took these conversations so seriously that she made notes, which she later revised to make sure she had not missed anything. When Lightfoot died, King George III bought his herbarium for Queen Charlotte for the grand sum of one hundred

Strelitzia Reginae, named in honour of George III's wife, Queen Charlotte (1744–1818), a keen botanist and flower painter.

guineas, confirmation of the couple's commitment to the new 'sciences' of botany and horticulture.

Queen Charlotte encouraged young women, especially her daughters, to immerse themselves in botany as an intellectual pursuit. For thirty years, inspired by John Lightfoot's lectures and instructed by William Aiton of Kew, the Queen collected plants, studied them under a microscope, dried them for her herbaria and categorised them in accordance with the system devised by Linnaeus. Charles Abbot, yet another clergyman, botanist and fellow of the Linnean Society, dedicated his volume *Flora Bedfordiensis* (1798) to Queen Charlotte, 'that august Patroness of the "*Hortus Kewensis*" whose scientific researches have justly obtained for her the character of the first female Botanist in the wide circle of the British Dominions'.[17]

To improve her horticultural knowledge Queen Charlotte studied the works of the great botanists and nurserymen of her time, and her interest was recognised when the Bird of Paradise flower from South Africa was named *Strelizia Regina*, its tall, striking and spiky habit entirely opposite to the small, homely and rather round domestic queen. She also brought over a variety of sweet apple, 'Borsdorff', from her native Germany, and it is quite possible that Apple Charlotte, the famous British pudding, is named after her as well.

HOME AND ABROAD

When the Duchess of Beaufort assembled her large herbaria – collections of pressed and dried plant material – her labels would have meant little to someone without a knowledge of Latin, nor did they have the scientific consistency to be understood worldwide. That was not her fault, for until the acceptance of the work of Carl Linnaeus in the mid-eighteenth century, the use of common, or 'soft', names changed from county to county, while 'hard' or botanical names were often cumbersome and illogical. The frustrations caused by the difficulties of naming species were petulantly expressed in a letter from Frances Boscawen to the flower mosaicist Mrs Delany in October 1773, after a recent plant-buying expedition.

I bro[ught] from [Mr Burrows] in my chaize a plant with a prodigious long Greek name, w[hich] I forgot before I got home, but the plant I hope (being well water'd with this morning's torrents) will take root and flourish. It is to be full of flowers all summer, and of berries all winter; its name begins with an M and is something like Mucephalus, but not just that; I think, perhaps you are acquainted with it; it is new to me at least by its hard name, and if it has a soft one the nursery man wou'd not trust me with it, lest I shou'd despise the plant and its owner; both wou'd be more considerable in my eyes, he thought, for bearing and pronouncing so long a name.[1]

Mrs Boscawen was not alone in finding the naming of plants confusing. 'Soft' names such as foxglove and bluebell were all very well in Britain but, as her conversation with Mr Burrows the nurseryman confirmed, they were increasingly associated with common British flowers deemed unworthy of being grown in anything other than a cottager's garden. They may have been easier for Mrs Boscawen to pronounce, but British botanists and horticulturalists were desperate for a surer and more scientific way of defining the different species and varieties of plants that were beginning to arrive in Europe from across the world.

During the late eighteenth and early nineteenth centuries, several competing systems of plant identification were in circulation, leading to considerable confusion. The system of plant identification created by the Swedish botanist Carl Linnaeus appeared to simplify the whole process. With his hierarchical scheme of genera and species, it was only necessary to look at the stamens and pistils of a flower (which could be equated with the male and female sexual parts), count their number and see where they were to know which plant 'family' they belonged to. This system led throughout the world to a closer study of plants in the second half of the eighteenth century, particularly of their reproductive systems.

In contrast, the natural system, devised by the Swiss botanist Augustin-Pyramus de Candolle, was non-sexual in its description of plant families and won wide support among the prudish in the early nineteenth century. His *Introduction to the Natural System* was published in 1830 and became an immediate success. De Candolle based his method on the morphology of plants, studying a plant's structure as a whole, and many of his terms, such as 'monocotyledons' and 'dicotyledons', are still in use today.

Amid this battle for scientific fame, women, enthralled by the 'botanomania' that gripped educated Britain, found themselves increasingly excluded from involvement in the male-dominated world of academic botany. This was largely due to the influence of John Lindley, the energetic Professor of Botany at the newly formed London University, who wanted to separate what he saw as 'drawing-room' botany from botany as an emerging natural science. He was a champion for the 'natural' system of plant classification, but the adoption of de Candolle's system was not his sole objective: Lindley's preference for the natural system was based both on his conviction that botany was a science that had to be studied professionally and on his belief that botany had been debased by the use of the Linnean system in Britain, becoming 'an amusement for ladies rather than an occupation for the serious thoughts of man'.[2] The future of the science of botany, he preached in his lectures (sometimes up to nineteen different ones a week), lay in the world of academia, which, given the educational system at the time, immediately excluded women. Thus Lindley slammed the drawing-room door firmly shut in the face of any female involvement in botany at an academic level.

It is perhaps not surprising therefore that when women were able to travel, those interested in plants took it as the perfect opportunity to develop practical botanical and horticultural skills with a freedom that was not available to them in Britain. As a result of colonial expansion and the increase in international trade during the eighteenth century, many women accompanied their husbands far from home and, as the British Empire grew, they found themselves in all the four corners of the earth. With their families left behind in Britain and their

Opportunities for women to grow and collect plants increased as the
study of flowers became an acceptable female accomplishment.

children sent home for education, some women found the loneliness
almost unbearable. There were also the rigours of disease, diet and climate to contend with. Luckily for some, this time away from home
enabled them to explore the native flora and gather up new horticultural discoveries.

The majority of the women who plant-collected across the world
are known to us merely as footnotes in horticultural dictionaries;
rarely do we have details about their lives or exploits. Yet even the
briefest mention gives a hint of the excitement and sense of adventure
that they must have felt in making these new discoveries. In about
1800, while Clive of India was carving his name in the history books, his
wife Lady Henrietta was exploring the area around Mysore, discovering new species including *Caralluma umbellata* and sending her specimens
to the Calcutta Botanic Gardens. Her love of horticulture was passed

on to her son Edward, 1st Earl of Powis, and her granddaughter, Lady Charlotte Florentina Clive, who became the first person to make the Kaffir Lily, *Clivia miniata*, flower in Britain. John Lindley may have wanted to keep women out of the scientific study of plants, but in 1854 it was he who named the plant after her.

Other intrepid women collectors were active in the same period, though many of their lives and activities are not as well recorded. In the early 1800s, a Lady Gwilliam (even her first name is unknown) was with her husband Sir Henry, a chief justice in Madras, where she collected Indian plants. In 1806 *Curtis's Botanical Magazine* carried an illustration of *Magnolia pumila*, the Dwarf Magnolia, stating that botanists in Madras had called it Gwilliamia in honour of her as a 'patroness of the science',[3] but this title was not upheld in Britain. Her sister, Miss Symonds, later brought back a tender pale pink flowering bulb given to her by Lady Gwilliam, then called *Trichonema pudicum*, which was also illustrated in *Curtis's* in 1809 after her death. Mrs Rachel Jameson travelled with her husband, Hugh, who was a deputy medical inspector in the Royal Navy. Her herbarium is now at Kew and shows that she collected over five hundred species from South Africa's Cape area, and twenty from the distant Falkland Islands. In 1840, when she had returned to England, she recorded her finding of a rare marsh gentian in Fulham, which had been thought to be extinct.

Lady Anne Maria Barkly collected plants while she and her husband were in Mauritius and the Cape, details of which are still held in the herbarium of the Natural History Museum and at Kew. Lady Emma O'Malley studied ferns in Jamaica and Hong Kong during her husband's terms of office as attorney general in the late nineteenth century. A collection of lichens from Natal and plants from New Zealand were received at Kew in 1867, having been gathered by a Miss

Armstrong three years earlier; who Miss Armstrong was and why she was travelling in the southern hemisphere are not recorded.

Charlotte, Marchioness of Bute and daughter-in-law of the keen botanist the 3rd Earl of Bute, who had encouraged Princess Augusta to establish the gardens at Kew, was clearly smitten by three varieties of dahlia she saw in Spain in the late eighteenth century. She sent them back to Kew in 1798 but they did not survive. Lady Holland had more luck six years later when she sent some seeds back to be cultivated in the greenhouses at Holland House, a mansion which dominated Notting Hill, then still a village looking down on London. Although she managed to get them to flower, these also perished, but from 1814 the peace in Europe made it easier to send seeds across the continent and within twenty years dahlias became, and have remained, a favourite decorative flower of the British summer.

Sarah Archer, Countess Amherst of Arracan, is best remembered for the variety of pheasant that she sent back to Britain during her travels with her husband in India when he was governor general of Bengal in the late eighteenth century. The countess was a thirty-eight-year-old widow when they married in 1800, the earl just twenty-seven. Nevertheless they produced four children, and she and her daughter, also Sarah, were passionate plant collectors, 'zealous friends and constant promoters of all branches of Natural History, especially botany'.[4] We are indebted to the countess for introducing that marvellous climber *Clematis montana* and the lesser-known *Anemone vitifolia* to Europe, both flourishing still, her clematis smoothing walls and fences with its pale pink flowers each spring, unlike her eponymous pheasant, which seems destined to become extinct in the United Kingdom since only one remains. *Amherstia nobilis* was named for her and her daughter by Nathaniel Wallich, the Danish botanist, reporting that the pair of ladies returned to England after five years in India 'with a large and very interesting collection of preserved specimens of plants, gathered and excellently preserved by their own skill and industry'.[5] The flower beds that Lady Amherst had planted during her time in Government House, Calcutta (Kolkata), were immediately ripped out by her successor, Lady Bentinck, who believed that 'flowers were very unwholesome'.[6]

It was often the duty of the incumbent's wife to oversee the gardens of whichever government residence the husband was posted to. For any woman who already had an interest in plants, such a responsibility could be a relief from the endless round of social events. Christian Ramsay, Countess of Dalhousie, came from a family of Scottish lawyers, and not long after her husband succeeded to his earldom in 1815, she accompanied him to Nova Scotia where he had been appointed lieutenant-governor. Once in Halifax, Lady Dalhousie became involved with agricultural and horticultural organisations through her philanthropic work and she was soon learning about the native plants, and sending seeds and living plants back to the gardens of Dalhousie Castle, near Edinburgh. She became so knowledgeable that she was able to present a paper on Canadian plants to the Literary and Historical Society of Quebec.

Not surprisingly, on their return to Scotland in 1824, the countess made elaborate plans to redesign the gardens at the castle. She won praise from her head gardener, a breed always notoriously difficult to please, who wrote in the *Gardener's Magazine* in 1826 that 'few . . . attained such proficiency as her ladyship in the science'.[7] Unfortunately, the family fortune suffered badly from the bankruptcy of their land agent and they were forced to move to India, albeit with the earl in the leading role of commander-in-chief of the British Army. While they were there, between 1823 and 1828, the countess did some serious plant collecting in and around Simla, and on their final return to Britain she presented her complete Indian herbarium of some 1,200 specimens to the Botanical Society of Edinburgh. This gesture resulted in William Hooker dedicating a volume of *Curtis's Botanical Magazine* to her, and Robert Graham, Professor of Botany at Edinburgh, then named the genus *Dalhousiea* for her, although one feels she deserved better than this not particularly interesting leguminous plant.

More recently, in the early twentieth century, Lady Catherina Macartney lived for seventeen years in even more remote Kashgar, in Chinese Turkestan, when her husband Sir George Macartney was posted there as British consul. During that time she designed and maintained a garden called Chini Bagh, or Chinese Garden. The Macartneys' home became a haven for European visitors during the First World War, but it was always a struggle for Lady Macartney to care for the garden in such extreme conditions and at such a high altitude. 'We could get only the hardier English kinds to grow. I think plants from England missed the rain and overhead watering, and probably still more a moist atmosphere.'[8] She did establish a wide variety of trees such as willow, elm, walnut, several types of poplar, and acacias that were grown from seed sent from Russia.

Lady Macartney also had magnificent mulberry trees which grew wild around the garden. This brought problems when it came to harvesting the delicious fruit since the juicy dark red berries are notorious for staining anything they come in contact with. On her arrival at Kashgar, she found that her gardener, who usually worked wearing the traditional white cotton trousers and top, had his own solution to the problem. She discovered him 'up the tree stark naked, with his clothes carefully hung on a bush', to be put on when he finished the job. 'I had to tell him that he must wear his oldest things and spoil them, and I would give him a new shirt and trousers to make up.'[9]

Although the study of plants was now an accepted accomplishment for young women of the middling sort, it was a long time before it was allowed to be anything more than an accomplishment to fit in alongside music practice, sewing sessions and painting classes. Indeed, there was a vital crossover between botanical studies and floral illustration, but as far as any professional involvement was concerned, women were excluded from horticultural and botanical societies (in the case of the Linnean Society until 1919) and thus unable to publish serious academic papers on their findings.

While many women welcomed the opportunity to travel with their husbands, others, for a variety of reasons, had little choice in the matter. Lady Anne Monson is just one of many educated women in

George Cruikshank's satire of the founding fathers of the Horticultural Society also included a caricature, purportedly of plantswoman Lady Anne Monson (c.1727–76), top right, whose life had already been rocked by scandal.

the eighteenth century who demonstrated their feistiness while enduring heartbreak. The eldest daughter of Henry Vane, 1st Earl of Darlington, Lady Anne had royal connections through her mother Grace, née Fitzroy, granddaughter of Charles II through his illicit liaison with Barbara Villiers, later Duchess of Cleveland. Although we know little about Lady Anne's upbringing, she was clearly no shrinking violet. In 1746 she eloped with a young widower, Charles Hope-Vere, though quite why they decided to elope is not clear as he seems to have been an eminently eligible husband. The second son of an earl, he had inherited large estates from his first wife after her death in childbirth. The elopement suggests it was a love match and she soon produced two sons, although the much-vaunted heir and a spare were already in existence from his first marriage. Their country life at this time would have been based on one of the family estates which Charles Hope-Vere oversaw, and as he did not view his responsibilities as MP for Linlithgowshire with any seriousness, he did not take much persuading to accompany his brother, the Earl of Hopetoun, and his uncle, the Marquess of Annandale, on the Grand Tour. Travelling through Europe via Lyon, Marseille, Nice and Genoa before visiting all the famous sights of Italy was in that era part of a young male aristocrat's education, and despite now being in his mid-forties Hope-Vere set off with his brother, leaving his wife and family behind. They were accompanied by the young architect Robert Adam, who was advising Charles's brother on the final stages of the building of Hopetoun House just outside Edinburgh.

This tour had a profound effect on the young Adam and his style of design, and it had a significant one on the life of Charles Hope-Vere and his family. When he returned to Britain two years later, it was to find that Lady Anne was pregnant. Shortly thereafter she gave birth to a son. Horace Walpole later wrote that there was some scandal about Lady Anne's early life but gave no hint of the dramatic scenes that must have taken place. A horrified Hope-Vere divorced his wife within the year, a very unusual event in the mid-eighteenth century and one that required the passing of an Act of Parliament. He continued her public humiliation by prosecuting her in the church courts for 'criminal intercourse and adulterous conversation with some person or persons unknown' and later being 'delivered of a Male Bastard'.[10]

For most women in her situation, banishment to the country would have followed, with little hope of re-entry into polite society, but Lady Anne took a different route. Within a year of her divorce, she had married George Monson, an army officer and administrator with a post in India. There is no proof that Monson was the father of her baby, but while Charles Hope-Vere was busy embellishing his estate at Craigiehall with a deer park and grotto, a temple or belvedere, and a bridge, all designed by the Adam brothers, his ex-wife was establishing a new life abroad.

Lady Anne would have had to leave behind her two sons by Hope-Vere and her illegitimate son, never to see them again, and there were to be no children from her second marriage. However the parting from her children may have affected her, we do know that she devoted herself to plant collecting and to cultivating friendships with some of the greatest names in the horticultural world of the time.

It is obvious that these men of horticulture and science were not interested in any scandal surrounding Lady Anne, although her personal affairs must have been common knowledge. To some extent there may have been an element of loyalty to Anne as a patron, but there is no doubt that strong friendships and affection were involved as well. She knew James Lee of the Vineyard Nursery in Hammersmith well before she went to India. According to Sir James Smith, founder of the Linnean Society and friend to both Lady Anne and Lee, it was Lady Anne who privately sponsored Lee's translation of Linnaeus's *Philosophia Botanica*. She had a good knowledge of Latin and was able to give him considerable help in preparing the book that was to be *An Introduction to Botany*.

It was Lee who later wrote on Anne's behalf to Linnaeus to thank him for naming *Monsonia Speciosa*, a plant she had discovered in South Africa, in her honour. On another occasion, Lee also wrote to him that Lady Anne had forgotten to warn Linnaeus that she was sending him some plants by ship and was concerned that they might die on the journey to Sweden. Transporting plants across the world continued to be a precarious venture until the advent of Dr Nathaniel Ward's sealed glass case in the nineteenth century.

Lady Anne obviously made a deep impression on the young botanists she met and entertained. Linnaeus would have been delighted to hear from one of his pupils, Clas Alströmer, that the first toast at every meal at her table was always to him. It was Alströmer who convinced Linnaeus that Lady Anne should have a plant named for her. She had a better botanical scientific knowledge than any other woman, he wrote to his master, 'not superficially – that is common with this sex – but in a close and profound way . . . The Duchess of Portland, a protector of Science, has not a thousandth of her deep insight.'[11]

Alströmer's entreaties worked, and Linnaeus, by no means immune to flattery, wrote in Latin to Lady Anne about her 'named' plant. If Linnaeus was aware of the scandal surrounding Lady Anne's first marriage, this flirtatious note would have been viewed as being somewhat indiscreet:

This is not the first time that I have been fired with love for one of the fair sex, and your husband may well forgive me so long as I do no injury to his honour. Who can look at so fair a flower without falling in love with it, though in all innocence? Unhappy is the husband whose wife pleases no one but himself. I have never seen your face, but in my sleep I often dream of you . . . Should I be so happy as to find my love for you reciprocated, then I ask but one favour of you: that I may be permitted to join with you in the procreation of just one little daughter to bear witness of our love – a little Monsonia, through which your fame would live for ever in the Kingdom of Flora.[12]

The note may in fact never have been sent as only a draft is in existence, and Lady Anne's reputation among scientists remained unsullied. When the young Danish entomologist and pupil of Linnaeus, John Christian Fabricius, met up with Daniel Solander who was then working at the British Museum, he wrote that he was introduced to 'all the learned persons in our department, [i.e. natural history] viz, Banks . . . Lee . . . Lady Ann Monson . . . Fothergill . . . Greville [the latter being one of the founders of the Royal Horticultural Society]'.[13]

On one of her voyages back to Bengal, where her husband was administrator, she met Carl Per Thunberg, a Swedish naturalist who was based in southern Africa. By this time she was nearly sixty but still full of enthusiasm for plant collecting. She had, reported Thunberg, 'at her own expense brought with her a draughtsman in order to assist her in collecting and delineating scarce specimens of natural history'.[14] She also used local artists and in 1775 was paying them three rupees a drawing.

Twelve years after her death in 1788, James Lee introduced *Monsonia filia*, or 'the Hairy-leaved Monsonia'. It is also probable that he named his daughter Ann, the botanical illustrator, after his patron. There was clearly great affection for this woman whose early reputation was tainted by scandal, who lost her children but retained her horticultural friends throughout her life. Her enthusiasm, wrote Lee's partner, John Kennedy, 'knew no bounds, and [her] liberal and fostering hand contributed more, perhaps, than any of her contemporaries, by her encouragement and example to the then incipient but not so prevailing taste for the study of botany'.[15]

The life of another Lady Anne, Lady Anne Lindsay, was somewhat different. She was the second of three daughters of James, the 5th Earl of Balcarres, who had married her mother in 1749 when he was sixty and she was twenty. Her mother was a martinet to eleven children, uncowed by the age difference with her husband, and her offspring once rebelled against her by trying to run away *en masse*.

As sibling after sibling left home, Anne found herself unmarried

Paul Sandby presents gardening as an inclusive family activity
in a cameo from a version of *The Artist's Studio* (c.1772).

and in danger of being left to look after her widowed mother in Edinburgh. Somehow she managed to escape her mother's clutches and went to live in London with her older sister, Lady Margaret, who had also been widowed. The sisters loved London society and London society loved them, so it was a great surprise when, at the age of forty-three, Lady Anne married Andrew Barnard, a bishop's son with no prospects and twenty years her junior. Lady Anne used all her influence with her well-connected friends to find her new husband a job. Eventually he was offered one, but it was not quite what Lady Anne had hoped for: Secretary of the Colony of the Cape of Good Hope. Her letters back to friends in Britain confirm the Cape as an exceptional place for plant discoveries. In one she wrote that at every turn there was yet another vista full of geraniums . . . 'I dug up a few bulbs . . . They change their colours, and what was scarlet last year may be yellow, blue, or white this. This green flower struck me as being singularly genteel.'[16] She was generous with her finds, sending what she could back to England. In 1799 she wrote, 'I have sent away so many of my bulbs as to leave me *bulbless*.'[17]

She travelled inland, ruing her lack of botanical knowledge but nevertheless collecting plants where she could. Her adventures came to an end when Britain lost the Cape Colony to the Dutch in 1802 and the couple returned to England. When the colony was reconquered in 1806, Barnard was given his job back and sailed immediately, but tragically died on his arrival. Lady Anne never returned to the Cape.

BEHIND THE MICROSCOPE

John Lindley's objections to women's academic involvement in the botanical sciences did not stop him writing a book on de Candolle's natural system for the female readership. In *Ladies' Botany, or a Familiar Introduction to the Study of the Natural System of Botany*, written between 1834 and 1837, he made it abundantly clear that this work was aimed at the 'unscientific reader'. Using the popular epistolary style of letters guiding a mother on how to teach her children the basics of botany, Lindley attempted to assist professional men in reclaiming botanical writing from the amateur females who were then dominating the genre. As Ann Shteir neatly phrases it, up to 1830 'women elbowed in but then were elbowed out'.[1]

Women were denied election to the Linnean and other academic societies until the beginning of the twentieth century, the only exception to this being a brief twenty-year window between 1836 and 1856 when the Botanical Society of London was formed and, as George White wrote to a friend, 'It has been proposed that *Ladies* should be admitted!!!'[2] During the society's existence, less than 10 per cent of the four hundred-odd members were women, but the institution did not flourish and the one forum available even to those few women disappeared.

In the sheltered world of scientific horticultural study, women were in some ways just as isolated as those women living abroad. Until well into the second half of the nineteenth century, few had access to a comprehensive secondary education, let alone one at university level, although some attempted to make a mark.

Ellen Hutchins, who was only thirty when she died in 1815, made a study of mosses and lichens, classifying them and then illustrating many of specimens she had discovered.

Lydia Becker, best known as a leader of the early suffrage movement, was a passionate botanist. She corresponded with Charles Darwin, was given a gold medal by the Horticultural Society in 1862 for her collection of dried plants, visited girls' schools to give botanical lectures and in 1866 published *Botany for Novices*.

The obstacles faced by Eleanor Ormerod were typical of many middle-class, mid-Victorian women. She was the youngest of a family of ten. All seven of her brothers went to Rugby to study under the illustrious Dr Arnold, but there was no question of Eleanor and her sisters being sent away to school. Instead, it was still the norm for girls of Eleanor's background to be educated at home by governesses or, more unusually, as in her case, by their mothers.

Eleanor was lucky – hers was a happy home and their father and much older brothers encouraged all the girls to be scientifically curious. Her mother taught her daughters Latin and her brother William used Eleanor to sort out his botanical specimens. She was fascinated by garden insects and soon began a collection of beetles which she attempted to identify through dissection, but first she had to kill them. She had been told that if beetles were dropped into hot water, death was instantaneous. However, she had not realised that the water must be boiling hot. 'Into the kitchen I went with a water-beetle,' she wrote. 'A large water-beetle which has great powers of rapid swimming – got a tumbler of hot water, and dropped my specimen in.' To her horror, the unfortunate insect 'skimmed round and round on the water . . . as if in the greatest agony'.[3] After that, she used chloroform.

Eleanor Ormerod's study of the insects found on garden plants became a lifetime passion. Working from the family home in Gloucestershire, enlisting workers on the estate to help her collect specimens, she supplied the Royal Horticultural Society with vital information, and her investigations enabled the RHS to establish a number of the causes of insect damage to plants.

She became close friends with the botanist and head of the Royal Botanic Gardens, Sir Joseph Hooker, and his second wife, Hyacinth, during their time at Kew. When she and her sister Georgiana moved near to Kew after their parents' death, she was allowed to slip into the Botanical Gardens at dawn to study the insects on the shrubs and plants. She was also invited to give lectures and papers there and at the Royal Agricultural College in Cirencester. These public appearances did not come easily to her, and Georgiana reported that on one occasion she had to be placed firmly between two professors on the stage 'for fear her courage should fail and she run away'.[4] At one venue, Lydia Becker loudly praised Ormerod, saying her work was 'proof of how much a woman could do without the help of man', but Ormerod was no feminist and was happy to acknowledge the assistance she had had from 'my friends of the other sex . . . Without their constant encouragement my poor efforts,' she responded, 'would have had no practical result in being of benefit to my fellow men.'[5]

Eleanor Ormerod was an exception in the late Victorian horticultural world. She quietly carved out a place for herself because of her diligent work and passion for meticulous research. She was rewarded by the RHS with its Silver Flora Medal in 1870 and elected a fellow of the society in 1878, but professional employment was not an option.

She did hold an honorary post at the Royal Agricultural Society of England for a few years, but eventually left because she felt that she was being taken advantage of. Her successor, a man, was paid an annual salary of £200. She was an examiner at Edinburgh University and the first woman to be awarded an honorary doctorate by the university. However, when a chair was established in economic entomology, her speciality, she was ineligible for the post because of her gender.

Even though many women were now doing research of a high academic standard, formal recognition continued to be hard to come by. In 1896 a nervous thirty-year-old woman attempted to submit research she had written up on spore germination of a rare form of fungi, *Agraicineae*, to the new director of the Royal Botanic Gardens at Kew, William Thiselton-Dyer, who had taken over from his father-in-law, Joseph Hooker, in 1885. Sent away with a flea in her ear, she later wrote in her diary, 'I fancy [Mr Thiselton-Dyer] may be something of a misogynist.' A later attempt, in 1897, to have the paper read at the Linnean Society also failed. The society still did not admit women and only papers that had been fully presented stood a chance of being published.

Instead the young woman returned to her private research and concentrated on her detailed watercolour illustrations of plant life. Her name was Beatrix Potter. One hundred years later, in 1997, when virtually every family bookshelf contained one of her children's books with her superb illustrations of both flora (just look at Mr McGregor's vegetable garden) and fauna, Miss Potter was honoured by the Linnean Society with a lecture from Professor Roy Watling of the Royal Botanic Garden, Edinburgh, entitled 'Beatrix Potter as Mycologist'.

With women's further education still in its infancy, the opening of the grand purpose-built Royal Holloway College for women, perched

Margaret Benson (1859–1936), head of botany at Royal Holloway, Egham, Surrey, shows obvious delight when 'turning the first sod' of her 'rather ambitious scheme' for an exhibition garden of hardy perennials.

high on a hill in the beautiful countryside of Egham in Surrey, was an exciting opportunity for young women to study all subjects, but particularly the sciences, without the inconvenient attentions of men and all the chaperonage that that still entailed.

Margaret Benson joined the staff at Royal Holloway in 1889 and within four years was promoted from lecturer to head of the botany department. Benson's journey had begun as a pioneer undergraduate at Newnham College, Cambridge. She had been tutored at home by her father, an architect with a passion for field botany, and her mother, a successful flower painter. After a spell of teaching to raise money, Benson finished her studies at London University, working under one of the leading botanical scientists of the day, F.W. Oliver.

One of her first projects on arriving at Royal Holloway was to create a botanical garden in the extensive grounds of the college. She had, she wrote to a friend, 'a rather ambitious scheme' to plant a selection of over seventy hardy perennials.

> I have written to the Director of the Gardens at Kew to see if I could get a few crumbs which perhaps would not be much loss to them . . . I thought perhaps I should get a few seeds – I hope you won't think I have done a very injudicious thing. Sir J. Hooker knows something of this place but Prof Ward thought I had better take the bull by the horns and go straight to head-quarters. I thought I would tell you what I had done in case you should be seeing Mr Dyer. I suppose he will hardly think it worthwhile to help a College he probably knows nothing about.[6]

Given Potter's opinion of Thiselton-Dyer as a misogynist, Benson may well have been right.

There is no record of whether her request was successful or not, but Benson had a reputation for getting what she wanted. 'Perseverance,' she wrote in a school essay aged twelve, 'is the prime quality of life. Men fail much oftener from the want of patient perseverance than from the want of talent. Youth is the best time to acquire this inestimable habit.'[7] Five years after she arrived at Royal Holloway, she was able to report that the garden had been enlarged to such an extent that a botanical gardener was taken on, a Miss Welsford who had trained at Swanley, one of the first horticultural colleges for women.

After the pioneering careers of Ormerod and Benson, botany was opened up to women and they led the field in many areas. Close on the pioneers' heels was Agnes Arber, to whom we owe a greater understanding of the form of the major groups of flowering plants. In 1946, when she was sixty-seven, she became only the third woman, and the first female life scientist, to be elected to the Royal Society.

Winifred Brenchley chose the agricultural route, extremely rare for women in the early twentieth century, and was the first female scientist to be appointed to any agricultural institution, in her case the Rothamsted Experimental Station in Bedfordshire, from where she published ground-breaking work on the importance of using less toxic herbicides.

Irene Manton was Professor of Botany at Leeds University for many years, where she specialised in the evolution of ferns, chromosomes, and the study of the structure of plant cells. Following in the footsteps of Agnes Arber, she was elected a fellow of the Royal Society in 1961 and served as president of the Linnean Society from 1973 to 1976.

Nowadays botany goes hand in hand with nature conservation, and the botanist Lady Anne Brewis spearheaded work to make the British Ministry of Defence aware of the damage that training on military land caused to local flora and fauna, a campaign which culminated in her being appointed as an adviser to the MoD's conservation committee.

Dr Daphne Vince-Prue is one of Britain's most noted botanists, having been Lecturer in Horticulture and Reader in Botany at the University of Reading before becoming a scientific adviser to the Agriculture and Food Research Council. Since her retirement she has acted as a member of the Science and Horticultural Advice Committee of the RHS.

Olive Hilliard, like Vince-Prue, is a holder of the Victoria Medal of Honour and a botanist who, throughout her life, has specialised in the native plants of South Africa, in particular of the Southern Natal Drakensberg. Based at Natal University for over forty years, she worked closely with British botanist B.L. [Bill] Burtt, producing ground-breaking work on Streptocarpus and Dierama. Demonstrating that the world of botany has its share of romance, they married in 2004, enjoying four more years together before his death at the age of ninety-five.

STOVES AND SOCIETY

Just as the world of botany became more academic and exclusive, the official gardening world also took a more formal turn with the establishment in 1804 of what was to become the Royal Horticultural Society. Women had to wait until the 1820s before they were 'invited' to take any part in it and even then it was only the privileged few, principally the wives of prominent fellows, who were allocated tickets to the annual dinners. However, there were other ways of becoming involved in the RHS, predominantly by displaying plants at their shows.

In 1824 Charlotte Marryat of Wimbledon, the American wife of a fellow of the society, Joseph Marryat, must have made an impression on the RHS since it was 'ordered' that she be given a plant of *Primula sinensis*, grown from the first batch of seeds sent from China by the society's own collector, John Potts. Why she was so honoured is a mystery, but her skill as a plantswoman was well known. Then in 1830 the council, having found that there was no actual clause which disqualified women from joining, proposed that five women, including Mrs Marryat, who were very keen to stand, should be elected fellows, and shortly afterwards she became only the third woman to be admitted as a fellow.

The elaborate flower garden at Wimbledon House with its 'Rustic Structure' and overflowing urns and pots was a small area of the huge garden cultivated by Charlotte Marryat in the early nineteenth century.

A description of Mrs Marryat's garden at Wimbledon House leaves one deeply envious at both its size and the varieties of plants she grew. A banker, Bond Hopkins, had established Wimbledon House and its hundred-acre grounds in the late eighteenth century. Joseph Marryat had bought the house and begun improving it before his death in 1824. Bostonian Mrs Marryat was left a wealthy widow and consoled herself as only a true plantswoman could. According to the great early-nineteenth-century horticultural writer John Claudius Loudon, she spared 'no expense in enriching and adorning the place, and more particularly in procuring the rarest and most beautiful plants'.[1]

All the necessities of the early-nineteenth-century garden were present: shrubberies, a 'very spacious ivy-covered summer-house', a rocky cascade studded with alpine plants, a grotto, a lake with two islands, a conservatory, an orangery. Hothouses abounded, with two devoted to grapes alone, another to greenhouse specimens and a fourth for Mrs Marryat's treasured collection of tropical plants which required a more humid atmosphere. Other areas were devoted to the forcing of fruits such as peaches, cherries, melons and strawberries, while the flower garden was a mere three acres.

Charlotte Marryat had fifteen children and some of them inherited their mother's horticultural passion. Her eldest daughter developed her own 'small but interesting garden, stored with British plants' at Wimbledon House, but it was another daughter, Fanny, later Mrs Palliser, who was to become an expert on ceramics and lace and supplied her mother with many rarities after her move to Italy. In the space of a single year she sent her mother around a hundred plants and seeds, of which about half had never been grown in Britain. These included Calendula from the botanic garden at Turin, a lithospermum from the rocks of Capri, *Morisia* from Sardinia, and a variety of *Stapelia* found by Italian plant collector Giovanni Gussone on the island of Lampedusa, the southernmost point of Europe, and all found success in the garden and greenhouses of Wimbledon House. Seeds of trees arrived as well, from Lake Fusara and the rocks of Tivoli, and a collection of 'curious species . . . of orange trees from the gardens of Count Camaldali' followed.[2] Mrs Palliser was horticulturally so well connected that there could not have been a botanical garden in Italy left undisturbed by her attempts to satisfy her mother's lust for new plants.

In May 1831 Mrs Marryat had started exhibiting plants, choosing, among others, a yellow azalea and *Boronia serrulata*, the 'Native Rose' of New South Wales. Subsequently many of the plants sent by her daughter from Italy and elsewhere were also shown, and portrayed for various horticultural journals such as the *Botanical Magazine* and *Botanical Register*. *Tacsonia pinnatistipula*, a beautiful passion flower with pale pink petals and purple corona filaments, was awarded a Banksian medal, and an anagallis was named for Mrs Marryat.

*

The lady who created the biggest upset among the bewhiskered gentlemen of the Horticultural Society was Louisa Lawrence. A great beauty, she must have created something of a stir when in 1828, aged twenty-five, she married William Lawrence, an eminent surgeon who was twenty years her senior. It was never going to be a conventional marriage. He installed her in a house with twenty-eight acres of land at Drayton Green, near Ealing in west London, while he remained at his central London home surrounded by his books and wine. It would seem that Mrs Lawrence thrived on these living arrangements, and set about refurbishing the house and garden at Drayton Green until it became, according to John Claudius Loudon, 'the most remarkable of its size in the neighbourhood of London, on account of the great variety and beauty which have been created in it'.[3]

By the time Loudon reviewed the garden in the *Gardener's Magazine* in 1838, Louisa Lawrence had been exhibiting at the Horticultural Society's show for five years and had gathered fifty-three medals. This is an astounding number until you read the list of plants under her care. The gardens and greenhouses contained four thousand different species, including five hundred varieties of garden roses, six hundred species of hardy herbaceous plants, and 227 varieties of stove orchids.

The description of Mrs Lawrence's orchid house in *The Ladies' Magazine of Gardening* in 1842 is astonishing:

[I]n addition to the usual orchidaceous plants, [there] are gigantic specimens of papyrus . . . widely-spreading ferns, a splendid specimen of *Nepenthes distillaria*, and in short, such a collection of those plants which only exist in shade, heat, and moisture, as is rarely seen. It was not, however, only with the beauty of the plants that I was so much delighted: it was the admirable arrangement of the house itself, and the effect produced by the deep shade thrown upon it by the gigantic leaves of the tropical plants, while the ear was soothed by the murmuring sound of dropping water. The contrast afforded by this house to the scene presented by the adjoining flower-garden, bright with scarlet *Verbenas*, *Salvia patens*, *Fuchsia fulgens*, and all the vivid colours of modern flowers, was very striking.[4]

Two years later her devoted, if distant, husband bought her an even grander house and garden at Ealing Park. Here she would entertain Queen Victoria and Prince Albert by candlelight when they came to admire her rare 'night blowing' cactus. She also brought *Amherstia nobilis* into flower in cultivation for the first time in Britain, sending the first bloom, as was reported in the *Botanical Magazine*, 'fitly . . . to Her Most Gracious Majesty', simultaneously putting the noses of the Duke of Devonshire and his famous gardener Joseph Paxton out of joint. They had had this beautiful tree for several years but had not been able to get it to flower.

Despite her success, Louisa Lawrence always came second to the duke whenever any expert mentioned the amherstia, and this was not the only time she felt that the gardening establishment dealt unfairly with her. It does not take much to imagine this pretty and extremely feisty little woman, with her fashionably wide crinoline skirts, waist tightly pinched in, stamping her foot in anger when the society she so strongly supported cut back the number of medals given in the orchid category. She later threatened to sell all her orchids if she was no longer able to enter them in competitions. She regularly wrote to the society's committee, and even in the dry minutes of the society's records one can sense the *ennui* when yet another of Mrs Lawrence's complaints had to be answered. Towards the end of her life (she was only fifty-two when she died), she complained of being ill-treated by the society's gatekeeper, who refused her early entrance to stage her exhibits. While defending the gateman, the society's secretary was wise enough to assure Mrs Lawrence that the next time she would be given a special early-hour order of admission. Imperious she may have been, but she was undoubtedly an extremely gifted horticulturalist, a talent that she passed on to her son, Sir Trevor Lawrence, who later became a highly effective president of what was by then the Royal Horticultural Society, and to her grandson, Sir William Lawrence.

Orchids were the ultimate status symbol for any Victorian gardener and proved that you had the income to buy and the skill to grow these delicate beauties. Louisa not only had the skill and the wherewithal, but also in those days of cheap labour the staff to manage such a collection. Nevertheless Loudon complimented her on the 'high order and keeping' of her grounds, 'effected', he said, 'by a smaller number of gardeners than might be expected . . . six, with one or two women for collecting insects and dead leaves, and during winter three'.[5]

On the other side of London, the Loddiges family's Hackney Botanic Nursery Garden was packed with tender orchids and palms. The tide was turning against native British flowers, and even among women gardeners, who had traditionally resisted the foreign introductions, there were signs that they were not going to allow themselves to be left behind in the challenge presented by these new arrivals. The first major female grower of these plants was Mrs Wray, whose garden near Cheltenham was the hub of her collection of orchids and other exotic plants. Her passion and skill were at their peak when she became the first person to get the beautiful but tricky white and bluey mauve *Laelia superba* orchid to bloom in 1844.

In contrast to Louisa Lawrence's modest regiment of six gardeners, Lady Dorothy Nevill, at her wealthiest, was in charge of twenty-three acres at Dangstein in West Sussex with thirty-four gardeners at her command, although the road to such abundance had not been

Lady Dorothy Nevill (1826–1913) made up for early indiscretions by devoting
her later life to acquiring a plant collection envied by Kew and from which
she donated specimens to Charles Darwin for his experiments.

smooth. The youngest, and favourite, daughter of the Earl of Orford,
Lady Dorothy had made a fatal mistake in her youth that was to affect
her life thereafter. Pursued by a well-known rake, she was discovered
to have spent half an hour alone with him in the family summer-
house. Rumours were rife that she had been 'compromised' and a fall
down a flight of stairs shortly after did little to quash rumours that she
had become pregnant and miscarried. Queen Victoria banned her
from court. The only option was a hastily arranged marriage and in
1847 she was united to an extremely wealthy but elderly cousin,
Reginald Nevill.

Still in her early twenties and excluded from court society, Lady
Dorothy resolved to develop the gardens at her new home at
Dangstein with a fervour that was considered unseemly in a woman.

Her well-placed male friends thought she should not worry her pretty little head with learning the Latin names of the plants going into her prodigious herbaceous borders, and thirteen – yes, thirteen – greenhouses, of which the peach, orchid and fern houses were irrigated by an elaborate network of aqueducts and heated, when necessary, with enormous furnaces kept going by a team of stokers.

Not surprisingly, such horticultural extravagance soon came to the notice of the gardening world, and before long Lady Dorothy, still just in her twenties, received a visit from the great Sir William Hooker, the first full-time director of the Royal Botanic Gardens at Kew. This was the beginning of an unlikely friendship between the young female gardening enthusiast and the seventy-year-old male botanical expert. He was clearly won over by Lady Dorothy's genuine but slightly dotty enthusiasms. How could he refuse her a few seeds when she offered him the pick of her three hundred ferns that amazingly included some that were not in the collection at Kew? 'I am more grateful than I can express,' she wrote to Sir William after one of his visits, 'for your offer of plants. I had meant <u>later</u> to remind you of your kind promise. The Musa Ansante? Would be gratefully received also if you had a duplicate of the Hibiscus alatus.' Sir William received additional incentives from his rich young admirer. 'I am shocked,' Lady Dorothy added, 'to find that you received only a brace of pheasants whereas on leaving home I desired two brace might be sent to you.'[6] Her collection of anoectochile orchids, one of the most difficult genera to grow, was built up in just six years, from 1856 to 1861, after which it reputedly contained virtually every species known at that time. A wing of the palm house was devoted to insectivorous plants while another section contained a tank for water lilies and other tender aquatic plants, all under the care of Lady Dorothy's head gardener, Mr Vair, and his thirty-three undergardeners.

Reginald Nevill appeared happy to allow his wife full rein with such horticultural extravagances, although occasionally her experiments did annoy him. When *Ailanthus glandulosa*, the Japanese Tree of Heaven, was planted at Dangstein the leaves gave off such a smell that even the rabbits would not touch them. An attempt to start a silkworm farm involved their London house becoming infested with caterpillars. The project was a failure, producing only enough silk for one dress, which itself was destroyed when Lady Dorothy's crinoline caught fire, although she saved herself by rolling in a ball on the floor.

In her late forties, Lady Dorothy's collection of plants was so extensive that when Charles Darwin was looking for specimens to conduct his research on orchid reproduction it was inevitable that John Lindley, then secretary to the Horticultural Society, suggested that he should ask Lady Dorothy if she could spare some from her magnificent collection. This she did willingly as she was already fascinated by Darwin's experiments. Not long after, she heard that Darwin was also in need of some insectivorous plants and again sent off the required varieties.

The unlikely pair began a correspondence and a friendship. Although Darwin never managed to visit Dangstein, despite regular invitations, Lady Dorothy did lure him to the London house and continued to send him seemingly endless supplies of specimens of everything from orchids to earthworms. One particular insectivorous plant she gave him, *Utricularia montana*, led Darwin to make an important link between the roots and bladders of epiphytics. Such was his excitement that he wrote quickly to Lady Dorothy, on 18 September 1874, 'I have hardly ever enjoyed a day more in my life than this day's work and this I owe to your ladyship's great kindness.'[7]

While she might still have been excluded from court society, she had established a new persona. Among her own 'court' of horticultural and political admirers was the future prime minister, Benjamin Disraeli. 'Lady Dorothy Nevill,' he wrote in a character sketch, '[is] a very clever woman; equal to Professor Hooker as a botanist, with without doubt the finest pinetum and conservatories and collections of rare trees in the world – all formed and collected and created by herself at Dangstein.'[8] Lady Dorothy had three children in her twenties, but when another son, Ralph, arrived ten years after the last, it must have been a bit of a surprise, particularly as he bore more than a passing resemblance to her great friend Disraeli . . .

Despite her undoubted femininity and wide circle of male friends and admirers, together with her expert level of horticultural and botanical knowledge, Lady Dorothy was acutely aware that she was excluded from many societies because of her sex, a fact which caused her to wish she had been born a man – something which may have seemed to her even more desirable when her long-suffering husband, Reginald, developed cancer. Britain was slipping into recession and he had already realised he could no longer support his wife's extravagances. When he died in 1878, she was faced with having to support herself on an allowance of £800 a year, about a tenth of her husband's income when they had married. It was not enough to maintain Dangstein and the treasury of plants there, which still rivalled those at Kew in its richness, and Lady Dorothy decided her only option was to sell them. Putting a brave face on the breaking up of her beloved collection, she wrote to Sir Joseph Hooker hoping that he would be able to 'puff the collection'. More realistically, she accepted that there would be problems finding new homes, especially for the large tropical palms and tree ferns, some of which were over three metres high. With the exception of some of the orange trees, which Lady Dorothy kept for her new home, the plants were all sold, many for knock-down prices. There is no record as to whether any plants went to Kew, but through private negotiations the prince of Monaco bought the tropical palms, and the king of the Belgians carried off enough exotics to fill his palace greenhouses.

Lady Dorothy was able to keep some of the small specimens for her new rented home in East Sussex, but she was never able to garden again on such a grand scale. Instead she turned her formidable energy to politics, always supporting her close friend Disraeli. After his death she became involved in the Primrose League, started to promote the principles of conservatism, and supposedly named for his favourite flower.

FROM SEED TO SHOW

There are two sorts of plant collectors: those who visit distant countries to find species that have never been seen before; and those who relish the satisfaction of hunting down a supplier for that rare variety which even the Royal Horticultural Society's *Plant Finder* does not list. One prime example of the latter group was the late-nineteenth-century consummate plantswoman Frances Jane Hope, of Wardie Lodge, near Edinburgh. 'To very many gardeners,' *Gardeners' Chronicle* wrote in their obituary of Hope, 'the garden is everything, the plants are mere accessories. This was not Miss Hope's way of viewing things; for her, the garden existed for the plants not the plants for the garden.'[1]

Long forgotten now, at the time of her death in 1880 Frances Hope evoked generous and emotional obituaries in both the *Gardeners' Chronicle* and William Robinson's *The Garden* magazine. Hope's legacy, they explained, was not to leave behind a grand garden but rather a passionate love for plants themselves. Her collection of hellebores, 'a tribe of plants' she was particularly passionate about, was reputedly larger than in any public garden. 'She spared no pains to add to her collection,' the *Gardeners' Chronicle* reported. She was supposed to have visited every nursery garden 'of importance' in England and Scotland,[2] and one suspects that she never came away empty-handed.

Hope wrote many short articles that were published collectively in 1881 as *Notes and Thoughts on Gardens and Woodlands*. A contemporary, Mrs Earle, commented that they were 'simply about gardening, but of the most intelligent and suggestive kind'.[3] Hope herself believed in getting to know a plant by growing it rather than reading about it. She explained that she preferred to take de Candolle's advice, 'to see the plants at all their ages, to follow their growth, to describe them in detail; in one word, to live with them more than with books'.[4]

These were sentiments which Mary Anne Robb would have agreed with. Robb came from a large, lively family. Her grandfather was Matthew Boulton, the Birmingham engineer who was part of the Lunar Society, the famous group of like-minded and gifted men which included Erasmus Darwin and Josiah Wedgwood. Mary Anne Boulton was the youngest of the family and lost her mother just after her birth in 1829, but she had a happy childhood and was surrounded by family friends who included the Darwins. She married a naval captain, John Robb, in 1856 and quickly had two sons, but she vanishes from history after her husband's death, reappearing only when in her early seventies, living in Liphook in Hampshire with a thriving garden filled with fine trees and shrubs. She had become friends with William Robinson, then at the height of his fame as a campaigner for more naturalistic gardening, and she also knew Kew's director, Thiselton-Dyer.

However, it was her friendship with a young E.A. Bowles that was to bring her horticultural immortality. Far from burying herself in the wilds of Hampshire, Mrs Robb was another intrepid female traveller. Some time in the early 1890s she visited Turkey, taking with her a suitably impressive wardrobe including, naturally, a hat. This bonnet was kept packed in a special box and was brought out only when she was in the company of Turkish pashas. On her journey through the countryside back to Istanbul, Mrs Robb spotted a euphorbia growing at the roadside. In those pre-plastic-bag days, she did what any serious plantsperson would do; she took the precious hat out of its box and used that to bring the plant back to Liphook. From there it went to Bowles's garden at Myddelton House in Enfield, where the plantsman himself may have nicknamed the new discovery 'Mrs Robb's Bonnet', a name that has stuck to this day.[5] It is a plant that you either love or hate; it will romp away where happy and few plants are as content in deep shade, even against a building wall, as *E. robbiae*.

This was not her only discovery. Bowles mentions having 'another of Mrs Robb's good things', a purple primrose she had spotted on Mount Olympus. 'Much to the annoyance of her magnificent dragoman [guide], who was dressed in a uniform richer in gold lace than that of the most distinguished general, she insisted on his dismounting from his horse and digging up some roots with a broken potsherd, the only weapon that presented itself.' Mrs Robb confessed to Bowles that the colour of the purple primrose always reminded her of the 'rueful face of that glittering dragoman'.[6]

Ellen Willmott was the daughter of wealthy parents, and the favourite of a childless god-mother who made her the sole beneficiary of a vast fortune. Around 1876 the family moved to Warley Place in Essex, the one-time home of John Evelyn, where he had written his famous *Sylva, or a Discourse of Forest Trees* in 1664. Her parents were interested in gardening, but it was only after they both died in 1891 that she was able fully to indulge her passion for plants.

She was no horticultural dilettante, however, and was soon appointed to various committees of the Royal Horticultural Society. A beauty in her youth, one can imagine the effect she had on the staid

The vast estate of Warley Place became a monument to the extravagance of plantswoman Ellen Willmott (1858–1934). Once looked after by over a hundred gardeners, it eventually lay in ruins.

men of the RHS when she swept in wearing a corsage of fresh rare flowers from Warley. It has been said that 'her delight in confounding those who could not identify the flower was only equalled by her genuine pleasure in finding those who could', although given her strength of character, she always expected due deference to her expertise.[7]

From her enormous wealth, Ellen financed plant-hunting expeditions to China, supporting the famous plant collector Ernest 'Chinese' Wilson, and to the Middle East, which made her a popular woman in the horticultural world. She is reputed to have grown six hundred varieties of narcissus at Warley Place, a garden which at one time was looked after by 104 uniformed gardeners. One year she grew every available variety of potato in search of the best. She created a rock garden on the grandest scale, with boulders, streams and a cave with a glass roof called the 'Filmy Fern Grotto', packed with New Zealand and British ferns. She also bought properties in the South of France and Italy and developed the gardens there. Plants were sent to and from the three gardens with wild extravagance, Miss Willmott keeping in touch with her three head gardeners by providing them with stamped, addressed postcards with which to contact her with updates.

Throughout this time, Willmott was regularly showing plants raised at Warley and winning medals from the RHS. Roses were her great love, although, like Gertrude Jekyll, her preference was for old roses and she complained that 'sad to say far too frequent among the newer roses ... the flowers are absolutely devoid of any fragrance whatever'.[8] Her legacy in print is the massive work *The Genus Rosa*, the publication of which in 1912 she financed herself. Economically it was a disaster, with the illustrations costing more than she ever earned in royalties, and under a third of the copies printed were ever sold.

Willmott had a seemingly bottomless pit of money with which she indulged her love of plants, yet her knowledge was beyond dispute and quickly recognised. In 1897 the Royal Horticultural Society inaugurated the Victoria Medal of Honour in celebration of Queen Victoria's Jubilee, but out of the sixty recipients only two were women, Willmott and Gertrude Jekyll. Other honours followed from the Linnean Society, Willmott becoming in 1905 the first woman to be elected a fellow.

'My plants and my gardens come before anything in life for me,' she wrote to Professor Sargent of the Arnold Arboretum at Harvard in 1906, 'and all my time is given up working in one garden or another, and when it is too dark to see the plants themselves I read or write about them.'[9] In addition to her acquaintance with Jekyll (whom she visited at Munstead), Ellen Willmott also enjoyed great friendships with the clerical horticultural supremos the Revd Charles Wolley Dod and Canon Ellacombe.

Given her lavish spending sprees with no one to rein her in, it was almost inevitable that the money would eventually run out and the dream turn sour. As early as 1907, after a fire at her uninsured house in France, she had to borrow money against Warley. Her rental income was erratic as tenants came and went, and eventually the houses abroad had to be sold. When the bank wrote threatening her with repossession of Warley, she retreated into the garden to weed. Only her faithful butler, Robinson, stayed with her until the end, by which time the money had gone and the garden had fallen into ruins.

After her death, her vast collection of horticultural books was sold. It took three days to get through all the lots, which also included some on her other interests of music and photography. A marked copy of the catalogue shows that the majority of her gardening books were bought by some of the most famous dealers of the day – Bernard Quaritch, Foyles and Maggs Bros, and she would no doubt have approved that they were to be acquired by people who loved gardening. Her name is now most commonly remembered for the sea holly *Eryngium giganteum* or 'Miss Willmott's Ghost', the seeds of which, it was said, she would sprinkle in other people's gardens as she swept imperiously through.

CULTIVATING THE NEW

The passion for collecting specific sorts of plants known as 'florists' flowers' has been strong since the seventeenth century. The earliest known meeting of such collectors, or 'Florist Feast', took place in Norwich in 1631. In those days, and until the late nineteenth century, the term 'florist' did not mean a professional flower arranger but a grower of one of eight types of flower which would be displayed at group meetings where prizes were awarded. Auriculas (*Primula auricula*) quickly gained a special status among growers and in the early 1800s prized forms were recorded as selling for up to £20 a plant – a sum to rival the prices paid during the 'tulipomania' of the seventeenth century. While there are few records of how and where florists' flowers were grown, we do know that women were involved in this particularly passionate form of plant cultivation. In her Battersea garden, 'Mistres Buggs' had collected auriculas, and her eponymous 'Her Fine Purple' was an unusual striped variety.[1] There are also records of a 'Mistress Austin's Scarlet'.

Then for over a century auriculas fell out of fashion as the imperious of the horticultural world looked down on florists' flowers as common, and it was not until the second half of the twentieth century

Traditionally, auriculas (*Primula auricula*) are displayed in outdoor
'theatres', maintaining the cool temperatures they prefer
but with protection for the farinaceous petals.

that they started to become popular again when Brenda Hyatt began
to show them at Chelsea in the 1970s. It is amazing now to realise that
auriculas had virtually disappeared as a garden plant until Brenda
came across them in the nursery where she worked. 'One day, a box of
show auriculas in full bloom arrived at the nursery and all thoughts of
the job in hand vanished . . . The delicate, porcelain-like flowers, with
their velvety greens, greys, reds, and purples, along with so many
other rich colours seemed like paintings come to life. Those first auriculas cast a lasting spell over me; from that day on my interest in them
became single-minded, almost obsessive.'[2]

Brenda's obsession was much helped when she was able to take
over the collection that had been built up by three generations of the
Douglas family. Many of the older varieties suffered from viruses, and

she worked with experts at Wye College, using the latest tissue culture techniques of propagation, to eradicate the disease. A down-to-earth, modest woman, by 1988 she held the National Council for the Conservation of Plants and Gardens (now Plant Heritage) National Plant Collection of fancy and green-, grey- and white-edged auriculas. Crowds used to cluster around her beautiful stand at Chelsea where she displayed her plants in the traditional manner against the backdrop of a black 'theatre' set, reawakening a pride in showing off single plants that had not been seen since the nineteenth century.

This was also the year that a small book, *Florists' Flowers and Societies*, was published which included an explanation of the former popularity of the auricula as a 'florist's flower'. The author was Ruth Duthie, a teacher who had developed a passion for garden history and in particular the group of eight traditional flowers that were grown – mainly by working men – in the nineteenth century for competitive showing. In her book Duthie explained that, in addition to the auricula, the tulip, the carnation, the polyanthus, the hyacinth, the anemone, the ranunculus and the pink were lovingly grown, then shown in pots and passed around in the back room of an inn to be judged among peers. The proud growers would award each other prizes, sometimes a silver spoon, sometimes even a kettle, in recognition of their growing skills. It was most probably this connection with florists and those with cottage gardens that contributed to the auricula's fall from fashion as the plant suffered from its association with the working man, just as the chrysanthemum to some extent still does. Dahlias, too, have only recently been rescued from the allotment. In 1993, the year that Ruth Duthie died, Brenda Hyatt was awarded the Veitch Memorial Gold Medal. While Duthie's work on the florists has never been surpassed, Brenda Hyatt led the way for an auricula renaissance. Her early death in 2001 robbed the gardening world of another plant heroine.

A less well known but equally passionate auricula enthusiast was Mary McMurtrie. A wife of the manse, Mrs McMurtrie began a small nursery at her home at Skene in Aberdeenshire in the 1930s, where she happily propagated saxifrages, primroses, pinks and auriculas in between looking after her husband, the parish minister, and four children. When they moved first to Aberdeen and then to Balbithan House, Kintore, not far away, the stock came too. Mrs McMurtrie began producing small plant catalogues and, having been to art school, accompanied these with delicate and highly prized watercolours which she exhibited along with her plants at the Scottish Rock Garden Club's shows. Fortified by a 'dram of sherry' from the bottle kept in her library desk, she gardened throughout the year, braving Scotland's coldest days to be outside watching over her precious plants. The garden, she wrote, 'was a *green* garden, and green is restful to the eye. Of course there is colour but on the whole it is gentle and restrained while, enhanced by so much green, the occasional vivid patch of brilliant colour is unexpected and stimulating.'[3]

By 1966, Mrs McMurtrie's nursery catalogue contained thirty different varieties of single primroses, including gems such as 'Blue Horizon', 'E.R. Janes', 'Sunset Glow', and seven forms of Garryard primroses, of which probably the only one remaining is 'Guinevere'. The hot summers of 1975 and 1976 were ruinous for the collection, and in her eighties Mrs McMurtrie moved in with her daughter but continued gardening enthusiastically for another fifteen years. Her artwork remained more in demand than ever, and in 1975 Roy Genders asked her to do some illustrations for his book *Growing Old-Fashioned Flowers*. She began writing and illustrating her own books, and just before she died in 2003, aged 101, she was given an award by the charity

Counsel and Care for the Elderly for being the oldest British working artist. *Old Cottage Pinks* was published in the same year.

As so often seems to happen, among women particularly, solace is found in gardening after some personal tragedy. Gwendolyn Anley lost her young daughter when she was in her forties and turned to gardening for comfort. She became captivated by the delicate but at the same time robust beauty of alpines and was soon showing her collection successfully. In 1938 she published a handbook, *Alpine House Culture for Amateurs*, which was later revised and enlarged. From her garden in Woking, Surrey, where she lived with her husband, Brigadier-General B.L. Anley, Gwendolyn also developed a passion for tall-bearded irises and began to breed them. 'Arabi Pasha', a mid-blue variety, was awarded the Dykes Medal for the best iris of the year. Such were her enthusiasms that she was a founder member of the Alpine Garden Society as well as editing the Iris Society's Yearbook, and undertook endless fund-raising for the Gardeners' Royal Benevolent Society (now called Perennial).[4] She was awarded the prestigious RHS Victoria Medal of Honour in 1968.

At their home at Keillour Castle in Perthshire, Mrs Mary Knox-Finlay and her husband Major W.C. Knox-Finlay grew other rare plants superbly. Delicate pale blue meconopses and rare nomocharis flourished in their woodland garden, which they started in 1938, adding to the original late-nineteenth-century garden. Crucial to their success, they always claimed, was old rotted-down sawdust which they dug into the soil. One variety is named for them, *Nomocharis finlayorum*, a fitting tribute to this passionate gardening couple, part of an elite club in which both husband and wife have been awarded the RHS's Veitch Memorial Medal.

However, when a couple were involved in breeding plants, it was rare for the wife to have greater recognition. In writing about Mrs R.O. Backhouse in 1940, twenty years after her death, the *Gardeners' Chronicle* stated that it was Robert Ormston Backhouse who 'assisted his wife' in developing the 'Backhouse' red-cupped daffodils, which with their vivid central colouring 'took the Daffodil world by storm'.[5] A small group of her daffodils had caused a sensation at the London Daffodil Show in 1920. She also hybridised lilies and colchicums, and to her we owe the Backhouse series of lilies, crosses between Martagon lilies and *Lilium hansonii*. The daffodil called 'Mrs R.O. Backhouse', which still divides gardeners with its unusual pink-coloured cup and white perianth, was shown by her husband just after her death and thus he always gets the credit for it.

It was her travels in several southern European countries that gave Pamela Underwood the taste for the silver-leaved plants that she became famous for in the 1960s and 70s. 'As a girl I had wandered over many of the foothills surrounding the Mediterranean and had often been sent clambering up cliffs collecting bits and pieces for the garden.'[6] Underwood started a nursery in the early 1960s at her home at Ramparts Farm near Colchester in Essex, infamously one of the driest places in the British Isles. Initially she grew carnations to sell to florists, but the Second World War hit this trade hard. Undeterred, she pioneered the growing of the drought-loving species that she had seen in the Mediterranean, plants such as unusual lavenders, artemesias, helichrysums and soft-leaved verbascums, many of which had been considered weeds before she introduced them to her nursery. Her book, *Grey and Silver Plants*, published under the name of Mrs Desmond Underwood – she had high social standards and preferred this traditional form of address – remains a classic.

Pamela Underwood also took inspiration from her immediate neighbours, Andrew and Beth Chatto, who were experimenting with drought-resistant plants, and with cuttings from their garden among others she soon built up a collection of over 160 different types of silver and grey-leaved plants. The nursery was by no means an instant success, since these were early days in the appreciation of foliage plants as opposed to 'a splash of colour', but Mrs Underwood's involvement with the flower-arranging industry led the way for a change of heart on the beauty of foliage for its own sake.

Tall, with a booming voice and usually a cigarette hanging from her lips, Mrs Underwood has been described as 'a woman of high standards and great courage', a euphemism for being rather terrifying in an English-country-lady sort of way. Beth Chatto calls her 'without doubt, a character'.[7] In 1977, when she was awarded her Victoria Medal of Honour, she was also asked by the RHS to provide the plants for their Silver Jubilee gift to the Queen – a silver foliage garden at Buckingham Palace which Mrs Underwood planted herself.

It is hard to imagine a garden now without a selection of drought-loving silver-leaved plants, though as ever they will go in and out of fashion. Equally, it is hard to believe that when Beth Chatto first showed hellebores in the 1970s they were nearly dismissed by the RHS as 'weeds'. Today it is not uncommon for people to swoon over the delicate lime and cream colours and the wide variations of pattern, from speckled icy white to near-black mauves and purples, of hellebores. These are flowers to be cut and floated in a dish of water to appreciate their beauty fully, and the fact that we do now appreciate them is down almost solely to one woman, Helen Ballard, thought by some to be the most remarkable plantswoman of the twentieth century.

Hellebores were Ballard's passion and as a perfectionist she was able to bring some control to bear on these most promiscuous of plants and develop astoundingly beautiful strains. An Oxford graduate, she was a teacher before devoting herself to breeding her hellebores. She is remembered in one strain of the flower, sadly hard to track down, and also for the *Aster novi-belgii* 'Helen Ballard', but her greatest legacy is in the plants she passed on to others. After her death in 1995, her collection went to Germany.

Elizabeth Strangman is another plantswoman who became captivated by the elegant hellebore. Her speciality is the double forms grown from the seed she collected on trips to the former Yugoslavia. It was Strangman who perfected a simple hybridisation technique, 'line-breeding' particular coloured strains, which she generously shared with readers in *The Gardener's Guide to Growing Hellebores*, the book she co-wrote with Graham Rice in 1993. One of her seed finds in Bosnia was *H. torquatus* from which she bred the 'Party Dress' group of hybrids, in particular *H. t.* 'Dido' and *H. t.* 'Aeneas'.

In the late 1950s Elizabeth Strangman had arrived at Washfield Nursery in Kent as a disillusioned horticultural student from Studley. She was bored with 'classroom botany', and when she visited the nursery with her father on a plant-buying trip she offered to work with the owner Hilda Davenport-Jones, known as 'Boss'. It was in these early days that she began her tentative experiments in hellebore crossing. When Davenport-Jones died in 1968, it was a natural progression for Elizabeth to take over the nursery. By then, she was also on the lookout for new introductions in a wide range of hardy perennials. In the early 1970s, she had discovered and nurtured *Origanum* 'Kent Beauty', still one of the most sought-after decorative origanums with stylish dangling pink bracts. Campanulas and hardy geraniums were favourites as well, with *Campanula* 'Kent Belle' coming from a chance seedling, as did *Geranium* 'Salome', a shade-loving variety without any of the sins of one of its parents, *G. procurrens*.

Strangman's talents for propagation meant that she was often given seeds to grow on and develop. The seed for *Campanula takesimana* came to her from Korea via the Royal Botanic Garden in Edinburgh, and in the 1960s Bertram Anderson gave her the *Pulmonaria longifolia* from a find in his Cotswolds garden that she was to name after him. This is a narrow-leaved variety, notable for its resistance to drought, with good spotting on the leaves and with dark blue flowers. It was typical of Strangman to describe what happened next in one of her memorable catalogues: 'One customer bought this plant, took it to the States where it found a partner, married and the child returned to Washfield.'[8] That light-blue-flowered child was named after that customer, *P.* 'Roy Davidson'.

The news in 1999 that Elizabeth Strangman was retiring and closing Washfield Nursery was greeted with complete dismay by gardeners across south-east England, leading them to make a final pilgrimage to Hawkhurst in the hope of getting hold of one of her exciting seedling discoveries. In her retirement Elizabeth Strangman continues to grow and breed her beloved hellebores, and seeds of her 'Washfield Doubles' are available commercially.

For regular visitors to the RHS's Vincent Square flower shows in London, the Fibrex stand is always a stopping-off spot. Depending on the time of year, beautifully arranged ferns and ivies catch the eye or pelargoniums, usually highly scented, tempt visitors to give the leaves a little squeeze to release their delicious, volatile perfumes. Still a family-run business, Fibrex Nurseries grew from Hazel Key's early passion for pelargoniums after she bought some at the Three Counties Show in the early 1950s.

Key's collection quickly outgrew the family greenhouse and the various sites that Hazel and her husband Dick subsequently acquired. With Hazel selling through shows and via mail order, Dick was always on hand to organise the ever-increasing space needed to hold their

stock. Hazel Key rapidly became one of the country's leading author-
ities on pelargoniums – the name she always insisted was used rather
than the more common but incorrect term, geraniums. She also travelled across America, South Africa and Australia, bringing new finds
back to the nursery but just as importantly making contact with
growers worldwide. By 1987 Hazel had established the National
Collection of Pelargoniums, which is still held at the nursery, with
well over two thousand varieties.

Hazel's second love is for ivies (*Hedera*) and hardy ferns (and she is
also another hellebore lover). While some gardeners might dismiss
ivies as dull and reminiscent of graveyards or dusty houseplants, Hazel
brings out their true beauty and variety, which are confidently displayed at the Vincent Square shows. Hazel Key's books on both
pelargoniums and ivies, in particular the RHS Wisley Handbooks, are
mines of practical and expert information.

In 1967 a young ex-teacher and farmer's wife, Beth Chatto, started the
Unusual Plants nursery at Elmstead, near Colchester in Essex, well
named since the plants she sold were just that. They were unusual not
because they were rarities but because they were unfashionable and
not considered colourful enough for the tastes of the time. These were
collections of euphorbias, geraniums, pulmonarias, and dozens of
hardy perennials that Chatto had refined until she was able to pass on
the finest specimens. It is highly appropriate that the first retrospective
exhibition held in the newly refurbished (and renamed) Garden
Museum at Lambeth in spring 2009 was to honour one of the great
women gardeners of the late twentieth and early twenty-first centuries. While it would be wrong to give Chatto all the credit for
changing what we grow in our gardens today, there is no doubt that
she has been one of the most influential in shifting the mindset away

Beth Chatto's mantra of the importance of choosing the right plant for the right place, and her eagle eye for the best new cultivars, has changed the way people garden today.

from the serried ranks of scarlet geraniums and hybrid tea roses stiff as flagpoles to the natural country look which so many gardeners now strive for.

In the 1970s, when Beth Chatto first exhibited at the Chelsea Flower Show, the public clustered round her stand, sometimes five or six deep, straining to get a view of her treasures displayed in the great marquee. Everyone scribbled furiously, covering pads with notes on the 'must-have' plants. Back then, the now famous gravel garden at Elmstead was still just a car park across which you would trundle your precious purchases. The early catalogues from Unusual Plants contained no photographs, just page after page of rarities divided into categories: dry soil, full sun; damp soil, full sun; damp soil and shade; and finally, that most treacherous of all combinations, dry soil and shade. Chatto, though, has solutions for all the awkward corners and one comes away from a visit to Elmstead almost wishing for a garden full of dry shady soil and large trees under which to grow her recommendations.

What Chatto makes look obvious and easy was the result of years of study and research. In 1943 she had married Andrew Chatto, a fruit farmer in Essex who had a passionate interest in the ecology of the land, most unfashionable at a time when everyone else seemed to be concerned with improving productivity with insecticides and artificial fertilisers. In 1960 the couple arrived at their new farm at Elmstead, where Beth despaired of ever being able to establish a garden. Nevertheless, she set to work, inspired by her husband's knowledge of plants and their soil requirements, as well as encouraged by the enthusiasm and eye of their friend, the painter and plantsman Cedric Morris.

A corner of the Beth Chatto Garden at Elmstead in Essex is devoted to a choice collection of succulents, happy to bake in the sun in one of the driest areas in Britain.

Nine years later, the Chatto farm and its farmland had to be sold because of Andrew Chatto's poor health but with the remaining land, then three acres (now expanded to fourteen), Beth started her nursery with the help of just one girl. Her first RHS show in 1975 was at the then fortnightly venue in Vincent Square. Beth drove up in a van full of hellebores, never having driven to London before. Rather than displaying her plants in pots, as was the norm at these shows, she created a woodland garden on her stand. It caused a sensation among the visitors and other nurserymen, and the rather nervous RHS judges awarded her a silver medal. There were rumours later that some thought she should have been disqualified for displaying 'weeds'.

The following year, Chatto made her debut at Chelsea in the great marquee, showing a microcosm of plants from the gardens at Elmstead, none of which had been forced as was the practice on so many other stands. It was awarded a silver gilt medal. The first of ten golds came the next year. Her record of ten consecutive gold medals from the late 1970s for displays at Chelsea was finally broken in 2006 by two women growers, Jekka McVicar, of Jekka's Herb Farm in Alveston, Gloucestershire, and Rosemary Hardy of Hardy's Cottage Garden Plants in Whitchurch, Hampshire. In 2009 McVicar (who in her youth sang with a progressive rock band called Marsupilami) rounded off her career in the giant marquee with her fourteenth Chelsea gold medal, bringing her overall RHS gold haul to sixty-two. Since she hopes to design an outdoor show garden in years to come, one suspects this may not be the last glint of gold she will see. The varied achievements of all these women show that the passion for plants continues unabated.

SHAPING THE LANDSCAPE

Having resolv'd upon a *Garden*, you must next
pitch upon its Situation, which must not be
incompass'd too close with High Buildings, but
laid open to the Air, and Sun, with a convenient
warm Wall, or Fence, about it ... The Walks in
your *Garden* are not to be limited, but rather drawn
out to your Fancy, in some Shape or Figure. But
be sure let there be a Fountain, Pump, or Rivolet
hard by, to furnish it with Water upon Occasion.[1]

Thomas Harris,
'The Lady's Diversion in her Garden' (1675)

THE GRAND DESIGN

In 1715 Stephen Switzer, the opinionated horticultural writer, turned his pen to thoughts on women in the garden. 'When Men are observ'd to busie themselves in this diverting and useful Employ,' he pontificated, ''tis no more than what is from them expected; but when by the fair and tender Sex,' he continued, 'it has something in it that looks supernatural, something so much above the trifling amusements of that Species of Rational Beings, that is apt to fill the Mind of the Virtuous with Admiration.'[1] Not for nothing was his book addressed solely to gentlemen and noblemen, for the thought of women being involved in the creation of gardens, rather than merely the cultivation of a few herbs and flowering plants, still appeared a strange concept to the educated classes.

Two years later another author, John Lawrence, writing under the pseudonym of Charles Evelyn, also questioned the role of women in the garden in, of all places, his book *The Lady's Recreation Or the Third and Last Part of the Art of Gardening Improved* (1717), the other two parts being written for gentlemen and clergymen. 'The greatest of men,' Lawrence wrote, 'used gardening as a time for unbending their thoughts and to retire from the world.' Ladies, on the other hand, were better suited to

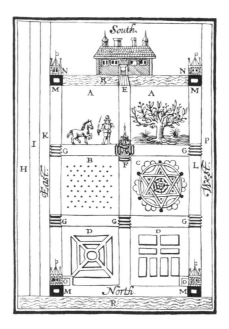

Designs for a sectioned garden from *The New Orchard Garden* (1618) by William Lawson
(1553/4–1635), the first person to write a gardening book specifically for women.

the management of the flower garden, 'where the Gardens are not very extensive, and the Inspection thereof doth not take up too much of their Time'.[2]

Despite the evidence that women had been collecting and growing plants for centuries, it is harder to find proof that they were involved in the grander task of designing the gardens they were working on. One of the earliest written references which suggests that women were involved in garden design comes in 1617 in William Lawson's *Country Housewife's Garden* and its sequel, *New Orchard Garden*.

Lawson, a clergyman from Yorkshire, was writing at the height of popularity of the knot garden, a square of ground planted with an intricate formal shape designed to be looked down on from upper reception rooms. Lawson includes illustrations of eight such designs, with explanatory names of their inspirations such as Lozengers, The Trefoyle, Cinkfoyle and Flower deluce. There was also a plan for a square maze, and he offered practical help on growing plants, written with an infectious enthusiasm. His plans were just a starting point, Lawson suggested, 'for special formes in square there are as many, as there are devices in Gentlemen's brains'. Because there were so many available designs of 'formes, mazes and knots', he was happy to 'leave every House-Wife to herselfe, especially seeing to set down many had been but to fill much paper, yet lest I deprive her of all delight and direction, let her view these few, choise new forms and note these generally, that all plots are squares and all are bordered about with Privit, Raisins, Fea-Berries, Roses, Thorn, Rosemary, Bee-flowers, Hysop, Sage or such like'.[3] We see here a clear invitation to women readers to try their hand at garden design if they were not already doing so.

By the second decade of the eighteenth century practical gardening was an accepted pastime for women, but one still has to look hard for women's involvement in changing the landscape. Stephen Switzer may have had reservations about the idea of women becoming involved in garden design, but he did make exceptions. He had praise for the Countess of Lindsey, formerly Lady Elizabeth Pope, about whom little is known except that, like the Duchess of Beaufort, she was a hands-on gardener at her home at Grimsthorpe Castle in Lincolnshire. Switzer, who had trained under George London and Henry Wise of the famous Brompton Park Nurseries in west London, and had worked alongside architects Vanbrugh and Hawksmoor, was surprised by her practicality, suggesting that this was not the norm among aristocratic women. 'This Lady was reputed to be a continual Attendant and Supervisor of her Works, without any regard to the rigid Inclemency of the Winter Season,' he marvelled, 'and not only so, but also in the measuring and laying out the Distances of her rows of Trees, she was actually employed with Rule, Line, etc.'[4]

We know a little more about Helen Hope, Countess of Haddington, who gardened in the fierce conditions of Scotland in the early eighteenth century. She was reputedly the main force behind the tree-planting programme at Tyninghame in the East Lothians. In addition to the planting of the eight-hundred-acre estate with over fifty species of tree, the countess oversaw the development of a 'pleasaunce' or wilderness area, and a bowling green that had fourteen walks emanating from its centre.

This arboreal lust had not won immediate approval from her husband, who was her first cousin, but he was won round and became a tree expert himself and supportive of the vast planting schemes proposed by his wife. Writing to his grandchildren in 1733 not long before his death, he admitted that in the early years of their marriage, he 'took pleasure in sports, dogs and horses but had no manner of inclination to plant, inclose or improve my grounds'. His wife, however, had other interests. 'Your grandmother was a great lover of planting, [and] she did what she could to engage me to it, but in vain. At last she asked leave to go about it, which she did, and I was much pleased with some little things that were both well laid out and executed, though none of them are now to be seen, for when the designs grew more expensive we were forced to take away what first was done.'

After her death, the countess was commemorated at least twice in verse for the legacy she had left to the East Lothians.

> While sylvan spirits hover bland,
> And verdant deck the lady's shrine,
> Who bade these canopies expand,
> In Gothic-fashion'd wreathes to twine.[5]

A history of the Haddington family, written at the end of the nineteenth century, quotes an even wiser verse, confirming that the best horticultural partnerships can sometimes take a while to grow.

Thus can good wives, when wise, in every station
On man work miracles of reformation
And were such wives more common, their husbands would
    endure it
However great the malady, a loving wife can cure it
And much their aid is wanted, we hope they'll use it fairish
While [until] barren ground, where wood should be, appears in
    every parish.[6]

By the mid-eighteenth century, the landscape of England's aristocratic estates was being resculpted by a new breed – the celebrity garden designer. Mrs Montagu, best known as the 'Queen of the Blue Stockings', was rare among eighteenth-century women in being able to commission such a garden designer directly rather than through her husband. When Edward Montagu died in 1775, she did as many widows did – she started spending his money to satisfy her own desires rather than those of her spouse. Although famous for her literary writing, such a reputation did not make Mrs Montagu independently wealthy, and during his lifetime it was her husband who controlled the family finances. On his death, she used her considerable widow's legacy of £7,000 a year to build a new London home in Portman Square, and to improve her country residence in Berkshire, Sandleford. Situated midway between London and Bath, Sandleford had always been a favourite place for the Montagus. Initially she was advised by her close friend, George Simon, 2nd Earl of Harcourt, who himself gardened at Nuneham Courtney, Oxfordshire. He had firm opinions on how a fashionable garden should be laid out and planted, and was only too willing to give Mrs Montagu the strictest of instructions.

The additional flower bed, or bosquet, over which I have placed a mark X appears to me to be totally useless, and that it would be better filled up with lilacs & other early shrubs NB: in London Bosquets, elder & even gooseberry & currant bushes are not to be despised, because the two latter come into leaf long before any other shrubs. – The roses should have no other bushes intermixed with them; but pinks & bulbous roots, may be planted round the clumps & between the several rose plants – Box well kept forms the neatest edging to flower beds. Round all the shruberies, (except the clumps of Roses) I would advise a thick hedge of privet & to be kept regularly clipt – it is almost an ever-green, & nothing grows so quick or looks more neat – Where there is not space to allow both shrubs & hedge, a very thick hedge clipt I should prefer. 4 feet is width sufficient, for the gravel walks – Mr Stuart has omitted the communications necessary between the different parts of the garden, but you will be pleased to observe madam that I have scratched out one from each of the allies on the side of the grand parterre – by the way, the large space in the front will be monotone if only filled with London Turf, I should therefore think a parterre of flowers absolutely necessary – the flower beds need not extend in the front beyond the projection of the hotel . . . I have ventured to alter for your decision 2 of the 4 long beds, in the garden where there are to be the arches of treillage, because I thought those 4 beds, exactly repeated, had an ill effect & were too much resembling pannels in a room – Remember Madam that your working Gardener must not have any Fancy, but must work with the compass & rule – I wish I may have explained myself clearly, if I have not, you know where your architect des jardins lives, and I hope you know likewise Madam, that he is at all times and on all occasions, happy to obey your commands.[7]

Mrs Montagu appears not to have taken offence at being so advised, as is obvious from a letter to her friend the literary hostess Elizabeth Vesey.

I am now very busy about the garden at my new house; Lord Harcourt has made a very pretty plan for it. I believe it will not be so stately as the garden of [jessamis, senesamis?]. nor perhaps as that where ye <u>sapient king with his fair spouse held dalliance</u>, but for these puny modern times it will be pretty well, & will grow laurels enough to crown Ld C—when he returns from his American expedition, I shall give you a merry merry Vauxhall when my trees & shrubs are in order. I assure you it will be a very pretty demi Saison garden, in winter it will not afford such shelter from storms as a Forrest of Pines, nor in summer shade like ye Groves of Oaks of our Druid; but it will serve as umbrellas & fans for Beaux & Belles.[8]

She planned to entertain even more lavishly at Sandleford than she had done previously. James Wyatt was commissioned to refurbish the house, while Lancelot 'Capability' Brown was engaged to 'improve' the garden. By the time Brown took on this commission, he was nearing the end of his illustrious career. He had established his reputation with the development of the grounds at Stowe in Buckinghamshire some forty years before. After that, landowners queued to have him take on and transform their estates. In the 1760s he not only completed more than sixty-five projects, including what many consider his magnum opus at Blenheim Palace in Oxfordshire for the Duke of Marlborough, but also was appointed royal court gardener at Hampton Court, and the palaces of Richmond and St James's in London.

Even though Mrs Montagu was a wealthy widow, she was still cautious about giving Mr Brown full rein to implement his notoriously lavish plans. In 1781, she wrote again to Elizabeth Vesey.

> It is a pity the noble genius of Mr Brown should be restrain'd by ignoble considerations & circumstances but you know I have some low plebeian sentiments which forbid my incurring debt so his improvements must not go beyond what my cash will immediately answer. I shall begin by embellishing what lies under the view of my new rooms, it is great satisfaction to me to find that he thinks great improvements may be made at small expense, & which has not cost me a farthing & yet is of the highest advantage & that is a perspective of giving you a Fete Champetre here next summer.[9]

Mrs Montagu was happy for the work to progress slowly as she wisely never, as she wrote, 'allowed my yearly expenses to exceed my yearly income, so that I go on softly'.[10] It was a good partnership, and one that Mrs Montagu did not want to get out of hand. 'We shall not erect temples to the gods, build proud bridges over humble rivulets, or do any of the marvellous things suggested by caprice, and indulged by the wantonness of wealth.' Brown understood the restraints she imposed, and later she was able to write, 'He is forming it into a lovely pastoral – a sweet Arcadian scene. In not attempting more, he adapts his scheme to the character of the place and my purse.'[11] Mrs Montagu and Brown got on well. She called him 'an agreeable, pleasant companion'.[12] Sandleford proved to be his last project and he did not live to see his designs there completed.

The siblings of the 2nd Earl Harcourt, the man who had given Mrs Montagu such detailed advice when she first planned her garden at Sandleford, were also keen gardeners. They may have inherited this from their mother Rebecca, née Samborne Le Bas, an heiress who grew up at Pipewell Abbey in Northamptonshire. In a letter she wrote in 1755 to George Simon, her eldest son, she enthused about a new horticultural venture at her home at Stanton Harcourt in Oxfordshire. 'I can't finish my Epistle without letting you know that we are making an alteration in the Flower Garden which I hope you will think an improvement 'tis by bringing the Flower Beds nearer to the Green House by which means that whole Room will be perfumed from the Flowers with out & the Tuberoses within which I have had this Year in some abundance.'[13]

Her daughter Elizabeth married Sir William Lee of Hartwell House, Buckinghamshire, in 1763, but little detail is known about the garden at Hartwell until the end of that century. In the 1980s the garden historian Mavis Batey discovered plans dating from 1799 which show that the Lees in their later years intended to remodel their garden. Or was it, as garden historian Mark Laird has speculated, 'the brainchild of . . . Lady Elizabeth Lee, exercising her prerogative over what was to become the traditional domain of the woman: the flower garden?'[14] Certainly, an earlier letter from her brother, the earl, written in 1771, appears to suggest this as he refers to 'our equally favorite Hobby Horse, the Flower Garden' and commiserates with his sister over the problems she has been having growing 'Lichnadeas' (Phlox).[15] Lady Elizabeth was, according to later reports, a 'highly accomplished and very amiable person' who was 'fond of her flower garden'.[16] The earl was generous not just with his advice but also with plants and supplied his sister with many from his own garden, including 'Nuneham Lichnedea' and 'Nuneham Hollyhock'.

Lady Elizabeth designed her flower borders to complement the house, a clear move away from the grand scale of landscaping that was so popular in Brown's time. One is placed 'near Door of Garden Room', another 'under parlour Windows', and a third 'under the Apple Tree at entrance into Garden',[17] not that these were small beds; they averaged thirty-two square metres in size. In planting, they were similar to an oval herbaceous border with taller plants in the middle graduating down to low plants around the edges, designed to be at their peak when the family was in residence in the early summer months. On the death of her husband in 1799, the year the plans were drawn up, Elizabeth took charge of the garden and put her own imprint on the land.

'MY LITTLE PARADISE'

'I have begun last Week to form a Plan about my Garden,' Queen Charlotte wrote to her son Augustus, Duke of Sussex, in 1791. 'The Person who Undertakes to render this Unpritty thing pritty, is a Clergyman from Yorkshire whose name is known to You,' she continued.

It is Mr Alderson who was formerly Protected by the Late Lord Holderness & to whom the King has given a fine living in Yorkshire. He is a Man of great Natural taste but not of the World. Lady Holderness did recommend him to me and sent him to Windsor. I have accordingly begun to Plant the 7th of this Month, & from thence I date the beginning of my little Paradise. The Green House is finished & built under the direction of Acton, & by all Connoisseurs allowed to be very Fine. My Chief Plants are to be Natives of England & all such foreign ones as will thrive in Our Soil, Curtiss Books of Botany, Lees Sowerby & Millers English Garden Calendar & Dictionary are to be my Chief Studies when there & the drying of Plants both Foreign and Natives & endless resource, of the Former I made a Collection and have hitherto gone on with great Success. Happy shall I feel when I can see You in my Garden.[1]

George III and Queen Charlotte were devoted to their large family and spent as much time away from the London court as possible. The Queen's favourite country home was the White House, or Kew House, on the site of what was to become the Royal Botanic Gardens, which they had inherited from George's mother, Augusta, the Dowager Princess of Wales.

Since the three Queen Eleanors had gardened in medieval Britain, several other royal wives had added to the strength of gardens in the royal palaces. Initially this was done through the influence of foreign garden designers. Anne of Denmark, wife of James VI of Scotland, later James I of England, invited the Huguenot inventor Salomon de Caus to Britain from France to work on the parterres and fountains at Somerset House, the sumptuous palace built on the banks of the river Thames. Celebrated designer André Mollet came to England from France at the request of Henrietta Maria, Charles I's wife, to oversee changes to her garden at Wimbledon House. She wanted him to soften the squareness of the garden that had been put in place by the previous owner, Sir Thomas Cecil, son of Elizabeth I's Lord Treasurer, and to introduce a more fashionable French style of design. Mollet was to return to England after the Interregnum to become royal gardener in charge of St James's Park.

Queen Mary, daughter of James II, went even further and, when her husband William was offered the thrones of England, Scotland and Ireland in 1689, she brought wagonloads of plants with her from Holland, of which four hundred were said to be new to Britain. During Mary's short reign – she died of smallpox when she was only thirty-two – her greatest triumph was the development of the gardens at

Hampton Court Palace, where she and William chose to live. In addition to the elaborate stove or hothouses Mary built for her valuable collection of rare plants, together with a series of small flower gardens, she and William worked with their designer, Daniel Marot, on the Privy Garden, much influenced by the Dutch style she would have come to know during her time in Holland. William was devastated by her death and lost enthusiasm for the project, and when Anne, Mary's sister, succeeded William on his death in 1702, yet different influences were brought to bear. Since Anne disliked not just William but also the Dutch style of gardens and the smell of box, she quickly cleared away the parterres and hedges and replaced them with grass-edged, narrow flower beds which were heralded as a revival of a more 'English' style.

Queen Caroline, the German-born wife of George II, also had a deep love of gardening; a passion she was able to indulge once she had been awarded the enormous yearly allowance of £100,000 when her husband ascended the throne on the death of his father. Caroline immediately began to develop the gardens of Hyde Park and Kensington Gardens. Her grandest and most ambitious scheme was the development of the grounds of her home at Richmond Lodge. Despite her staunch Germanic background, she invited famed designers Charles Bridgeman and William Kent to create a *jardin anglais*, which included a Gothic-style cave complete with hermit, and waxworks of famous fictional and past British heroes. Eventually the estate covered four hundred acres and stretched from Richmond to Kew. Queen Caroline was happy for the public to wander through the grounds when the royal family were not in residence, but the gardens were never completely finished and what was achieved drained her generous allowance to such an extent that she was in debt when she died.

Despite not getting on with her eldest son – a regular occurrence in the Hanoverian monarchy – Caroline had passed on her love of plants to Frederick, Prince of Wales, and also to her eldest daughter, the Princess Royal. When Robert Furber published his beautifully illustrated *Twelve Months of Flowers* in 1730, both the Prince of Wales and his sister were the leading subscribers and patrons. Gathering subscribers was a common way to raise money for publications and the female fascination with plants is highlighted by the fact that nearly 30 per cent of the book's subscribers were women, from duchesses down to a plain 'Miss'.

To avoid close contact with his parents, Frederick acquired a house at Kew, just a mile from Richmond Lodge. For the next twenty years he worked on establishing an informal garden, which ultimately was the death of him, since he developed a fatal chill after a spell outside in the winter of 1751. Once again, it was a husband's death that allowed his widow Augusta, another German princess, to work seriously on the development of the gardens at Kew with her adviser – possibly also her lover – the Earl of Bute. They not only extended the landscaping of the grounds, adding the famous Pagoda, but also built up a plant collection, particularly of exotics and trees, to rival any in the country. Bills from the 1760s show purchases ranging from hundreds of bulbs to orange, mango and cinnamon trees, and a 'Lott of New American Plants'.[2] A true plantswoman, Augusta insisted on the laying out of beds with plants in order of genus along Linnean principles. This collection of rare plants and trees at Kew was to form the basis for what became the Royal Botanic Gardens, the foremost institution of its type in the world.

For Augusta's daughter-in-law, Queen Charlotte, such an example gave her the opportunity to follow her own passions for plants and flowers. In 1798 she was reporting to her son Augustus on how busy she was with a new building project at Windsor.

According to your desire, Frogmore is no more called so but goes by the Name of the Queens Cottage, which is to be build there one

A sketch of a canna by Charlotte, Princess Royal (1766–1828) from 1783,
after John Miller, showing her skill in botanical drawing.

Day or other. The size of this little territory of mine is increased by
the King's goodness who has given me the long Elm Walk which
used to lead to Shaw Farm. It is now pailed in & the Plantations
begun, 4,000 Trees are already Planted & I hope to plant 2,000 more,
of my Spring Plantations I have lost but five Trees & every thing
thrives well. Wyatt the Architect has made me the prittiest plan
imaginable for a Gothic Cottage. It consists of the 4 rooms upon a
Floor besides the Towers of which there are 4, which will make 8
Closets alotted for Books, Plants, China, & one for the Flower
pieces painted by Miss Moser. There will be a Colonade the whole
length of the House which will make a sweet retirement in the
Summer all dressed out with Flowers. My imagination carries me
a great way & though I do not intend to begin building very soon,

yet do I fancy myself frequently in the new House, . . . and that
you find delight in looking over the Plants you sent, the last cargo
of which I received about a fortnight ago by Sir Henry Ingelby.[3]

Her philosophical nature when it came to the vagaries of the British
weather are to be envied. 'We have the mildest Winter possible,' she
told Augustus in February 1791, 'no Frost nor Snow, & everything in
Blossom, the Hazels, Lilacs, Primroses, Wall Flowers, Polyanthus, are
all out this present time, in Kew, Richmond & Windsor Gardens which
the Generality of People lament as they fear that April & March,
Easterly Winds will kill all the Blossoms. I am however of oppinion
that the best thing is to enjoy what I have & not to make myself
uneasy about things in which no human Power can direct.'[4]

The 'Generality of People' were right to be worried as not long
before this letter was written, Mrs Lybbe Powys wrote about the met-
eorological disaster that had befallen her garden. 'Our gamekeeper
measured a piece of ice from the pond on the 29th [January 1776]; it was
nine inches and a half thick. The beer and ale froze as they drew it, and
the cream was forced to be put in the oven to thaw before they could
churn it for butter, all my tender greenhouse plants died, did not save
one geranium, the oranges and myrtles not hurt, or any shrubs or
flower-roots out of doors, the snow no doubt preserved them.'[5]

The tough German princesses who married into the British royal
family did not allow such climatic extremes to deter them, and there
is no doubting the influence they had in laying the foundations for
Great Britain to become the leading nation in the world for gardens
and horticulture.

FOR THE LOVE OF GARDENING

One of the biggest social changes in eighteenth-century Britain was the emerging reality of leisure time for a far wider proportion of the population. Among the middling sorts, the home was now the centre of material consumption as domestic ornaments such as mirrors, china and paintings came within the price range of many families, as did garden design. While large estates were landscaped, smaller domestic gardens were laid out with beds to the side containing mixed plantings of perennials and shrubs. At the upper end of the social scale it was no longer just the aristocracy who could display the 'exotick' plants that were arriving in the country from the new world. The cultivation of these 'curious' varieties was taken up by the next tier of society – or rather by 'gentlemen', as women were thought not knowledgeable enough to be interested in them.

This attitude of exclusivity in gardening matters is just one example of the low status of women generally at that time. Whatever their social rank, women had few rights, and virtually none concerning their children and property. Divorce was rare and resulted in the woman being ostracised from society. Similarly, a wife who used separation as a means to escape an unhappy or abusive marriage normally found herself exiled to the depths of the countryside, where 'polite' people would not be forced to keep company with her. It is not surprising therefore that one such woman sought solace by creating a garden where she had to spend her enforced 'retirement'.

Henrietta St John had been forced into an arranged marriage in 1727 when she was twenty-eight, then thought a 'dangerously "mature"' age.[1] This was a common practice in upper-class families where such unions were agreed for dynastic or financial gain, and when the emotions of the bride were never considered. Henrietta did her duty and bore her husband, Robert Knight, later Lord Luxborough, two children, then struck up an unfortunate 'platonick' friendship with a young poet, John Dalton. This was seized upon by her husband as a reason to banish her to Barrells House in deepest Warwickshire

Henrietta, Lady Luxborough (1699–1756), found solace in gardening, having been banished to the country by her jealous husband.

without access to her children, with little money and, initially, without even contact with her friends.

The house at Barrells was virtually derelict and the garden was known only for 'the thistles and nettles that adorned this savage place'.[2] But Henrietta (or 'Heriott' as her favourite brother, Henry Bolingbroke, called her) had grown up among gardening women in Battersea, where her grandmother and mother had cultivated flowering plants familiar to us today, such as honeysuckle, larkspur and hollyhocks. This area south of the Thames was then in the countryside, well away from the hustle of central London, and the family had space for hotbeds to grow melons and walled gardens for peaches and apricots. Using the horticultural knowledge acquired in childhood, Henrietta went to work at Barrells and gained fame in gardening history by being probably the first person to use the simple but explicit term 'shrubbery'.

She used the word in a letter she wrote to the poet and gardener William Shenstone, on Easter Sunday in 1748. While shrubs were well known to nurserymen and gardeners, they were then generally referred to as 'flowering plants',[3] but within a few years Henrietta's term was in common use among those who could afford the outlay. Lady Mary Gregory, a close friend of Jemima Grey who gardened at Wrest Park, north of Luton in Bedfordshire, tells of a 'Mr Potter [who] had laid out £1200 on a shrubbery'. Creating such an area on your land had, she said, 'become a national disease',[4] and some grand examples were laid out at that time, including those of William Kent at Rousham House in Oxfordshire and Charles Hamilton at Painshill.

Despite her coining the term, Henrietta's own scheme was not on such a scale, and while the idea of a '*ferme ornée*', or ornamental farm, was popular, she wittily referred to hers as a '*ferme negligée*'. In addition to her 'few cows, sheep, etc', she also kept 'Turkies, ducks and chickens and guinea-fowl', and a varied vegetable plot, often from seeds provided by her brother, who always remained loyal to her. Lettuce, melon and cucumbers were a regular success.[5]

William Shenstone corresponded with Henrietta, encouraging her in her work at Barrells, from his famous garden at The Leasowes, Halesowen. The Revd Dr A. Carlyle described him as a 'large, heavy and fat man' who wore fashionable but completely impractical clothes for gardening, comprising a white outfit with silver lace, and his grey hair fashionably powdered and tied back. He appeared shy and reserved on first acquaintance, but opened up when encouraged into conversation, which was no doubt welcome to Henrietta on his occasional visits to Barrells.

Out of the wilderness Henrietta created a substantial garden. She had a ha-ha built to keep out encroaching animals, she marked out trees to create a visually exciting landscape while making no sacrifices in the space needed for flowers and fruit, she relished the challenge of placing a seat – or 'eye traps' as she called them – although she had few visitors to enjoy her vistas. She was no lover of 'exotics', which may have been as much to do with her limited budget as her personal taste, but she still managed to fill her beds with a long season of flowers, including a collection of florists' auriculas which she displayed on a fashionable 'theatre'.[6] She loved her guelder roses, which flowered in June and reminded her during one cold summer of snowballs, and equally enjoyed the flowers that she encouraged in her coppice, often using the word 'embroidery' to describe the carpet of cowslips, primroses, ragged robins, wild hyacinths in blue and white, and violets that would appear in the spring.

Lady Mary Coke was another woman who came to gardening as a result of a marital rift. A duke's daughter, she was married off in 1748, aged twenty-one, to Edward, Viscount Coke, heir to Thomas, 1st Earl of Leicester, of Holkham in Norfolk. The pair were seriously mismatched and the marriage was a disaster from the wedding night. Lady Mary was eventually given permission to live with her mother until Edward's death, which, luckily for her, happened just five years later. She never remarried, but enjoyed travelling and court life, the latter through her friendship with George II's daughter, HRH the Princess Amelia.

When she was fifty-one Lady Mary, who had been living near Windsor, bought the lease of a relatively modest villa west of London, Notting Hill House. On one side it was bordered by the home of the influential Fox family, Holland House, on another by the Uxbridge Road, giving good access to London; elsewhere Notting Hill was surrounded by fields. Lady Mary immediately set to work, opening up the views towards Hampstead and Highgate by having trees cut down, and she reinstated the kitchen garden which, according to her journal, was 'occupied by as large a crop of weeds as I ever saw'.[7] She was also unhappy with the carriage drive to the house, where 'you w'd not believe there had ever been gravel'. She blamed the gardener who came with the property, a Mr Lloyd, 'a most good for nothing Creature', and immediately hired a woman weeder to come in to tidy things up. This was nothing to do with sisterly unity but rather that she would have been the cheapest labour available for the task.

Having had things put in order, Lady Mary was determined to be a 'hands-on' gardener. This resulted in some all-too-familiar injuries such as splinters from rose thorns buried deep in her fingers. Always one to take advantage of her social connections, Lady Mary showed them to the eminent Dr William Hunter, best known as an anatomist but also obstetrician to Queen Charlotte. Having attended the Queen during many of her fifteen deliveries, Lady Mary thought that 'he might be as skilful in delivering one of a thorn, as he was on some other occasions'.[8]

Lady Mary's delightful journals show that she was as frustrated by gardening problems as any of us today. She complained, 'There's a thing called couch grass that plagues me excessively; it has overrun the border of shrubs in my North Walk.'[9] Notting Hill House was set high on Campden Hill and she lost newly planted shrubs to vicious easterly winds that swept across her gardens in the spring of 1768. Lady Mary was rather more patient than many gardeners would have been when one of her cows broke into the garden and ate almost all the young shrubs. "Tis vexatious, but these things are triffles.'[10]

Even more 'vexatious' were garden thefts, which goes to show that nothing much is new. One year all her plums were taken, 'of which I had great quantities', and the following year, while she was away, she was upset to get a letter from her gardener reporting that 'my Garden has been robbed, the frames broke open, three & twenty Tuberoses taken away, all my bell glass & other things'.[11] Tuberoses were much sought-after tender plants brought into the home to scent the air.

Neither was she simply a fair-weather gardener. 'Perpetual showers of rain' one spring did not stop her getting on with her planting. 'I am now so accustomed to be wet that it does not give me cold.'[12] However, she had to learn to be circumspect after she was reprimanded for working in her garden on the Sabbath. '[I] walked in my Garden till dinner & cou'd not help watering some sick plants, but I was quite afraid of being seen.'[13]

While she dressed for court in formal gowns of silk, such as the pale pink mantua that she wore for the portrait by Allan Ramsay in 1762, at home she was much more relaxed. This led to a panic one

June evening in 1769 when she saw the approaching coach of her friend Princess Amelia. One can almost hear her breathlessness: 'Thinking it might be HRH I threw off my working apron, ran up the Walk, & just in time enough to receive the Princess as she got out of her Coach.'[14]

Lady Mary's main supplier of plants was James Lee, who had started the Vineyard Nursery at Hammersmith. 'I have planted a hundred perannual flowers,' she confided to her sister in 1768, 'that I had this morning from Mr Lee.'[15] Since Lady Mary lived alone except for her staff it was natural that she should deal directly with nurserymen. It was, however, not uncommon in other households for the wife to do this, in addition to handling payments for seeds and plants together with gardeners' wages. At Belhus in Essex, for example, while Capability Brown and the owner, Lord Dacre, oversaw the big picture of the landscaping, Lady Dacre kept detailed records of seeds bought from James Gordon's shop in London's Fenchurch Street and plants from Samuel Driver in Lambeth.

Eventually it appears that Lady Mary was worn down by the continuing vandalism in the Notting Hill area and she moved to Chelsea, leaving the Notting Hill house empty until the lease expired two years later. No doubt the garden reverted to the neglected state it had been in when the lazy Mr Lloyd was in charge.

The biographer Jane Brown describes Henrietta, Lady Luxborough, as 'truly a gardener'[16] and the same could be said of Lady Mary Coke. Another woman of rank not content to leave the practical business of gardening to hired hands was Mary Lepell, Lady Hervey. In her youth, Lady Hervey and her husband John, 1st Earl of Bristol, had been leading courtiers to George I, but in later life, particularly after the death of her husband, Mary Lepell spent more time at the family home of

Ickworth in Suffolk. From there she wrote frequently to her friend the Revd Edmund Morris, confiding in him about her fondness for her garden: 'For these last three weeks, or indeed a month, I have been stuck as deeply in my garden as any of the plants I have set there, and I wish they may flourish half as well; for though I can't say I have run up in height, yet I have *spread* most luxuriantly.'[17]

She was writing in 1747, two years after her husband's death, when she took control of the design of a completely new area of the garden. Rose breeding had begun in earnest in the late seventeenth century when the Dutch and other new varieties became readily available from nurseries to tempt British gardeners. 'I have made a rosery; perhaps you will ask what that is: it is a collection of all the sorts of roses there are, which amount to fifty.' (Some seventy years later the editor of her letters thought that there were by then nearly five hundred varieties of rose available to buy, but there was in reality probably double that number on offer after the Dutch, and later the French, became enthusiastic rose breeders. Most are now lost to us.) The work involved in creating this new-fangled garden was clear: 'This rosery perhaps may bring me to an untimely end, but it is a very pretty thing: I have made the whole design of it myself. In the middle of it, raised above all the others, is one of the most *beautiful kind*, who, conscious of the right to possess that place, does not *blush* in doing so.'[18]

Gardeners often have strong likes and dislikes, and Lady Hervey was no exception. 'I approve of flowers and sweet shrubs for your garden,' she wrote to the Revd Morris in 1745, 'but pray what have you to do with exotics? They are things of little beauty, great expense, and only matters of curiosity. Pray stick to what will make your parterre gay to the eye and sweet to the nose.'[19]

Henrietta Luxborough's and Lady Hervey's dislike of exotics puts them out of step with horticultural fashion. These newly discovered species were beginning to flood in from the Americas and further afield, many of them tender and requiring the added expense and bother of stove and hothouses. This need for specialist treatment meant few women had the resources to grow them – and in some cases perhaps their attitude to these newcomers was more a question of what you have never had, you do not desire.

In the eighteenth-century salons of Mayfair there was usually more talk of politics than plants, but even here gardening was not seen as a mere 'accomplishment'. Intellectual writer Catherine Talbot (1721–70) wrote to her friend, the bluestocking Elizabeth Carter, about the joys of horticulture. 'Gardening is [one] of my delights; and I can amuse myself with projects for improving a quarter of an acre as much as if his Majesty had given me the care of Kensington Gardens. Our little spot has been so gay with flowers, it was enough to inspire one with good humour to look into it.'[20]

However, as so often happens, a gardener regularly frustrated her horticultural ambitions: 'I have but three creatures in the world over whom I have a right to exercise any government, a foolish dog, a restive horse, and a perverse gardener . . . In this my small dominion I meet with as many difficulties as ever indolent monarch did. The dog uncontrouled is for ever running after sheep, or jumping upon me with dirty paws; the horse will by no possible persuasion go over the same ground twice; and the gardener is demolishing my beds of flowers, which I meant to have had enlarged.'[21]

Elizabeth Carter's reply is one that still resonates with anyone who has ever crossed swords with that most truculent of breeds, the jobbing gardener. 'As to your gardener,' she wrote, 'he being a perverse human creature, I am utterly at a loss to give you any advice how to proceed with him, and you may rest satisfied no kind of argument you

Thomas Rowlandson's cartoon of 'Dr Syntax' and a catastrophe in the conservatory (*c.*1816), with the lady of the house having to deal with 'a foolish dog' for a change instead of the 'perverse gardener'.

can use, will ever convince him that you know better how to dispose the flower-beds than he does.'[22]

While the relationship between jobbing gardener and owner was often fraught, the relationship between garden owner and designer involved different degrees of deference. After the death of Capability Brown, the next designer to make a name for himself on the British landscape, albeit with a different style to Brown's, was Humphry Repton. Whereas Brown was as much a contractor as a designer, Repton, a talented artist, would present his clients with a 'Red Book' of before-and-after illustrations, enabling them to see his suggestions materialise instantly by the clever use of overlays. This imaginative sales pitch brought him fame, although few of his designs were ever realised. In 1789 Lady Salusbury, having control of the family purse after her husband's death, invited Repton to her London home in Upper Harley Street to discuss designs for a garden surrounding her new country home, Brandsbury, just outside London in the village of Willesden. Repton's description of their first meeting leaves little doubt as to who was in control of the interview:

> I was conducted to a room on the 2nd floor. No sooner was the door opened than I was salutd by the barking of half a dozen pet dogs, pups, lap dogs and spaniels all joined in a chorus with not less than 20 birds of various kinds exciting their lungs to their utmost pitch — thus surrounded I found one of the most dignified but pleasing ladies I ever beheld, her age was about 70 and she was dressed in the richest brocade — with treble ruffles of costly lace. She received me with all the kind and gracious manners of le vielle couer and she explained to me that she had lately purchased a little land in Middlesex, with a small house — and requested my opinion on paper, how the place could be improved by planting — for it was naked and wanted shade.[23]

This was an early commission for Repton and his initial reaction was to open up vistas towards the nearby hilltop villages of Hampstead and Highgate and down towards the City of London and Westminster, but this was not at all what Lady Salusbury had in mind. Could she please, Repton later noted, have 'more shade and less prospect'? More recently, it has been suggested that Repton's designs were too 'statesmanlike' for Lady Salusbury and her companion, Mrs Maud, and that it was necessary for him to adapt them to 'a more horticultural, ladylike landscape',[24] one implication being that, at the end of the eighteenth century, it was women who were interested in detailed planting whereas men were more concerned with the bigger picture.

For many, involvement with and a love of gardening often began in childhood, when, just as in adulthood, a garden can be a place in which to escape. Maria Edgeworth, best known as an author of children's literature and books on their education, is said to have had an unhappy childhood in which her father ignored her in favour of his new wife, whom he married in 1774 when Maria was six. Before she was twelve, Maria was gardening at the school she attended in Derby before the family's move to Ireland and, once settled there, Maria's father, Richard Lovell Edgeworth, gave each of his children a plot of their own. Maria's was so close to the house that she could see it from her bedroom window. She tended it with devotion, and became a committed gardener for the rest of her life.

One of Richard Edgeworth's close friends was John Foster of Collon in County Louth, who was a keen plantsman and instrumental in the opening of the (Royal) Dublin Society's botanical garden at Glasnevin. Maria began corresponding with Foster, who was also a keen collector of 'new' plants from America, and he sent her twelve rhododendron plants 'in perfect health and most freshness', which she hastily planted. Despite the risks associated with transporting plants, Maria's later letters are peppered with requests to her friends to help her out with new supplies.

After her father's death, Maria had even more time for her own garden, and her enthusiasm was obvious: 'Never was Bess Ruxton [her cousin's wife] more red-hot about any new fancy as I am at this moment about my garden . . . I am very happy building castles of flowers in it.' Even crises led to new solutions. 'All my everblowers [roses] have perished for want of something to support their backs – and I am now making a spick and span new trellis – digging up, trenching, manuring my garden – a total revolution.'[25]

Edgeworth was keen to learn about planting schemes. We know that she owned a copy of Maria Jacson's book, *The Florist's Manual: Hints for the Construction of a Gay Flower-Garden*, which she generously sent to her friend and gardening correspondent Lady Granard at her home, Castle Forbes, in County Longford, in return for gifts of china roses, double-flowering periwinkles and scarlet *Lychnis chalcedonica*.

In addition to the plants sent by Lady Granard, Maria collected carnations, roses, highly prized camellias and many more. Several American friends sent her seeds which she swapped for yet more with John Foster, now Lord Oriel. He sent her a Chinese double pink tree peony, seeds of which had originally been brought to Kew by Sir Joseph Banks in 1789. It came with helpful advice on its culture and delighted Edgeworth with a profusion of flowers every year; it was a gift she never forgot. 'My peony tree is the most beautiful thing on earth,' she wrote to her aunt in 1830, '9 flowers will be in full blow next week. Poor dear Lord Oriel gave it me and his own is dead and he is dead. But love for him still lives in me.'[26] Towards the end of her own life, Maria Edgeworth still had the true gardener's optimism that she would see her plans come to fruition, drawing them up while on her sickbed, and then, aged seventy-eight, going out into the garden in February to plant roses.

AUTUMN FLOWERINGS

The traditional view of nineteenth-century women and gardening is often of an extremely passive pastime. They were frequently portrayed sitting in their gardens, often reading, sometimes talking, and occasionally even asleep. It is all very sedate and ladylike and rarely shows any active participation in the physical work of creating the gardens they are pictured in, but this belies what was actually going on in domestic gardens. While many women in the burgeoning middle classes would undoubtedly have had paid help from the likes of a jobbing gardener to deal with the heavy work, the success of books aimed at female gardeners suggests that women were active participants in the creation of their gardens.

There is no doubt that money, family connections and good partnerships have created some of the best gardens, and one great example of this truism is Biddulph Grange, near Stoke-on-Trent. Its owner was James Bateman, the scion of a wealthy family. He had been known as a bit of a dandy during his time at Oxford in the early 1830s, but it was there that he became passionate about the orchid, then a relatively new introduction to England. By the time he married Maria Warburton in 1838, he had already used some of his wealth to start work on one of the biggest horticultural books ever published, *Orchidaceae of Mexico and Guatemala*, and his wife was an expert botanist, the sister of Peter Egerton Warburton, who had created the garden at Arley Hall, Cheshire, and she had her own passion for hardy plants.

In 1840 James Bateman bought the estate of Biddulph Grange and set about building the requisite enormous mansion, and he also began with Maria to establish a sumptuous garden. They knew Edward Cooke, an artist and gardener who was the son-in-law of one of the greatest nurserymen of the time, George Loddiges, whose Hackney nursery was famous for its quantity and quality of rare plants. Together with Cooke, James and Maria Bateman created the gardens across the fifteen-acre site, incorporating a dahlia walk, a Chinese temple surrounded by Japanese maples, a grotto and subterranean passage, and 'masses of evergreens'. Eventually the upkeep of Biddulph became too much even for this passionate pair and they passed the estate to their son and retired to Worthing, where, both in their seventies, they created a new – smaller – garden.

While there were few major gardens created solely by women in the mid-nineteenth century, all that was about to change as a result of the efforts of just one woman who came to dominate garden design for the rest of the century and beyond. Although the details of her life are well documented and thousands of words have been written about Gertrude Jekyll, only a handful of her gardens still survive. Her achievements stay alive through her own writing, together with her detailed border plans and sketches, all of which are a reminder of her feistiness and strong opinions.

When writing about Jekyll, it is hard not to resort to all the usual clichés. Anyone with even the slightest interest in horticulture knows about her myopia, her talent for painting which had to be channelled into gardening, and her friendship with Edwin Lutyens. It is not surprising that when one mentions women and gardening history the first name to be uttered, even by non-gardeners, is Gertrude Jekyll. Her style of planting in swathes of colour and form still influences our borders, a seemingly infinite legacy. Beth Chatto claims that Jekyll was one of the three greatest influences on her own gardening life (the other two being the painter Cedric Morris, and her friend and sparring partner Christopher Lloyd). The television gardener and Chelsea gold medal winner Chris Beardshaw admits to tracing over Jekyll's detailed, beautifully coloured plans to allow him to absorb her talent for 'flow' in a border. Her books, most written well over a hundred years ago,

Gertrude Jekyll (1843–1932) in Deanery Gardens, Sonning, Berkshire, a perfect partnership of her planting and the house, built in 1901 by her friend Edwin Lutyens.

remain relevant and readable, causing any serious gardener, when considering a new plant or placement, to think, 'I wonder what Jekyll thought of this, what was her experience of growing that?'

When Gertrude Jekyll first published her famous work, *Wood & Garden*, in 1899 it was subtitled 'Notes and Thoughts, Practical and Critical, of a Working Amateur'. She was an amateur in the strictest sense of the word as she had received no official training in horticulture, simply because there would have been none available to her; however, she was making it acceptable for respectable women to become professional by earning money, not just by writing about gardens or illustrating plants but also by designing beds and borders and whole garden schemes.

Jekyll was used to wearing the yoke of 'amateurism'. As a young woman she exhibited embroideries of fruit and flowers that were so highly admired by Lord Leighton that he found it hard to believe they were the work of an 'amateur' and presumed the designs 'must have been borrowed'. 'I want very much to know ...' he continued, 'whether Miss J does these things solely for her delight (being as I understand a lady of independent means) or whether they are accessible to outside admirers.'[1]

There was no malice behind Lord Leighton's comments; he was genuinely impressed by the outstanding detail and colour composition in Miss Jekyll's work. A commission for an embroidered tablecloth followed and this 'lady of independent means' might well have continued as a talented artist and embroiderer had not her eyesight failed her, forcing her to turn to a wider canvas and begin a career in garden design. This, together with her writing, places her almost without criticism at the head of the gardening 'royal family', the Queen Victoria of horticulture. Her friendship and professional partnership with Lutyens, twenty-six years her junior, is justly famous.

Her biographer, Jane Brown, catalogues 112 gardens they worked on jointly, a list that does not include several hundred others not associated with Lutyens. Her designs were really detailed planting plans, as her income came from the sale of the suggested list of plants which she would supply to her clients from her nursery at Munstead Wood, rather than from design fees. In 1910, for example, over twelve hundred plants were sent to Sir George Sitwell's garden, and the following year six hundred went to Roger Fry's.

Although there is a tendency to think that Jekyll turned to gardening only when her sight started to fail, she had been collecting plants since a family visit to the Mediterranean when she was twenty. She met William Robinson, horticultural author and critic of Victorian bedding practices, some ten years after that, but as later planting plans showed she did not entirely approve of his 'wild' gardening theories.

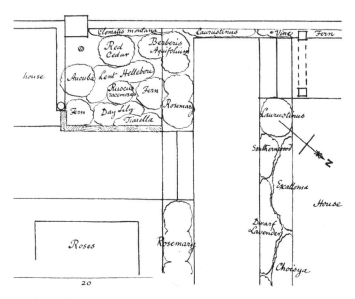

A section of Gertrude Jekyll's characteristic border plans for Millmead, Bramley in Surrey. Jekyll never charged for her designs but provided the plants from her nursery.

This notwithstanding, she was happy to contribute articles to his magazine, *The Garden*, from 1881 and she carried on with her journalism for the rest of her life. In her early forties, Jekyll took up the new hobby of photography, and no doubt took pictures of her award-winning flower arrangements at the RHS shows. She also began to enter plants she had raised herself for awards.

She loved the Mediterranean and it was on the way back from a trip to Capri in 1883 that she bought the pair of 'Balmoral' gardening boots in Paris which were to be immortalised by the artist William Nicholson in 1920. Called 'Balmoral' because they were supposedly the style favoured by Prince Albert when he was at the Scottish castle, the pair lasted Miss Jekyll for fifty years. She had them regularly repaired rather than have to wear a new pair in. 'I suppose no horse likes a new collar; I am quite sure I do not like new boots.'[2]

In 1995 Margaret Thorne wrote of her memories of meeting Miss Jekyll when she was a young horticultural student just after the First World War. A group of pupils from the School of Nature Study and Gardening near Worthing were taken to Munstead to meet the great lady. They were welcomed by the housekeeper, who told them they were to go round the garden and each pick something that interested them. Accompanied by the gardener, 'a dear old man in a bowler hat', they did as they were told. Later that afternoon, the girls found Miss Jekyll sitting just as she did in her famous portrait, by this stage completely blind. 'One by one we put our bits of plants in her hands. She felt them and smelt them and then without hesitation named them and told us about them. It was an unforgettable experience.'[3]

'Does your sister *never* remember time [when she's] in the Jap Garden?' Andrew Lang complained to Alice Stewart about his friend Ella Christie one day when he was hungry for his lunch.[4] It is a familiar refrain from any gardener's spouse or companion, as time can disappear when one is in the grip of an obsession, whether it proves glorious or ruinous. Isabella – Ella – Christie's obsession was the Japanese garden which she created in the grounds of her home at Cowden Castle, Perthshire.

Ella and Alice were born in the 1860s, daughters of a wealthy Scottish coal-mine owner whom Ella looked after when her mother died. He repaid her care by leaving everything to a local orphanage after his death, but she and Alice, by then a widow, contested the will on grounds of insanity and they eventually settled on sharing the estate with the orphanage. Ella had travelled a great deal with her parents to Europe, and once freed from any ties at home she became an intrepid traveller. Arriving in India in 1904 with her maid, Humphries, and armed with letters of introduction to the wealthy and influential, Ella began something of a royal progress across the Far East, moving on to Ceylon, Malaya, Kashmir and Tibet. Sheltering from the snow at the 16,700-foot Chorbat Pass where her party camped, she kept warm by wearing all her available clothes, hugging a hot-water bottle and drinking cherry brandy, which, one hopes, she shared with her hapless maid if not with her bearers.

However, it was a trip to Japan, which she visited as well as China and Korea in 1907, that changed her forever. She was captivated by the Japanese style of gardening and determined to recreate its beauty and serenity back home in Perthshire. Writing from the Imperial Hotel in Kyoto, she described to her sister some of the plants which had stunned her. 'The Belgian Legation,' she noted enviously, 'has an azalea garden just coming into a blaze of red, and this morning I went to see a temple on which is a show with wistaria, the flowers about eighteen inches long and trained on verandahs over the water.' Here Ella illustrates that it was the plants as well as the form of the gardens with their controlled trees and carefully placed rocks that so entranced her.

> I think the great secret of the Japanese talent for gardens lies in their superlative powers of imitation. The gardens were first copied from the Chinese, and then improved upon the lines of nature till one can scarcely see where the artificial and natural join. I have seen one in the making and it is most curious, out of a villa strip to find in a month that the whole thing is laid out with all the marks of positive antiquity. Not a plant looks as if it had ever been moved and the mossy stones go on mossing, whereas with us if one disturbs such you know the effect is a withered look within a few days.[5]

Christie was not the only British woman to be enthralled by this highly stylised and, to many Western eyes, artificial way of gardening. The du Cane sisters, Ella and Florence, unusually independent female travellers, were there at the same time, complete with easels and paintbrushes, capturing the very look that Ella Christie so admired. This resulted, when they got back to England, in a book, *The Flowers and Gardens of Japan* (1908). They were to follow this with similar volumes on the flora of Madeira and of the Canary Islands. They also knew of Ella Christie's plans for when she returned to Scotland. 'If feasible,' she schemed, 'I shall bring a Jap home to lay out my pond. It could be made a dream of beauty . . .'[6]

When she got back to Perthshire she started to turn the dream into reality, having invited a female Japanese designer, Taki Hionda from Nagoya's Royal School of Garden Design, to assist her. Ella later described the process of creating the garden out of a marshy field that flooded in winter. First a lake was formed by damming an offending ditch. 'For six weeks [Hionda] toiled and planned while shapeless mounds arose and stones were sought for and placed in the orthodox grouping . . . No mis-shapen or broken stone was made use of, and in the same manner no mountain stone was used near water . . . This grouping was a work of art, based on the strict observance of nature's methods and a conventional rule.'[7]

Ella imported a large stone lantern from Nippon which arrived with a letter from the shippers pointing out that 'the moss with which it is well covered will be dry after the long journey; kindly thoroughly wet this with warm water in which enough raw rice has been washed to make the water look milky'.[8] A Shinto shrine was added, and the essential tea house placed on an island in the middle of the lake where Ella would entertain her friends and the gardeners who visited her from across the world.

Christie was advised on the upkeep of the garden by a well-known expert, Professor Susuki, on his occasional visits to Britain to root-prune Kew's Japanese shrubs. With dwarf specimens his advice was to 'plant them first in a big pot, then smaller and smaller by gradually winding roots smaller up [sic]'.[9] The professor's credentials were impeccable as he was the Eighteenth Hereditary Head of the Soami School of Imperial Design. He approved of the design at Cowden with one proviso: 'My learned friend who visited the garden declares it is best in the Western world, except for bridge, which he thinks is just like flaw in precious gem. It is matter of regret to me to leave even one thing wrong in garden that I concerned . . . I leave it to you to consider alteration of wrong to right.' Not surprisingly, Ella altered the offending bridge across the lake, changing it from a straight run to a zigzag design known as 'Yatsuhashi'.[10]

Ella Christie looked after the garden herself and in the cold weather could be found working away outside, wearing her garden coat lined with 'the tummies of her own grey squirrels'.[11] She eventually found a Japanese gardener, Matsuo, willing to live what must have been a very isolated life maintaining the garden. He was with her for eleven years until his death. Although Matsuo had little English and Ella no Japanese, they still somehow managed to communicate through a series of 'signs and wonders'.

Ella Christie died in 1949 and Cowden Castle was demolished in 1952. The garden was vandalised in the 1960s when the bridges and tea house were burned down, and although it has never been restored, her great-nephew, Sir Robert Stewart of Arndean, has plans to clear the overgrown lake. Christie would have been heartbroken to see the garden in such a state, but she would have recognised that her obsession could in turn be both glorious and ruinous.

By the time Jekyll and Christie had died, a new generation of 'amateur professionals' – talented gardeners with no formal training – were carving out careers for themselves, and in several cases became world leaders in garden design. One of these, Norah Lindsay, like many women, discovered her interest in gardening after the birth of her children, Nancy, born in 1896, and David, in 1900. The garden at her home at Sutton Courtney in Berkshire should have conformed to the sort favoured by Gertrude Jekyll, with controlled groupings of herbaceous plants, but Lindsay was happy to let seedlings lie, despite her sister Anne's disapproval. 'We found Sutton looking very pretty, masses of roses and poppies and lilies and delphiniums, but all very untidy. I never think they make the most of that lovely garden, it ought to be a blaze of colour, very bright and rather formal, where it is always too thin and weedy.'[12]

During the Edwardian period, Norah Lindsay gardened against a background of high society and a whirl of entertaining. She was intelligent, amusing and beautiful and could easily have stayed on the

The pool and fountain of the Long Garden at Sutton Courtney, home to garden designer Norah Lindsay (1873–1948), as it appeared in *Country Life* in 1930.

society pages but for the almost inevitable marital problems that came out of the traumas of the First World War. By 1918 the Lindsay marriage was over and the couple separated, with Norah being allowed to stay on at Sutton Courtney. Her finances were so precarious that she turned to the only marketable talent she had, which was for garden design. She began offering her services to her society friends in 1924, when she was fifty-one, which led to her being involved with over one hundred gardens in the course of her career. She usually advised on the planting of herbaceous borders, but unlike Jekyll she was not prepared to draw up plans for gardens she had never seen. Instead she accepted retainer fees from her clients before travelling across the country to view the sites, usually taking public transport to save money. An Edwardian *grande dame* she may have been, but she was also an individualist whose style was greatly admired and, such was her eye for colour, she was soon being asked to help with the planting schemes of gardens such as Trent Park, Blickling Hall, Cliveden, Gleneagles and Mottisfont Abbey. Vita Sackville-West was reputedly jealous of Lindsay's skills.

Norah's closest friendship was with the reclusive Lawrence Johnston at Hidcote in Gloucestershire, where they worked together developing his garden throughout the 1930s. After the Second World War, Johnston wanted to retire to the South of France and was in the process of giving Hidcote to Lindsay when she died suddenly in 1948. Instead, it became the first garden to be acquired by the National Trust, which now keeps Hidcote in an immaculate condition, although one suspects that the gardens might have developed very differently had Lindsay lived longer. She described the 'relaxed' untidiness of her own garden in one of only three short pieces of writing she ever published, which appeared in *Country Life* in 1931: 'In a garden where labour is scarce and the soil beneficent, all manner of tiny seedlings get overlooked till, lo and behold! A handsome clump has established itself in the most unlikely position, claiming squatter's rights and in nine cases out of ten succeeding in establishing its claim.' She goes on to describe the cooling influence of water features in a garden. 'All the walks at Sutton Courtney end in pools or fountains with near-by seats to enjoy the different music's. How delicious on a boiling June day, after an arduous hour of tying-up the heavy and contrary heads of the regal poppies, to relax and merely sit and listen.'[13]

Norah Lindsay's daughter, Nancy, an eccentric of a different sort, looked after the garden at Sutton Courtney for a while but then, according to Jane Brown, she sullied her reputation on a plant-hunting expedition to Persia 'when she was delayed too long in a silken tent'.[14] She was a skilled gardener and plantswoman but her lifestyle took its toll of her horticultural talents. After her mother's death, she sought to advise the National Trust on the garden at Hidcote but disagreed with them over its upkeep, and reputedly burned the records that her mother and Johnston had kept of the planting plans. She then retreated to her home at Manor House Cottage in Sutton Courtney, where she continued to grow old roses, many of which she had collected during her time in Persia.

Lawrence Johnston continued to keep himself very much to himself after Norah Lindsay died, seeing only a small circle of gardening friends, including Phyllis Reiss, who had been his near neighbour at Dowdeswell Manor near Cheltenham. In 1933 she moved with her husband to Tintinhull in Somerset and there created a garden to her own taste.

Tintinhull is a seventeenth-century hamstone house to which a handsome frontage was added on the garden side in the eighteenth century. Although Mrs Reiss had no formal gardening education she had travelled widely, especially in Italy, and looked at her garden with the eye of an architect rather than a plantswoman. The shape of the garden at Tintinhull was already laid out, but she refined this, carving out compartments using yew hedges and choosing plants for all aspects of their habit, not just shape and colour but leaf density as well. In the weeks before the start of the Second World War, Mrs Reiss's talents were well enough known for her to be invited by the BBC to make two broadcasts on the design and development of Tintinhull. The death of a nephew in the war caused her to create a memorial to him of a garden set around a canal water feature flanked by one pale-coloured and one 'hot' border, her last major addition to Tintinhull.

By the 1950s, the garden at Tintinhull was gaining great acclaim from the gardening *cognoscenti*. Lanning Roper called it 'no ordinary garden' and landscape designer Sylvia Crowe was also full of praise for the way Mrs Reiss's skilful planting design tricked the eye into thinking it was larger than the two acres it actually covered. Crowe had watched the garden and Mrs Reiss's talents develop while she was working for Mrs Reiss's father after graduating from Swanley Horticultural College. In 1954 Mrs Reiss gave Tintinhull to the National Trust, but continued to live there until her death in 1961. Since then the garden has been cared for by a variety of tenants, but it thrived particularly under the stewardship of the garden designer and historian Penelope Hobhouse between 1980 and 1993. Together with her husband, Professor John Malins, Hobhouse worked with special care on the planting of the large terracotta pots, and on developing an arboretum beyond the kitchen garden in the old orchard.

Many women have been drawn to garden design after raising their families, and Rosemary Verey is one of them. She had had to break off from her degree course at University College London in 1939, then marriage and children followed quickly after the war. She settled into the family home of Barnsley House in Gloucestershire, ready for a life of hunting and horses, never imagining that in her seventies she would be one of the world's most highly regarded garden designers, working with pop stars and royalty, moving between European palaces and the west coast of America.

As Verey's children grew, so did her interest in the garden, grassed over by former occupants. She was much encouraged by her husband, David, an architectural historian, and by a fortuitous present from her son, Charles, in 1962 — membership of the RHS. Armed with another gift in the shape of a garden diary from her daughter, Davina, and a copy of Russell Page's *The Education of a Gardener*, she began the transformation of the main borders around the house. Verey was influenced by the Lindsay borders at Sutton Courtney and used ideas from there for her first two plantings, although the second one was based more on her own ideas. She is a great believer in keeping records of plantings and her notebooks proved invaluable over the years as her ideas changed and matured.

It was a visit in 1975 to Villandry in France with its medieval-style walled gardens that inspired her best-known contribution to gardening fashion, the 'potager', a design of a captivating mixture of flowers and vegetables, which Verey makes deceptively simple to produce. In 1979 work began at Barnsley on what was to become a seminal garden design, and the following year Verey co-authored *The Englishwoman's Garden* with her friend and neighbour Alvilde Lees-Milne, which became an instant hit. It was one of the first books to combine knowledgeable writing with a beautiful array of inspiring photographs of gardens.

When the garden opened to the public, it was clear that Verey had achieved something special and Barnsley spawned thousands of small-scale imitations, few of which succeeded because the genius of a true innovator is to disguise the amount of hard work which lies behind their creation. High-profile design commissions followed, including helping HRH the Prince of Wales at Highgrove, which in turn undoubtedly helped Verey secure much overseas work. To many she was the queen of gardening during the 1980s and 1990s, so influential in garden design and planting choice that her name on a book or as a speaker guarantees success.

BREAKING NEW GROUND

In the more specialised branches of garden design such as landscape architecture, women made few inroads in the first half of the twentieth century, although there are exceptions. Lady Marjorie Allen was the first woman to be elected a fellow of the Institute of Landscape Architects in 1930, but her devotion to the rights of children and the development of playground areas led her away from mainstream horticulture. However, two graduates from Swanley Horticultural College, the first of the women-only institutions, did have a wider public impact than could possibly have been imagined even a decade earlier. Brenda Colvin and Sylvia Crowe met at Swanley just after the First World War. While Crowe worked as a garden designer for a nursery in Barnet until the Second World War, the more wide-reaching scope of landscape architecture immediately attracted Colvin, and she started her own practice in 1922. After the war Crowe also moved towards landscape architecture, working alongside but not with Colvin. They both not only achieved enormous success in their careers but became hugely influential among the profession, ignoring any barriers and letting their work speak for itself.

Brenda Colvin went to Swanley in 1919 after a peripatetic education in India and England, and in France where she had taken art classes. Her first horticultural interest was in growing fruit, but once at Swanley she became intrigued by Madeline Agar's classes in garden design. Here, she realised, was the opportunity to bring together her taste for design and the outdoor life, and in her second year she switched courses and became absorbed and stimulated by Agar's ideas.

Agar, who was a pioneer of landscape design and had had to go to America to study it, was by now busy with her own practice, and an inexperienced student not much older than her classmates replaced Agar at Swanley, much to the horror of Colvin and her fellow pupils. 'The last straw for our small group of garden design students came when our youthful tutor produced, instead of . . . instruction on triangulation, a bowl of water and some Plasticine and set us to kindergarten exercises in model making.'[1] The students, led by Colvin, rebelled and took private tuition from Miss Agar.

Soon afterwards Colvin joined Miss Agar as a clerk of works and site assistant on the war memorial garden at Wimbledon, and before long Brenda found that friends and relatives were offering her small freelance jobs so that a 'small but satisfying livelihood was available' despite the very low fees.[2] After two years learning at Miss Agar's side, Colvin left to establish her own practice. It eventually thrived, though she was the first to admit that the early 1930s were difficult, and by 1939 she had advised on some three hundred gardens, including some in America.

One of Colvin's largest projects was an addition to the Archduke Charles Albert Habsburg's garden at Zywiec in Poland in the late 1930s. In a marvellously sweeping statement in 1979 she explained how the fate of this garden pushed her towards designing open spaces for public and industrial organisations. '[I] have heard . . . the place was over-run by German troops and later became a Russian barrack, so regard it as typical of what happens to private garden work.'[3] Hardly the fate of the average suburban garden, but enough to make Colvin feel that public garden work had a 'greater hope of survival'.[4] Her move into the public sector after the Second World War is rightly lauded, and she remained adamant that the private work of the landscape designer is often lost through changes of ownership or by pure neglect.

Unlike the working gardener, the job of a landscape gardener changed from day to day and required a much broader knowledge than mere horticulture. Colvin and Crowe remembered that their work ranged from 'the design of window boxes to the planning of school grounds in a county . . . Candidates for our profession require a sound knowledge of such diverse subjects as drains, hydrangeas, gravel pits, roof gardens, slag heaps, herbs and bulldozers.'[5]

Sylvia Crowe had gone to Swanley the year after Brenda Colvin, but they shared an early interest in fruit growing. Sylvia's father had retired to grow fruit in Sussex and the family travelled to Europe a great deal. One of Sylvia's earliest memories was of spending her fourth birthday in a forest in Corsica, sitting and 'revelling in a carpet of wild cyclamen',[6] and by the time she was seven she knew she wanted to be a garden designer, quite an unusual aspiration for an Edwardian child. After Swanley, Sylvia spent four years in Italy with her parents, then undertook two years' training with landscape gardener Edward White (which included making Plasticine models of contoured landscapes), after which she was able to realise her ambition.

A job as a garden designer at William Cutbush's nurseries in Barnet brought Sylvia the chance to show at the Chelsea Flower Show, where she won a coveted gold medal in 1937 with a design of a bluebell wood and a stream running into a pond. Given the formality of interwar, and much post-war, garden design, Sylvia's plan appears to have been ahead of its time in anticipating the joy of the 'naturalist' schemes to come.

After the war Crowe set up her own practice, sharing offices with her old friend Brenda Colvin. They were never formal partners, but together occupied cramped rooms in Gloucester Place, near Baker Street, with their young assistants and sheets and sheets of design documents. Crowe was heaped with honours from British, American and Australian landscape institutions. In 1973, she was made a Dame of the British Empire, the first landscape designer to have been so honoured since Sir Joseph Paxton, famed creator of the Crystal Palace, received his knighthood 122 years earlier. Needless to say, she was the first woman to achieve such recognition. Rather shamefully, it took the RHS nearly twenty more years to award her the Victoria Medal of Honour, when she was eighty-eight.

Many of the projects that Colvin and Crowe worked on, such as Harlow New Town or industrial landscaping around the power stations at Stourport and Rugeley, seem light years away from the gentle and genteel advice given to lady gardeners by Jane Loudon, the most important female horticultural writer of the early nineteenth century, or even from the designs of Gertrude Jekyll, yet they are all linked by one common ideal. In old age, Dame Sylvia Crowe said, 'I have enjoyed being a landscape architect; I would not have wanted to be anything else.'

Such a sentiment would have been understood by Kitty Lloyd Jones, although she was never to achieve the success of Colvin or Crowe during her long career as a garden designer. Lloyd Jones had started her training at the Practical Gardening School of the Royal Botanic Society in Regent's Park just after the First World War, following that with a B.Sc. in horticulture and a National Diploma in horticulture, both from Reading University. Despite being a prize-winning and exceptional student, she was unable to find work as a professional gardener when she graduated in 1925, so she took on a job teaching the daughter of one of the Balfour family. This apparently lowly position did lead to her making other connections within the political world, and brought Lloyd Jones a commission from Lady Gladstone to design a hundred-yard-long, twenty-foot-wide border at Dane End House in Hertfordshire, which also brought the use of a cottage close by where she was able to live for the next six years.

Once she had got her foot on the ladder, it was not long before other well-connected families began to ask her to design and supervise garden projects for them. This was a two-edged sword, however, for while the offers invariably came with invitations to stay at their homes (Lloyd Jones's writing case was full of engraved notepaper from grand addresses across the country), often her hosts expected advice to be given in exchange for little more than free board and lodging, and the owners of these grand houses often claimed the credit for the work themselves. However, Lloyd Jones did work throughout Britain and abroad, from the gardens at Achamore on the Island of Gigha to the chateau of Courances near Fontainebleau. She also contributed a design for a rose garden at Greys Court near Henley-on-Thames.

Lloyd Jones was not good at keeping accounts, but it has been estimated that she had an annual income of between £200 and £400 a year, similar to a female college gardener at Cambridge at that time, but without the security or accommodation. She was always having to chase payments and ran a small nursery to augment her consultancy fees. As with so many women who chose horticulture as a full-time career, she never married, although she is reputed to have had a close friendship with Sir James Horlick, owner of Achamore. Her modesty has meant that little of her work was properly recorded, but her achievements during her lifetime were admirable.

A GROWING LEGACY

It would be impossible to name all the women who work professionally in horticulture as designers or garden creators today. Female students always outnumber male at garden design schools, and a new generation of women continues to push the boundaries forward, most with excellent qualifications. Some have to resort to pure grit and determination, as the Duchess of Northumberland did when her plans for Alnwick with its eclectic mixture of bamboo labyrinth, poison garden and twenty-first-century grand cascade initially met with fierce opposition.

The duchess aimed to create something on a scale not seen for over a century. Armed only with the experience of a three-week garden design course at John Brookes's Denman garden near Chichester, and the creation of two modest gardens at her previous home at Chatton Park, sixteen miles north of Alnwick, she realised that she would need to commission a professional designer for the new garden. After many false starts the job finally went to the Belgian designers Jacques and Peter Wirts, and Louis Benech from France. But it was the duchess's personal dream together with inspiration and perspiration that finally brought the Alnwick Garden into reality, making it one of the most visited in Britain, with half a million visitors during 2008.

However, garden visiting is not a new pastime. Since the mid-eighteenth century the gardens and grounds of large properties such as Painshill, Charles Hamilton's estate in Surrey, and William Shenstone's The Leasowes near Birmingham had welcomed visitors. Such was the popularity of these visits that Mrs Joel-Henrietta Pye wrote a short guidebook, *A Peep into the Principal Seats and Gardens in and About Twickenham*, in 1775. She aimed her book at young women in particular as she felt that garden visiting for them was the equivalent of doing the 'Grand Tour' for 'our young gentlemen', and she expressed concern that they tended to do so 'without answering any other end than barely saying they have been there; but neither receiving any instruction from it themselves, nor rendering their conversation more amusing'.[1] Visiting other people's gardens was then, and is even more so now, one of the best ways to learn about plants and design, and today more open their gates to the public each year.

One garden which has been a place of pilgrimage since 1938 is Sissinghurst, Vita Sackville-West's creation in Kent, which attracts hundreds of thousands of visitors every year from all over the world. Such numbers were not imagined at its first opening, when the entry fee was a shilling per head and over £25 had been raised by the end of the day, leading Vita to name the new stream of visitors 'the shillingses'.

Sackville-West has left such a legacy to gardening history that it is impossible to think about garden development in the twentieth century without her; like Gertrude Jekyll, she is synonymous with British gardening at its best, but her early life gave no hint that she would establish such a reputation. She had hoped to inherit Knole, the magnificent Tudor estate in Sevenoaks, Kent, where she was brought up, and was devastated when it passed to a male cousin on the death of her father. After her marriage to Harold Nicolson they acquired Sissinghurst Castle, complete with derelict garden and sixteenth-century tower, moving there when she was thirty-eight. As with many gardening couples, the work was shared, Nicolson concentrating on the design and his wife on the plants, aiming to achieve 'the strictest formality of design, with the maximum informality in planting'. Possibly her most famous creation was the legendary White Garden, planted with *Rosa mulliganii*, phlox, agapanthus and lilies, and a carpet of grey- and silver-leaved plants which has inspired thousands of 'white' gardens and 'gardens with rooms' across the world. The Rose Garden is justifiably renowned for its collection of long-lost favourites, including the delicious *R.* 'Souvenir du Docteur Jamain' with its confection of velvety-maroon cupped blooms, which Vita discovered in an old nursery.

While Sissinghurst spawned the fashion for pastels and purples, in spring its Cottage Garden has always been ablaze with the hot colours of wallflowers and tulips, and the gardeners there are courageous: 'You want to have it jam-packed, as solid as we can get it. And get every shade if we can. We simply don't worry if this doesn't go with that,' says deputy head gardener Wendy Tremenheere. 'It is important that it doesn't end up all yellow. But it doesn't matter where things go, because they are all within that same orange, yellow and red range.'[2]

Sackville-West, already a successful poet and author, brought her gardening experiences to life in her column in the *Observer*, which appeared regularly between 1946 and 1961. These popular weekly articles, many reproduced in four collections, have similarities to a modern gardening blog. Sackville-West herself admitted that she 'quailed at their incompleteness, their repetitiveness, and also at the haphazard way they had been dotted about the years',[3] but what her reading public

Vita Sackville-West (1892–1962) in 1960, by which time her reputation
as an inspirational gardener and writer was established.

loved was her practicality and 'down-to-earthiness', writing about
plants which ordinary gardeners longed to try themselves. She received
a continuous stream of enquiries – one week she received two thousand after one particular article – the letters arriving neatly tied with
string in bundles of fifty. Many of her readers struggled to find the
plants she was describing, one writing to her in frustration that 'I tried
to get *Metasequoia glyptostroboides* in the horticultural department at the
Army and Navy Stores, but they didn't seem ever to have heard of it,'[4]
which led Vita to include in the later volumes lists of specialist nurserymen, some long gone but some familiar to this day.

In my own well-thumbed copy of *More for Your Garden*, the third collection of her articles published in 1955, a previous owner of the book
has written some stanzas from Sackville-West's poem 'The Garden' on

the inside cover, suggestive of her hold on the imaginations of her devoted readers. Perhaps even more than Jekyll, reams have been written about Sackville-West the gardener, and even more about the complexities of her private life. Both aspects of her character prove her to have been a risk-taker, a woman of aristocratic hauteur striding around Sissinghurst in jodhpurs and laced riding boots, but it is the confidence with which she planted her extraordinary garden that has been her lasting legacy.

Although Sackville-West came from one of the oldest English landed families, there was little wealth attached to this status and while money never guarantees a great garden, it can go a long way in helping to create one. This was the case with Bodnant, a sprawling estate just outside Conwy in North Wales.

In 1895 Laura McLaren, Lady Aberconway, by then in her early forties, inherited Bodnant from her father, Henry Pochin, a highly successful industrial chemist who had realised the tremendous potential of this site. Laura's mother had been an activist for women's rights, and Laura herself was proud of having attended as a child the very first public suffrage meetings, and her enthusiasm for the suffrage movement continued throughout her life.

Lady Aberconway was a passionate and gifted gardener, particularly knowledgeable about herbaceous plants, especially native flora, also roses and peonies, and she developed an exceptional gardening partnership with her only surviving son, Henry McLaren, later the second Lord Aberconway. While Henry took over the day-to-day running of the garden from 1901, it was Laura who developed the semi-formal borders close to the house and she was the prime mover in the design of the famous west-facing terraces. Her skill and vision were recognised by the Royal Horticultural Society in 1931 when she was presented with their Victoria Medal of Honour, and after her death she was described as 'one of the foremost horticulturists in Europe ... To watch Lady Aberconway walking round her gardens with her son was to see two beings as near to complete happiness as is given in this world, and to be able to create and to leave behind such a heritage of beauty is a rare and precious legacy indeed.'[5] She passed on some of her horticultural magic to her son and grandson, both of whom were to serve as presidents of the Royal Horticultural Society and were recipients of the prestigious RHS Victoria Medal of Honour, in 1934 and 1961 respectively.

Lady Aberconway had the advantage that her father had begun the creation of the garden at Bodnant, as starting a garden from scratch is somewhat different to cultivating one. Many people have reflected that if they'd known it was going to be that hard they wouldn't have begun. Such a sentiment occurred to Helen Robinson of Hyde Hall in Essex, but like all keen gardeners she did not give up. Gardening guru Fred Whitsey called Helen and her husband 'the most enthusiastic gardeners in the land',[6] which they needed to be given the conditions they were battling with.

Hyde Hall is in the area of England with the lowest rainfall, and when the couple arrived to start clearing their farm estate in the mid-1950s, they found two-foot-high rye grass, a slag heap of rubbish including beds and fireplaces – and a pampas grass. By travelling across the country from garden show to garden friend in their camper van, the Robinsons amassed not just an enormous collection of plants but also an enthusiasm for gardening. The sharing of that zest and knowledge grew like Topsy in the same proportions as their garden, which gradually spread into the surrounding farmland.

Viburnums became a particular passion and by 1982 their collection had national status, although it is a mistake to pick out just one plant to associate with Hyde Hall, since there is such a variety growing there. Inevitably the garden began to attract visitors. Anyone, myself included, who has gardened in East Anglia can only marvel at what has been achieved on such arid soil. In 1976 the Robinsons set up a Gardens Trust, then in 1993 it was decided to offer the garden to the RHS, which now keeps it open all the year round.

Always modest about her achievements, Helen Robinson was never a committee woman but nevertheless agreed to serve on several RHS and Royal National Rose Society bodies. Numerous awards followed, including the Gold Veitch Memorial Medal, and the RHS Victoria Medal of Honour in 1995. At home her house overflowed with foliage plants and in one upstairs room she installed fluorescent lighting for hundreds of African violets. Eventually Mrs Robinson moved to a smaller garden nearby but, true plantswoman that she was, she continued propagating furiously into her eighty-sixth year.

Some might say that the RHS has been lucky with its leading female supporters. Down in the West Country, another RHS outpost was donated to the society by a passionate woman gardener. It was thanks to a bout of measles in 1959 that Lady Anne Berry (previously Palmer) became interested in gardening. Her father, the last Earl of Orford, had bought Rosemoor in Devon as a fishing lodge in 1923. By the 1930s the garden was, by Lady Anne's own admission, 'dull and labour-intensive, typically Victorian with a great use of annuals in beds round the house'.[7] However, a chance meeting with Collingwood 'Cherry' Ingram in Spain, where she was convalescing from her bout of measles, led her to discover what could be created with the right planting and, once back in England, Lady Anne organised a 'raid' on Ingram's garden in Kent. So much was acquired that the plants filled a Land Rover and accompanying trailer. A pale pink *Rhododendron griersonianum* 'Infanta' and a red *R.* 'Timoshenko' are still growing in the gardens, remnants of gifts from Ingram. He also bred a cistus that he named 'Anne Palmer' for his friend.

Lady Anne developed her garden slowly with the help of designer John Codrington – and no help from her over-enthusiastic Labrador puppy, who once dug up a newly planted *Paeonia mlokosewitschii* – the highly desirable 'Molly the Witch' – which, despite being notoriously shy of flowering at the best of times, miraculously survived and flourished, as did the rest of the garden. By 1979 Rosemoor had been significantly enlarged and was home to a mouth-watering array of rare plants, many available for sale at the garden's nursery. Six years after the death of her husband, Lady Anne made the generous decision to donate the property to the Royal Horticultural Society and in 1986 it became the 'Wisley of the West'. Handing over the reins of Rosemoor allowed Lady Anne more time to travel and on revisiting New Zealand in 1990, a country whose trees she had studied, she made a second visit to the Hackfalls Arboretum. Later that year she married its creator, Bob Berry, and settled permanently in New Zealand.

Lady Heathcoat-Amory was one of Lady Anne Palmer's mentors. As Joyce Wethered she had been one of Britain's champion female golfers, winning the British Open three times in the 1930s, and after her marriage she and her husband, Sir John, created a stunning garden at Knightshayes Court, near Tiverton. Surrounding the late-nineteenth-century house, built by Sir John's grandfather who had made his fortune in lace, the garden is famed for its rhododendrons, azaleas and alpine plants. Lady Heathcoat-Amory was inspired by the writings of Sylvia Crowe, and sought to make her designs blend with the surrounding countryside. For many years the couple worked the twelve-acre garden themselves, with help only in mowing the lawn, but by the 1960s extra staff were needed and in the early 1970s the running of the garden was taken over by the National Trust.

Lady Heathcoat-Amory continued to be involved in the garden and was awarded the Victoria Medal of Honour in 1981, fifteen years after her husband became a holder of the same award. 'A garden need never have an off-season, particularly if the beauty and contrasts of ever-green foliage are understood and not forgotten,' she insisted. 'A rule we have always kept, which I think is a good one, is that if a group of plants is continually passed, or bypassed without being looked at, then this area is obviously dull and must be altered to attract attention.'[8]

It is not only a partnership of husband and wife which has created some of the greatest gardens, and among the most enduring of fre-quent, not to mention fascinating, mother-and-daughter gardening partnerships is that of Heather Muir and her daughter Diany at Kiftsgate Court. Heather Muir arrived at Kiftsgate, literally just over the road from Hidcote, in 1918 and extensively reworked the gardens over the next thirty-five years. It is a tricky site with steep slopes, but yew hedges and the Yellow and Rose Borders give it shape and her plantings have correctly been called courageous. Graham Stuart Thomas said of them in 1951 that they were 'the finest piece of skilled colour work that it has been my pleasure to see'.

When Muir's daughter, Diany Binny, took over the garden in 1954, it took her four years, in her words, 'to pluck up enough self-confidence to alter my mother's plans'. Among other things she added a grey foliage border and it was Binny who built the swimming pool, an unimaginable intrusion to anyone who has not seen it but a sensitive addition to those who have. There is not a blue tile in sight; instead, with its enviable views and positioning, it was a precursor to the cur-rent vogue for natural swimming. Now the mantle has passed to Diany's own daughter, Anne Chambers, who continues to maintain this beautiful garden, retaining its unique charm so that it is never overshadowed by its National Trust neighbour.

Just as gardens mature, so gardeners change and develop varying interests in different aspects of horticulture. This is what happened to Penelope Hobhouse, the *grande dame* of planting colour and garden history. Self-taught and possessed of a fierce intellect, Hobhouse was in her late twenties when she got to know Phyllis Reiss at Tintinhull, near her home in Somerset. 'It hit me like a bombshell that gardening was about beauty,' she remembers.[9] At that stage she was less interested in design than in the plants. She listed every one she came across and it became a competition with herself to make as many notes as possible and to be able to name all the plants she saw.

When, in the late 1960s, Hobhouse and her family moved to Hadspen, near Castle Cary, she already had a firm breadth of knowledge on which to base her ideas about design and colour. She became a member of the Garden History Society, an interest she shared with her friend and the woman she considered her greatest gardening mentor, Jean O'Neill, and it was through the society that Hobhouse met her second husband, John Malins. A new life of shared interests began for them in 1980 when she became the tenant gardener at Tintinhull, which Phyllis Reiss had left to the National Trust on her death in 1954.

Hobhouse's early books concentrate on colour and design and have become gardening classics, putting her in great demand as a designer both in Britain and especially in the United States. She has since given up design work, although the mantle of being a 'colourist' will, somewhat to her regret, be with her for ever, and she is now recognised as a world expert in garden and plant history, particularly of Persian and Mughal gardens. Her hero now is Babur, the sixteenth-century Mughal ruler who brought formal gardening to India. Among many other accolades Hobhouse was awarded the RHS Victoria Medal of Honour in 1996, the year before her good friend Rosemary Verey received the same award. It is the one that she is most proud of, though she confesses, 'You're supposed to wear it to anything to do with the RHS but I always forget.'[10]

Kiftsgate Court and National Trust gardens such as Sissinghurst, Bodnant, Tintinhull and Knightshayes Court, together with the RHS gardens at Hyde Hall and Rosemoor, attract hundreds of thousands of visitors annually, but in addition to these famous places thousands of enthusiasts visit far less grand gardens every weekend throughout the summer, usually clutching a well-thumbed *Yellow Book*, the annual bible of the National Gardens Scheme.

A hundred and fifty years after Mrs Pye wrote her little guidebook to the horticultural secrets of Twickenham, garden visiting has become a British passion, facilitated by a movement begun on the death of Queen Alexandra, widow of Edward VII. At that time it was only grand gardens that were open to the public, but the Institute for Nurses, which funded endowments for district nurses, decided to open an appeal in memory of Queen Alexandra. The effects of the General Strike shortly after her death in 1925 meant that raising money was difficult and in 1927 Miss Elsie Wagg, a member of the institute's council, suggested that it might be a good fund-raising idea to have a National Garden Week. She persuaded several lady members of the rather aristocratic council and their friends, including Hilda, Duchess of Richmond and Gordon, to open their gates to the public. The committee lobbied railway and charabanc companies to lay on special transport, and the gardening writer Marion Cran mentioned the openings in her Friday evening radio programme. The first week was an astounding success.

Sixty gardens opened initially and more joined later in the week. Nine hundred visitors turned up at Ham House in Surrey when only a hundred had been expected, each paying one shilling for entry. By the end of the year, over six hundred gardens had agreed to open and £8,000 had been raised – a lot of shillingses.

Although Elsie Wagg did not join the scheme immediately, by 1929 she had been persuaded to open her own garden, The Hermitage in East Grinstead, although she apologised that it was a mere four acres. Since the open gardens in the first years included those of the King, the Princess Royal, nine dukes and numerous lords, and others were attached to properties named Grange, Hall, Park or the Manor House, her modesty is understandable. She was rewarded with an MBE in 1934 for having initiated the scheme.

The Duchess of Richmond was by now chairman and brought in her friend Daphne Heald to help on the committee. Lady Heald remembered that the idea of opening gardens to the public was considered 'a rather radical thought at that time'.[11] The scheme was only a little diminished by the war, and she became the national chairman in 1951, a post she held for twenty-eight years, helped by her friend Rachel Crawshay.

Lady Heald's own garden was at Chilworth Manor near Guildford in Surrey on the site of an eleventh-century monastery, and although she claimed to have known little about gardening when she and her husband moved there, relying on the gardener to keep her 'firmly in order',[12] it soon became a passion. However large a garden was, she believed there should always be 'little treasures' to be shared with visitors: '"first aconites, then scillas and all the heavenly little anemones [that] come peeping through the cold ground"'.[13]

As with many upper-crust women – she was born and grew up at Knebworth, where she frequently got locked into rooms because the doorknobs were so high – Lady Heald's 'career' was her effective involvement with numerous charities in addition to the National Gardens Scheme. She loved meeting her visitors and saw gardening as 'a great leveller'. Capturing the essence of the now famous *Yellow Book* scheme, Lady Heald thought 'gardeners all talk the same language and always feel they have something to share'.[14] This is a sentiment which drives the success of the National Gardens Scheme and its *Yellow Book* for 2009 lists 3,500 gardens to visit in England and Wales alone (Scotland and Ireland have their own successful sister schemes). In 2008, £3 million was raised for the various charities which the National Gardens Scheme supports.

Penny Snell is the NGS's current national chairman, and she was for many years the regional organiser for the vast London area. She regularly opens her own exquisite garden in Cobham, Surrey, complete with topiary and beehives, and strongly believes that

Penny Snell in the abundant conservatory at her home in Cobham, one of the hundreds of British gardens opened annually for charity.

women do have a special affinity with gardening, together with a willingness to share their gardens with others. 'As someone who has turned a maintenance-free garden into a labour intensive one, it is a priority [for me] to allow visitors to enjoy it!'[15]

MOTHER EARTH

'I had not intended saying any thing about
the kitchen-garden, as it hardly comes within
a lady's province.'

Jane Loudon,
The Lady's Country Companion (1845)[1]

'HERE'S AL FINE HERBS
OF EVERY SORT'

Late one April evening in 1605 Lady Margaret Hoby reached for her diary, inkpot and feathered quill pen as she had done many times before. At thirty-four she was the mistress of Hackness, a Yorkshire estate, and the small pages of her diary were covered with an italic hand, sometimes bold, sometimes tiny but always neat. It was, later editors agreed, 'the calligraphy of one well accustomed to the use of the pen'.[1] But on this night she was weary and her devout conscience pricked her. 'This day,' she wrote as though addressing her confessor, 'I bestowed to[o] much time in the Garden, and therby was worse able to performe sperituall duties.'[2]

The garden that Lady Margaret could not tear herself away from was a few miles inland from Scarborough, and Hackness is still a peaceful hamlet where the river Derwent runs through the village, purple heather covers the moors behind and rolling dales surround it. Nothing remains of her home, but it was most probably built from the stones of the small monastic settlement that existed there until its dissolution in 1539, and her family may have acquired the monks' own gardens and orchard.

Lady Margaret lived at Hackness for forty-four years. Three times married but childless, her 'family' consisted mainly of the household, the people who lived and worked on the estate around her. Growing herbs, vegetables and fruit was among the earliest forms of gardening that women of all classes would have been involved in, and it was Margaret's duty to provide for those around her. There were supplies from the orchard; carrots, parsnips, leeks and cucumbers grew in her garden alongside a variety of herbs. Although wealthy, she was immensely practical and was always busying herself cooking sweetmeats, preserving fruits such as damsons and quinces for the winter months, and collecting the honey from her bees.

A deeply religious woman, Lady Margaret practised her skills of housewifery and husbandry conscientiously. Since the dissolution of the monasteries the study of herbs, or 'the art of simpling', had become secular and Lady Margaret was adept at the making of herbal remedies. She often mentions consulting her 'arball',[3] which may well have been John Gerard's famous *Herball or General Historie of Plants*, first published in 1597. Gerard worked for William Cecil, 1st Baron Burghley, and Margaret's husband had family connections to them. The book was originally a Belgian herbal and, knowing there was nothing like it available in English, Gerard decided to produce a translation. He also took the advice of his wife, Anne, and believed that it should be 'principally intended for gentlewomen'[4] as these were the people who gathered the herbs and organised their use in the home.

William Lawson was another seventeenth-century author keen to instruct women on how to organise their gardens. Disapproving of the 'cottage garden' or 'potager' style which combined flowers, vegetables and herbs grown together, instead he recommended that:

Herbs are of two sorts and therefore it is meete (they requiring divers manners of Husbandry) that we have two gardens: A garden for flowers and a kitchen garden: or a summer garden and a winter garden: not that we meane so perfect a distinction, that the Garden for flowers should be without herbs good for the kitchen or the kitchen garden should want flowers nor on the contrarie: but for the most part they would be severed; first, because your Garden flowers shall suffer some disgrace, if among them you intermingle Onions, Parsnips etc. Secondly, your Garden that is durable, must be of one forme: but that which is for your kitchin use, must yield daily roots, or other herbs, and suffer deformity. Thirdly the herb of both will not be both alike ready, at one time, either for gathering or removing.[5]

He had a point, not least because potager-style gardens are notoriously difficult to maintain. This was the time when the utility or kitchen garden was first considered distinct, a garden in its own right. However they were set out, Lawson provided practical advice that might seem obvious to a practised gardener but is always helpful to the beginner. 'Place your herbs of biggest growth, by walles or in borders as Fenell, and the lowest in the middest, as saffron, strawberries, onions, etc.' He also counselled care in the design of the plot 'yet must you have your beds divided, that you may goe betwixt to weede . . .'[6]

Lawson lived less than thirty miles from 'that honourable Lady at Hackness' across the North Yorkshire moors, and it is reasonable to suppose that he not only knew her but that they also swapped thoughts on gardening.

Lady Anne Clifford was wealthier than Lady Margaret – much wealthier, having fought lengthy court battles to claim her inheritance of large landed properties in Yorkshire and Westmoreland.

Woodcut from 1533 of a couple gathering plants in a herb garden. Herbs were vital in the preparation of medicines by the women of the house.

Settlement came in 1643 when she was fifty-three, but before this she had been mistress of grand homes and gardens at both Knole in Kent and Wilton in Wiltshire, and in 1650 it was estimated that she had an annual income of £8,000. Despite her riches, she took pleasure from simple things, her diaries revealing how she spent her time picking cherries and making quince marmalade. Lady Anne was unusual in having complete control over so many properties and their gardens, and we know she gardened at Appleby Castle in Westmoreland in the 1660s, and made a large garden at Brougham Castle around the same time, where it is likely that she grew the white lilies she asked to be sent to her when she was staying at her other properties close by. As well as her diaries recording the details of her life, her account books give tantalising clues as to how she organised her gardens, including the fact that large amounts of seeds were purchased.

Although there is evidence to suggest that both Lady Anne and Lady Margaret got their hands dirty, custom and clothing dictated that any hard digging was still left to paid male help. A little weeding was recommended for 'gentlewomen' by botanist William Coles, writing in 1656 in *The Art of Simpling, or, An Introduction to the Knowledge and Gathering of Herbs*, 'if the ground be not too wet' when they 'may doe themselves much good by kneeling upon a Cushion . . .'[7] As any gardener knows, hand-weeding one's own garden if one has the time can be a satisfying occupation and there is no doubt that over the centuries many a redundant cushion has been saved from the rubbish heap to protect creaking knees. Coles also thought a bit of weeding was a good way for 'both sexes [to] divert themselves from idleness, and evil company which oftentimes prove the ruin of many ingenious people'.[8]

'Simpling', the growing of herbs for medicines and other remedies, was an important part of any housewife's gardening, and it was essential for weeds to be kept at bay. Sixteenth-century horticultural writer Master Fitzherbert pointed out, 'as ofte as nede shall requyre [a garden] must be weded, for else the wede wyl overgrowe the herbes',[9] and William Lawson had also recommended that 'a Mistress' do her own weeding or encourage her maids 'to take the opportunity of a shower of rain'. However, he strongly advised 'the Mistress either to be present her self, or to teach her maids to know herbs from weeds'.[10]

Although William Lawson recommended distancing the flower garden from the kitchen garden, it was hard to separate them when so many plants were relied upon to enhance recipes. The ingredients of the delicious-sounding rose and cowslip preserves made in Lady Anne Clifford's kitchens no doubt drew on her gardens' own plentiful supplies, for, despite its northerly position, Brougham's gardens provided the kitchens with cherries and quinces in addition to the expected apples, together with a variety of herbs and vegetables, including artichokes. Both Brougham and Appleby produced soft fruit such as strawberries, and her sweet pies were filled with plums and varieties of *ribes* which had dried to currants.

Such a selection of produce from a kitchen garden would not have been unusual for properties of this size, and women always played a key role in organising the growing of it all for their kitchens. Until the eighteenth century, stillrooms – so called as it was where herbs were 'distilled' – also had to be supplied with plant material for both medicinal and culinary use. In the 1600s 'Goodwife' Cantry, a gardener and herbalist and the wife of a Puritan yeoman, tended a colourful garden at her Northamptonshire home full of larkspur, spiderworts and lupins, and she concocted ointments from the fennel and camomile in her herb plot. Few women, however, had the skills of Grace, Lady Mildmay, of Apethorpe in the same county, one of whose early-seventeenth-century recipes for a balm required 159 different seeds, spices, roots and gums.

Within most marriages there was a clear demarcation of territory when it came to being in charge of the various areas of garden. The orchard was the man's province, while the kitchen and flower gardens were women's territory, which may have been because the cultivation of fruit trees involved heavier work in the form of pruning and harvesting. However, with Britain's increased industrialisation during the eighteenth century, market gardens sited just outside the major towns began to take over the supply of fruit, herbs and vegetables, and the need to maintain kitchen gardens diminished since none but the largest estates were able to be completely self-sufficient.

Smallholdings which specialised in growing herbs were often worked by women, who then sold their produce at one of London's markets such as Covent Garden, Honey Lane in Newgate or Fleet Street. The market at Covent Garden had been established in 1670 and there was also a herb market near Leadenhall. Until 1737 the Woolchurch Market was on the site of what is now the residence of the City of London's Lord Mayor, the Mansion House. From the records of markets such as these we find the names of over fifty women who traded as market gardeners and herb sellers. It was not an easy way to make a living, especially with the strict rules of entry to the City of London which had been designed to control country traders, as various comments in these records attest: Mary Hillyard, who had a smallholding in the country, had to sign a declaration promising that she would not compete against larger, better established traders. 'I do agree . . . to take a standing for Greens to come on after the Gardiners are gone, to enter at Midsumer next and to comense Rent at Michaelmas next at 1/6 per week, witness my Hand this 19 June 1740.'[11] Herbswoman Elizabeth Gobby fell into arrears for the rent for her stall at the Newgate Market in 1737 after her husband died and she became lame, and such was the competition for a place in these markets that she lost her position even though she offered to pay off her arrears at 2s a week.

Tough though life must have been for these women, there was no lack of demand for their 'greens' since every home used herbs not only for medical remedies but also for household cleaning and cooking. Scented plants had long been employed in homes to ward off illness and to bring sweet-smelling scents to cover up some of the unpleasant odours associated with poor sanitation. This was an age-old practice, as a visitor to Britain in the late sixteenth century recorded. 'Their chambers and parlours strawed with sweet herbs . . . their nosegays finely intermingled with sundry sorts of fragrant flowers in their bedchambers and privy rooms with comfortable smell cheered me up and entirely delighted all my senses.'[12]

While 'strawing' or 'strewing' was a habit which began to die out in the eighteenth century as the supply of water improved in domestic homes, it remained a lucrative source of income for herbswomen with contracts to supply businesses and the royal palaces. Between 1660 and 1836 six women held the official post of King's Herb Strewer, a position they held for life. Bridgett Rumny, the first to hold this title, laid claim to it because of a warrant she held from 1647. She had paid a high personal price during the Civil War and it seems that Charles II rewarded her with 'the office of providing Flowers and Sweet Herbs for the Court granted by the late King to herself and her late mother who, with her own two sons, was killed in the Battle of Naseby'.[13] By the start of the nineteenth century the King's Herb Strewer had become a symbolic role, but until then it had been a well-paid position, guaranteeing security for the provider of a variety of aromatic plants to scent the royal 'privy lodgings'.

One of the famous Roxburghe Ballads, better known as the 'Cries of London', gives a delightful hint of what these women grew and offered on the streets:

Here's fine rosemary, sage, and thyme!
Come buy my ground ivy.
Here's fetherfew, gilliflowers, and rue,
Come buy my knotted marjorum, ho!
Come buy my mint, my fine green mint.
Here's fine lavender for your clothes,
Here's parsley and winter-savory,
And hearts-ease, which all do choose,
Here's balm and hissop, and cinquefoil,
All fine herbs, it is well known.
   Let none despise the merry merry Cries
   Of famous London Town!
Here's pennyroyal and marygolds!

Come buy my nettletops.
Here's water-cresses and scurvy-grass!
Come buy my sage of virtue ho!
Come buy my wormwood and mugwort,
Here's al fine herbs of every sort.
Here's southernwood that's very good,
Dandelion and houseleek.
Here's dragon's tongue and wood sorrel,
With bear's foot and horehound.
    Let none despise the merry merry Cries
    Of famous London Town![14]

As the nineteenth century progressed, the increasing middle classes established a different way of life enhanced by improved house-building and transport. The ever-expanding market gardens took away much of the pressure on women to grow their own supplies, since vegetables were more readily and cheaply available locally. There was also less reliance on domestic apothecary skills as medical care became 'professional', and thus a male province where women's remedies were no longer considered reliable.

Later in this era, women working in horticulture at the lowest end of the social scale also had to come to terms with changes in society. Cities across Britain were expanding at dramatic rates; railway lines ran like rivers across the country, enabling fresh food to be moved from farmland to market at speeds previously undreamed of; and London's market gardeners were being forced further and further from the centre of the city as land was bought up for suburban housing, swallowing up the acres previously worked by smallholders.

The female herb growers were among those hit the hardest; they had already lost the market for strewing herbs, the medical profession no longer needed their goods for remedies, and now they could not compete with commercial nurseries which were able to transport their produce across long distances.

As the 1800s progressed it was only in the kitchen that herbs were used regularly, and by the start of the twentieth century only a handful of them were to be found in gardens: mint, parsley and perhaps some lavender, still occasionally used for its moth-proofing qualities among the linen sheets of the upper classes. Vegetable production, however, became big business, and while women were still helping to run nurseries, particularly within family businesses, they received little credit or money for this. As national demand for fruit and vegetables grew, nurseries expanded and women were often employed in the propagating houses for the most routine jobs, but without qualifications or connections it was hard to progress to more rewarding work.

Women's involvement with growing the food they ate became restricted to the most rural areas, where 'cottage' gardening continued in its simplest form until it was 'rediscovered' by gardeners in the mid-twentieth century. Although Jane Loudon, writing on gardening for women in the mid-nineteenth century, includes chapters on the kitchen garden they are very much an adjunct to the main business of growing flowers. 'I had not intended saying any thing about the kitchen-garden, as it hardly comes within a lady's province,' she states firmly in a book written for women newly moved to the country on 'how to enjoy a country life rationally'.[15] Her instructions on growing vegetables appear to have been included with some reluctance and little enthusiasm. A few decades later Edith Chamberlain did not suggest that her gentlewomen readers work in the kitchen garden at all, although she bemoaned the fact that the art of distilling herbs had been taken over entirely by the specialists, meaning that women took 'no trouble to find out things for ourselves'.[16]

DAUGHTERS OF CERES

In 1809 Mary Ann Brailsford, eldest daughter of Charles and Elizabeth Brailsford, moved with her family to a new home in the village of Southwell in Nottinghamshire. One day Mary, tired of helping her mother with the endless round of cooking, decided to sow some pips from an apple being used for a pie; one germinated and soon grew too large for its pot. Mary planted it out in a corner of their cottage garden just near the village church, but four years later, when the tree was still too young to fruit, Mary married and left home and thought no more about it. Twenty-five years later, when her tree was producing exceptionally large apples, she inherited the family cottage but was happy to sell it to a butcher, Matthew Bramley.

Mary Brailsford died in 1852 and it was not until five years later that a local nurseryman got to hear of butcher Bramley's apples and started propagating cuttings from the tree, so she had no intimation that her little seedling was the origin of the Bramley that was awarded a first-class certificate by the Royal Horticultural Society in 1883. Since then it has been cultivated across the United Kingdom, producing the choicest cooking apple available.

In spite of Mary Brailsford's lack of interest in her plant-growing experiment, it is gratifying that it is her name rather than Bramley's that is recorded for posterity in the *Oxford Dictionary of National Biography*. She is rare in having that distinction, as few women have been directly associated with developments in fruit and vegetable production, despite the fact that women have always had such a key role in organising the growing and then purchasing of the produce for their kitchens.

For most of the twentieth century, the vegetable plot was traditionally seen as a male domain, typified by the fact that it was Mr McGregor whom Peter Rabbit had to watch out for around the cabbages, not Mrs McGregor, she being busy in the kitchen heating up the pot. This was the suburban ideal: the man working on the allotment and the woman cooking or growing flowers with which to make the house beautiful for her family. Since the aim of a kitchen garden is to produce fresh fruit and vegetables for families to eat, it would be natural for women to want to be involved in growing them, yet they were surprisingly absent from the vegetable garden throughout the nineteenth century until several women helped to change this attitude.

On 14 February 1927 Hilda Leyel, a forty-seven-year-old divorcée, opened the Culpeper Shop in London's Baker Street, convinced that the British public would want access to natural products and herbal remedies. 'The whole business,' she later wrote, 'was to be extremely English in character, so on all the wooden bins and spotless white jars were painted the old familiar names of many English flowers and plants.' Mrs Leyel had had a passion for botany since she was four. 'Although . . . [I was] too young to enjoy searching in the heat for such rare plants as Ladies' Tresses and Green Hellebore, the names of the plants, like the dates of the English Kings, were impressed upon my mind so vividly that it has been impossible for me ever to forget them.'[1] She would probably feel at home in the shops which bear the Culpeper name some eighty years later.

The original Baker Street shop sold wholesome sweet-scented distillations of plants in various forms of medicines, perfumes, lotions, superior soaps and creams, the latter made from such healing flowers as lilies, roses and cowslips. Culpeper's also offered many of the simple tisanes, such as camomile and lime-blossom tea, 'so popular abroad,' wrote Mrs Leyel, 'but at that time almost unknown in this country'.[2] A male visitor to her new shop was entranced.

A certain new establishment which I was tempted into the other day is radiant and alluring with its green facade, its barrels and jars and bottles, and not a little of the atmosphere of the garden about it – not merely the physic garden, but the garden of the flowered walls, and birds and spaniels and lawns. Yet to my eye it is the words on the jars and bottles that are the most attractive feature of this new herbalist. On the herbalist's labels I found words that, if not actually new to me, had been long forgotten, and just for that reason came back with added charm: such words as Comfrey and Agrimony, Eyebright and Melilot, Borage and Basil, Silverweed and Marjoram, Betony and Lovage.[3]

Hilda, or Mrs C.F. Leyel as she was always known, was the public face of herbalism in the interwar years. She was the force behind the Society of Herbalists that was founded a year after the first Culpeper shop opened. Later she battled successfully against the government's proposed Pharmacy and Medicines Bill of 1941, which threatened the livelihoods of herbalists by preventing them from prescribing dried herbs. She wrote on the history of the herbs available in her shop and also some of their more eccentric uses. She repeated at length, for example, and without apology, a recipe given by an English medieval herbalist, Gilbertus Anglicus, who was 'celebrated for his puppy-dog ointment' that involved taking 'a very fat puppy', skinning him, stuffing him with herbs, boiling him, and making an ointment from the resulting grease,[4] which was not something one would associate with the genteel atmosphere of her sweetly scented Culpeper shop.

Another influential herbalist was Maud Grieve, who only became interested in herbs at the start of the twentieth century when she was in her fifties. She grew medicinal and culinary herbs in her garden, The Whins, in Chalfont St Peter in Buckinghamshire. She was the local representative for an organisation called 'Daughters of Ceres', dedicated to improving employment opportunities for women in agricultural jobs. At the outbreak of war in 1914 she began to give lessons from her home on cultivating herbs and set up an association of herb growers, writing pamphlets on the uses of various plants. When some of these arrived on the desk of Hilda Leyel she suggested to the publisher Jonathan Cape that they should be published. He agreed, with the proviso that Mrs Leyel edited the book and that Grieve also included American herbs, to give the book a wider potential audience. The resulting volume, *A Modern Herbal*, which came out in 1931, was the first to be published on the subject since John Lindley's *Flora Medica* in 1838. As Mrs Leyel rightly pointed out, 'Surely it makes a garden more romantic and wonderful to know that Wallflowers, Irises, Lupins, Delphiniums, Columbines, Dahlias and Chrysanthemums, every flower in the garden from the first Snowdrop to the Christmas Rose, are not only there for man's pleasure but have their compassionate use in his pain.'[5]

Maud Grieve advertised her school at The Whins as a 'Vegetable Drug Plant Farm and Medicinal Herb Nursery'. During the First World War, when medicinal herbs were recognised as essential to the war effort, she was particularly concerned that the gathering of them was done in the correct way, something she wished could be taught to village children across the country. Without care in their harvesting, herbs succumbed to mildew or were so thoroughly bleached by the sun that little or no medicinal properties remained. 'Unless herbs are properly gathered and made ready for the market, as they were in Germany before the war,' Grieve wrote in 1916, 'they had better be left alone till gatherers are taught how to gather, or there may soon be no herbs to collect if they are pulled up by the roots and none left for seeds.'[6]

In 1926 Grieve's great friend Dorothy Hewer needed little encouragement to start a herb farm at Seal near Sevenoaks when the onset of deafness forced her to give up teaching. From there she sold herbs by mail order, and later from a West End shop in Mayfair's North Audley Street. Margaret Brownlow (whom Dorothy always called 'Little Margaret') later took over this business and ran it until her death in 1968,[7] when, thanks mainly to this group of women, herbs were fully rehabilitated into modern gardening.

Organic gardening, on the other hand, was still considered a foolish and eccentric fad at the time of Margaret Brownlow's death. Britain was in the grip of intensive, highly mechanised farming methods as a result of post-war legislation, and no one had any desire to stop using the pesticides and fertilisers which helped produce such perfect fruit and vegetables. At home, in the back garden or on the allotment, amateur gardeners followed the general horticultural trend of buying any available aid to kill off unwanted bugs, pests and diseases.

One of the very few voices of dissent against such methods came from Lady Eve Balfour, niece of the Edwardian Prime Minister. Unusually for someone of her position and sex, Eve Balfour had always been passionate about agriculture, lying about her age to be part of the

Women's War Agricultural Committee in 1918 when she was only twenty. She ran a small farm in Monmouthshire with a team of female conscripts brought in to replace men on agricultural land, while she herself was adept with a horse plough and regularly milked cows by hand. During the interwar years she rented her own farm, acquired a pilot's licence, and wrote detective thrillers in what little spare time she had.

Lady Eve also read widely on sustainability, which led her to run her own experiments in organic farming. In 1943 she published *The Living Soil*, and it quickly became the 'classic text for the organic movement'. Three years later she became a founder member of the Soil Association, which published a campaigning and advisory journal, *Mother Earth*, which for unknown reasons was later changed to *Living Earth*, a more accurate title but less of a tribute to Lady Eve.

Miriam Rothschild was another committed woman who throughout her long life across the twentieth century campaigned for causes that she believed were right and just. 'Nobody has really thought about what is so satisfying in nature,' she said, 'but people really do benefit from contact with plants, animals, birds and butterflies. Without them we are a deprived species.'[8]

Dame Miriam's greatest contribution in the horticultural world was to open gardeners' eyes to the disappearance of the many wild flowers which were the ancestors of the highly cultivated plants grown in every back garden. 'I realised with dismay that wild flowers had been drained, bulldozed, weedkillered and fertilised out of the fields, and that we now had a countryside reminiscent of a snooker table.'[9] This was only one of the many causes Dame Miriam campaigned for, but it had the greatest impact among gardeners. Having produced a seed mixture she called 'Farmers' Nightmare' to re-establish her own fields as meadows, Dame Miriam was asked by the Prince of Wales to advise on doing the same to a large field close to his country home of Highgrove. She also encouraged the planting of cowslips and primroses on roadside banks, and sponsored seed distribution to schools. A pioneering campaigner against the use of pesticides on farmland and in gardens, she was ahead of her time but her values should strike a chord with any gardener: 'I garden purely for pleasure. I love plants and flowers and green leaves and I am incurably romantic – hankering after small stars spangling through the grass.'[10]

After the 'dark ages' of the nineteenth and early twentieth centuries when women's involvement in fruit and vegetable cultivation seemed to disappear, there were those whose work had a lasting effect on growing plants for food, although their identities remain invisible except to insiders. One such woman was Joan Stokes, a student from

Joan Stokes was the tiny powerhouse behind the gold-medal-winning strawberry exhibits at the Chelsea Flower Show.

Waterperry Horticultural School, near Oxford. After graduating Joan stayed on the staff and specialised in growing and preparing the famous Waterperry strawberries that were displayed at the Chelsea Flower Show every year and which have won fifteen gold medals. Head and founder, Beatrix Havergal, at first found it hard to believe that the diminutive and modest Stokes had the strength to be a good gardener, but Joan found her niche preparing the school's display of strawberries for Chelsea and it was due to her dedication that they won such a crop of medals. Each August she would layer six hundred plants in pots, half of which would eventually be considered worthy of display, then the plants were put outside until November, when Joan covered them in straw to prevent the frost from cracking the pots. In January she put them under glass and the real work of producing champion strawberries began. She would feed the plants regularly with solid fertiliser, blood, manure and potash, then once the small fruits began to grow, she would thin them down to seven or nine to a pot and then wait anxiously for the fruit to ripen. The displays were painstakingly created, each strawberry hanging from the three hundred plants supported by a tiny hazel-twig crutch so that visitors to the show could see the fruit to its best advantage. 'We followed our noses all the way to your strawberries,' the Queen reputedly told Miss Havergal on one of her annual visits to the show.[11] Her Majesty was the only person invited to taste a succulent specimen. In 1968 Stokes was only the third woman to be awarded the RHS Associate of Honour reserved for horticultural professionals.

Far better known is Joy Larkcom. Nowadays we take for granted the easy availability, at a price maybe, of organic or unusual vegetables and salads, but this is something that has only happened because of the influence of a few lone voices in the wilderness. Joy Larkcom's first achievement was to induce British seed companies to include

Lollo Rosso lettuce in their catalogues, the first of many battles which Larkcom fought in her attempt to improve the nation's palate. In the early 1970s the idea of 'cut-and-come-again' salads and herbs was unheard of and now they are on every supermarket shelf, due in part to Larkcom's inspiring books and her 1992 revision of the RHS's *The Vegetable Garden Displayed*, which up until then had been a solid and reliable tome with a hint of mud on its boots and string around its waist.

Joy Larkcom had struggled with botany as a student at Wye College in the mid-1950s, and it was a spell with her parents in Thailand that sparked her interest in unusual vegetables. Returning to England and later settling in Suffolk, Joy began her career as a journalist while experimenting with growing vegetables on an allotment. Her marriage to Don Pollard came about after she had expressed the need for a bag of pig manure and he bought one for her, and her first book, *Vegetables from Small Gardens*, was based on their experience of working on her allotment. In 1976 she and Don with their two children set out in a caravan on what she called their 'Great Vegetable Tour', to see how vegetables were grown in continental Europe, and it was this adventure which inspired Joy's interest in salads unseen in Britain, including the Lollo Rosso lettuce and red chicory (radicchio). Her first sighting of the lettuce was in a market garden near Turin where the grower called out, "'Lollo! Lollobrigida!" . . . [with] sweeping, busty gestures in the air'.[12]

A steady stream of books, continual pressure on supermarkets and seed companies plus the fledgling interest of television gardening programmes in organic growing gradually helped establish these unusual vegetables in British salad bowls. Larkcom's later visits to China encouraged producers to introduce varieties of Asian vegetables unknown in this country, although they have never become as popular as her earlier cut-and-come-again salads. She has also worked tirelessly with heritage tomatoes, ensuring that there is now an alternative to the tasteless Dutch ones which were once the only choice for growers and consumers.

Now retired to southern Ireland, Joy Larkcom modestly feels she has always been a bad gardener and 'cack-handed', but the legacy of her books on vegetable growing firmly refutes that. She changed the British salad from a limp lettuce leaf and a slice of thick-skinned cucumber to a colourful medley of luscious leaves and sweet cherry tomatoes, though one suspects she would not approve of them having been flown in by jumbo jet from another continent. She was aware of climate change long before it became a fashionably correct concern. 'Radical thinking', she feels, is urgently needed, something she is no stranger to.[13] She predicts that we will need to develop new strains of edible plants which can be grown in shorter seasons. In addition to wanting to find ways of saving water, Larkcom is concerned about the resources which animals consume. While she recognises that rearing fewer animals for food and concentrating more on crops might seem to mean creating a lower standard of living, she strongly believes that this is the way of the future.

THE FLORAL ARTS

'A flowerless room is a soul-less room.'

Vita Sackville-West,
In Your Garden (1951)[1]

'EMBROIDERED SO WITH FLOWERS'

In February 1741 Mary Pendarves, an inveterate letter writer and skilled embroiderer who later came to be better known as Mrs Delany, the flower mosaicist, wrote to her sister to describe a court dress she had just seen worn by her cousin, the Duchess of Queensberry. 'The bottom of the petticoat [had] *brown hills* covered with all sorts of weeds, and *every breadth* had an old *stump of a tree* that ran up almost to the top of the petticoat . . . round which twined nastersians, ivy, honeysuckles, periwinkles, convolvuluses and all sorts of twining flowers . . . the robings and facings were little green banks with all sorts of weeds, and the sleeves and the rest of the gown loose twining branches of the same sort as those on the petticoat.' An expert needle-woman herself, Mary declared that she had never seen 'a piece of work so prettily fancied, and am quite angry with myself for not having the same thought, for it is infinitely handsomer than mine'.[1]

For centuries the transferring of floral designs on to fabric and furnishings was another indication of the widespread love of plants and flowers, not just in Britain but across the world. During the six-teenth century it was common to see flower motifs used on clothes and in home decoration among the English elite; the fashionable blackwork of Elizabethan times with its complicated patterning of outlined flowers and fruit on white linen is strikingly reminiscent of the knot gardens and mazes popular at that time. Grace, Lady Mildmay is best remembered for her herbal potions, but she was also a keen embroideress: 'every day I spent some time in works of myne own invention without sample [sampler] or pattern before me . . . to drawe flowers and fruit to their life . . . all which varietie did greatly recreate my mynde, for I thought of nothing else but what I was doing'.[2]

As with all portraits of that age, the ones of Elizabeth I are thick with symbolic representations, but they also display her love of flowers. Her elaborate gowns and stomachers are shown strewn with stems and petals like a flowery mead, including depictions of the white and red roses of York and Lancaster and the Tudor rose, and also Elizabeth's particular favourite, the tiny purple herbal viola, 'Heart's ease', or what Oberon in Shakespeare's *A Midsummer Night's Dream* calls a 'pansy' from the French *pensée* or thought. Few women had the skills of Lady Mildmay, who was able to produce designs without a pattern, and professional embroiderers took designs from the early herbals, pricking out the pattern so that it could more easily be transferred to canvas or silk for stitching. These patterns were then sold on and appeared as embroidery on curtains, cushions and bed hangings, as well as on more personal items such as nightcaps and gloves. William Turner went even further in his *Newe Herball* of 1551 by suggesting that sprigs of lavender should be quilted into a cap to ward off diseases and comfort the brain.

Some women did have enough plant knowledge to create their own designs, including Elizabeth Talbot, or 'Bess', Countess of Shrewsbury. She had spent much of her vast wealth during the second half of the sixteenth century building not one but two halls, or great houses, at Hardwick in Derbyshire. The old hall is now a ruin, but the newer hall remains a monument to her sense of style. Although we know little about the gardens surrounding the halls in Bess's time, the intricate and exceptionally detailed flower embroideries which decorated her grand home, many done by her own hand with her initials 'E.T.S.' subtly stitched in, show that she had an intimate knowledge of flowers and plants.

The Stuarts took their joint love of flowers and embroidery one step further to create fantastical stumpwork boxes with raised representations of complete garden scenes. Tapestries, too, became vivid representations of plants indoors, while outside parterres were likened to embroidery by Sir Thomas Hanmer in his 1653 *Garden Book*. The highly

Silks designed and woven by Anna Maria Garthwaite (1688–1763?) brought almost botanical accuracy to dress fabrics in the mid- to late-eighteenth century – part of society's obsession with plant material.

accurate depictions of native flowers so beloved of the Tudor and Jacobean aristocracy fell out of fashion during the late seventeenth century, and rich damask silks took their place. However, such was the passion for nature in the Georgian age that flower motifs found their way back onto home decoration as the eighteenth century progressed, in particular onto fabrics used for silk mantuas, court dresses and men's coats and breeches.

It was during this period that Anna Maria Garthwaite was active, and her designs are so naturalistically accurate that it is now assumed she must have worked from real plant material rather than from books. Little is known about her life other than the legacy of her beautiful designs, many of which remain in the Victoria & Albert Museum's textile collection. There is a suggestion that Garthwaite had a relative who was a naturalist and belonged to a local botanical society, and it is a fact that after coming to London to live in the Spitalfields area with her widowed sister, Mary, Garthwaite produced hundreds of drawings and designs – sometimes as many as eighty a year – between 1726 and 1756. Many of these featured the new exotic plants that were arriving in England, and some of her silk fabrics even found their way to North America, but how she got access to her plant material remains a mystery.

A keen knowledge of flowers was an absolute requisite for any woman who did her own embroidery, and Mary Pendarves knew her plants, working them up into exquisite embroidery designs which she was generous in giving to friends. She is possibly the first person to have embroidered the pelargonium, which she did onto a black petticoat, or underskirt. Shortly before Mary Pendarves's marriage to Patrick Delany in 1743, she sent a pattern to Elizabeth Robinson, later to be the Mrs Montagu who would commission Capability Brown, who wrote to her sister describing it:

Mrs Pendarves has sent me a pretty pattern . . . in black & white only outlines, it consists of Auriculas Anemonies a poppy roses & buds Orange flowers & lilies of the Vally[.] To help me in shading she lent me the Prints of the flowers which my Pappa said would be admirable directions if they were coloured but I have only black [and] white, now what I should be infinitely obliged to my father & you would be to get me a pattern done by Mr Hately of Auriculas in abundance Convalvalens (that is the blew flower we work up in the print in the facing) the lillies you mention, poppies & tulips (of which I have painted ones very fine) as likewise Convalvalens is a picture, lillies I would have too & narcissus's & anything else to make out the pattern . . . The Dutchess would have me work upon a black ground because it wont dirty, but if my Pappa thinks another ground prettier I will chuse it.[3]

Few women had the artistic skills of Mrs Delany, but this did not hinder the eighteenth-century passion for floral designs. While many would have bought their silks from a professional such as Anna Maria Garthwaite, the mistress of botanical accuracy, others blithely trod their own amateur path. The writer Hannah More observed in 1770, after attending a party, that she had seen women with 'on their heads, an acre and a half of shrubbery, besides slopes, grass plots, tulip beds, clumps of peonies, kitchen gardens, and greenhouses'.[4] More may have been a witty critic, but she was herself a keen gardener, once confessing that 'I work in my garden 2 or 3 hours every day, . . . I am rather proud of my pinks and roses . . .'[5]

Although Mary Delany was a highly gifted embroiderer, her more generally known soubriquet 'the flower mosaicist' comes from her skill at painstakingly cutting out minute slivers of paper and gluing them together in accurate depictions of plants. King George III and

Queen Charlotte were among the many who marvelled at the 'paper mosaics' she created, which they saw on visits to Mary's close friend, the Duchess of Portland, at her home at Bulstrode. Through her edited letters we know Mary Delany gardened throughout her life, accumulating the botanical knowledge needed to produce her miraculous flower pictures. The detail in them is so precise that only a person who not only adored flowers but also knew them botanically and intimately could have created them. The accuracy of Mrs Delany's mosaics was such that the eminent botanist Sir Joseph Banks, in charge of the Royal Botanic Gardens at Kew, was reputedly able to identify each plant 'without the least fear of committing an error'.[6]

Although socially well-connected, Mary Delany's fortunes were mixed. Her first marriage in 1718, when she was just eighteen, to a much older MP, Alexander Pendarves, had been unhappy. He was a jealous man and kept Mary away from her friends and relatives. After his convenient death just six years later, she enjoyed the relative freedom that widowhood brought and travelled widely in England and Ireland, staying with family and friends. It was in Ireland that she met the Protestant cleric Patrick Delany and there was an immediate attraction; however, Delany was already engaged and took the honourable path by marrying his rich widowed fiancée. Mary Pendarves returned to England and waited. Eleven years later Delany's wife died and, after a suitable time had elapsed, he came to London finally to claim Mary. They married in 1743. They had twenty-five happy years together at their home, Delville, at Glasnevin on the outskirts of Dublin, where Mary enthusiastically cultivated her eleven-acre garden and continued to develop her keen knowledge of plants. From here she wrote regularly to her sister, describing their garden's progress.

I wish I could give you an idea of our garden, but the describing it puzzles me extremely; the back part of the house is towards a bowling-green, that slopes gently off down to a little brook that runs through the garden; on the other side of the brook is a high bank with a hanging wood of evergreens at top of which is circular terrace that surrounds the greatest part of the garden, the wall of which is covered with fruit trees, and on the other side of the wall a border for flowers and the greatest quantity of roses and sweet briar that ever I saw.[7]

Nearly two years later, when she was due to visit England and see her sister, she wrote again enthusiastically describing the garden's progress.

Our garden is now a wilderness of sweets. The violets, sweet briar, and primroses perfume the air . . . I have been planting sweets in my 'Pearly Bower' – honeysuckles, sweet briar, roses and jessamine to climb up the trees that compose it, and for the carpet, violets, primroses and cowslips. This year I shall not smell their fragrance, nor see their bloom, but I shall see the dear person to whom the bower is dedicated, I hope, and I think I shall not repine at the exchange.[8]

When Patrick died in 1768, Mary Delany returned to England, where her friendship with the Duchess of Portland and the King and Queen meant she was at the heart of the royal circle who shared their interests in plants and botany. Summers were spent at Bulstrode, where the two women were surrounded by all the exotic flora and fauna that the duchess had in her collection.

Mrs Delany was seventy-two when she started work on her

A stem of *Rosa gallica*, the damask rose (*c.*1780), created from
tiny slivers of coloured papers by Mary Delany (1700–88).

exquisite *Hortus siccus – a paper garden*. In the ten years between 1774 and
1784 she completed nearly one thousand flower and plant pictures,
painstakingly sticking tiny slivers of paper onto a black background,
which was most probably discarded wallpaper. She may have chosen a
dark base to make it easier to see the minute pieces of paper and, as
Thomasina Beck, the embroidery historian, has noted, she must have
had razor-sharp scissors as well.

Writing to her niece in 1782, Mrs Delany admitted that her eyes 'serve
me with some difficulty to attempt a flower now and then, wch I can
better see to do than to write, as the white paper dazzles my eyes, and at
this moment it obliges me to break off till I recover a new ray of light'.[9]
Erasmus Darwin was so impressed by Delany's skill that he included this
verse in his poem 'Loves of the Plants', part of *The Botanic Garden*.

So now DELANY forms her mimic bowers,
Her paper foliage, and her silken flowers;
Her virgin train the tender scissars ply,
Vein the green leaf, the purple petal dye:[10]

While many others attempted to make paper mosaics, no one had the brilliance of Mary Delany, but Darwin does mention another ingenious lady, Mrs North. She also created a *Hortus siccus*, about which he wrote, 'she executes on a ground of vellum with such elegant taste and scientific accuracy, that it cannot fail to become a work of inestimable value'.[11]

The majority of Mrs Delany's work is now in the British Museum, but Mrs North's has not survived. An album of flower collages by Mary Wise, a young woman who lived in Bath in the mid-nineteenth century, is in the Rachel Lambert Mellon collection at the Oak Spring Garden Library in Virginia.

The daughters of King George and Queen Charlotte also tried their hand at these collages. The Princess Elizabeth did some for her younger brother, the Duke of Sussex. 'I shall enclose two or three of my cuttings out, and if you like them I will send you more but,' she warned him, 'you must remember that I do not draw figures and cut out these without drawing them before.'[12] The princess was being modest as she was a talented flower painter, and decorated the Cross Gallery at Frogmore with panels of painted flower garlands and extremely delicate paper cut-outs.

Despite her royal connections, Mrs Delany's two marriages had not left her a wealthy woman. The Duchess of Portland had had to lend her £400 to buy a house in St James's Place. In her later years she relied a great deal on the friendship of the duchess, but notwithstanding her own immense wealth, she left Mrs Delany only three small pictures (two of which were of mice) and her 'small blew and black enamel snuff-box'.[13] She was treated far more generously, and with great esteem, by the King and Queen after the Duchess of Portland's death. They gave her a house close to Windsor Castle and an annual allowance of £300, a sum apparently tucked into a pocket book that the Queen presented to Mrs Delany twice a year.

Mrs Delany had no family to inherit her talents for paper mosaics and embroidery, but such botanical skills became unnecessary with the arrival from Germany in 1830 of a new form of embroidery kit with a printed cross-stitch chart of detailed floral designs. A Mr Wilks of Regent Street had spotted these kits some twenty years after they were first available in Germany and seen the potential for selling them to the flower- and embroidery-mad middle classes. The colourings of Berlinwork designs with black backgrounds and gaudy threads using the new strident aniline dyes discovered by William Perkin in 1856 were a world away from the delicate embroideries of Garthwaite and Delany, but their popularity was immense and a testimony to just how much spare time Victorian middle-class women had on their hands. They also confirm the continuing fascination for flowers in home décor, though no one could claim they had much botanical or artistic merit, and Perkins's dyes, perhaps thankfully, faded rapidly.

It took the intervention of the socialist William Morris to change attitudes towards design in the home. In 1882 in his famous work *Hopes and Fears for Art*, he attacked the fashion for vulgarity and asserted that the decorative arts in the home were 'in a state of anarchy and disorganisation, which makes a sweeping change necessary and certain'.[14] He felt the public needed to be reminded of the joy of simplicity in flowers. 'Don't be swindled out of that wonder of beauty, a single snowdrop; there is no gain and plenty of loss in the double one.' He detested the exotic plants being grown in greenhouses and conservatories across the country:

> plants, which are curiosities only, which Nature meant to be grotesque, not beautiful, and which are generally the growth of hot countries, where things sprout over quick and rank. Take note that the strangest of these come from the jungle and the tropical waste, from places where man is not at home, but is an intruder, an enemy. Go to a botanical garden and look at them, and think of those strange places to your heart's content. But don't set them to starve in your smoke-drenched scrap of ground amongst the bricks, for they will be no ornament to it.

He reserved his greatest venom for the fashion for strong colour in flowers: 'there are some flowers (inventions of men, i.e. florists) which are bad colour altogether, and not to be used at all. Scarlet geraniums, for instance, or the yellow calceolaria, which indeed are not uncommonly grown together profusely, in order, I suppose, to show that even flowers can be thoroughly ugly.'[15] The peak of Berlinwork coincided with the time when florists' flowers and their associated feasts became the preserve of the mainly northern working classes. It is a puzzling anomaly that Morris chose one of the last florists' flowers to be adopted and one which is certainly no native to Britain, the chrysanthemum, as the focal point of one of his most popular and enduring fabric designs.

The link between gardening and embroidery continued into the twentieth century, a trend encapsulated by Lady Ottoline Morrell. In the early 1900s she was a noted society hostess, entertaining both political friends of her MP husband and artists such as Augustus John, Henry

Lamb and Mark Gertler at their home at Garsington just outside Oxford. During the twelve years they lived there, from 1915 to 1927, Lady Ottoline created a garden, the charm of which, says her biographer Miranda Seymour, was 'its lack of ostentation and the use of space'.[16] Box-edged beds were packed with the hot colours of summer – montbretia, zinnias, marigolds, sunflowers and the like – while away from the grey stone seventeenth-century manor house, the grass tennis court was edged with soft lavender and pale yellow roses. The Italian garden with its tall clipped yews like Italian cypresses remains as a reminder of the Morrells' trips abroad and their love of statuary. 'Is the air ever normal at Garsington?' queried Virginia Woolf, a regular visitor. 'No, I think even the sky is done up in pale yellow silk.'

Silk was a key component of Lady Ottoline's other great passion, her embroidery lying rolled up behind a sofa ready to be worked on at a moment's notice. For ten years Lady Ottoline worked on an embroidered floral bedspread, 'a brilliant jungle of silk leaves and blossoms',[17] and she described in her memoirs the pleasure this gave her in the dark days of war when she started it in 1916, helped by her daughter's governess and a young Belgian refugee.

> I sat in my special chair under the lamp with a piece of embroidery and all my coloured silks spread out around me . . . How much is woven in that coverlet! How intense the feelings as we worked at it. What interesting and vital ideas were blended with the silks and woven into the pattern of gay flowers. Some flowers must still be bright with poetry, some dark and smudged with war; others vivid and bizarre with thoughts of life; and a lovely rose will always speak of the fragile beauty of love and friendship, and a sunflower was like one that grew in the garden with thoughts of Blake's 'weary of time'.[18]

The war was to change many things in women's lives, leaving less time for indulgences such as embroidery. The connection between garden and home did not weaken, however, and in the interwar years flowered chintzes supplied by companies such as Colefax & Fowler became the hallmark of the upper-class home. Despite having lost all her money in the crash of 1929, Sibyl Colefax moved in high society circles and knew the garden designer Norah Lindsay. Her collaboration with John Fowler led to one of the most important design partnerships of the twentieth century, and together they were responsible for the revival of the English country house style. Beautifully coloured and often botanically accurate fabrics, reminiscent of eighteenth-century designs, were their hallmark.

After the Second World War one woman more than any other was associated with flowery prints. Laura Ashley was inspired by the delicate floral muslin prints of the early nineteenth century and began by printing headscarves on her kitchen table in the 1950s. By the 1970s, the success of the company meant that the Laura Ashley style of tiny prints for cotton dresses, curtains and on wallpaper was instantly recognisable. It fitted in perfectly with the hippie and earth mother look of the time. Even before Ashley's untimely death in 1985, the fashion for floral designs with botanical accuracy had faltered, only to re-emerge in the new millennium in the more stylised form of Cath Kidston's fabrics. Today, gardening has become only one of the ways to bring flowers and plants indoors.

EVERY LADY HER OWN
DRAWING MASTER

In a letter dated 1751 to her friend the bluestocking Elizabeth Carter, Catherine Talbot wrote, 'I have lately got the advantage of an excellent master in the art of flower-painting, the head gardener of the physic-garden.'[1] Such was the passion for plants in that era that even an intellectual writer such as Talbot did not think it beneath her to learn how to paint flowers.

In the eighteenth century, certainly among the gentry, most female pastimes were seen as 'accomplishments', skills to be practised in between more essential duties. Embroidery, painting or playing a musical instrument were considered practical talents that might improve a young woman's marriage prospects, unlike reading too much fiction, which might give a girl unsuitable ideas. Botanical painting was one such 'accomplishment', seen as a genteel – and gentle – pastime for ladies in drawing rooms. It is hard to imagine that any drama could take place as the artist examined the details of a petal or seed pod, beyond an anxiety that the plant might expire before the painting was completed. However, Elizabeth Blackwell, the first woman known to have produced a work of botanical illustration in

Britain, practised her undoubted skill under extraordinarily stressful circumstances.

Blackwell married her second cousin, Alexander, when she was twenty-eight, possibly moving to London from Scotland in the mid-1730s. Alexander was from a Scottish family of highly esteemed medics and he had trained to be a doctor, but in London he decided he wanted to open a print shop. With ambitious enthusiasm and no qualifications he quickly ran into trouble and was sent to the debtors' prison for two years. With no income, the Blackwells' debts mounted even more quickly.

In desperation his wife turned to the only skill she had, which was drawing, in particular botanical drawing. Through her husband's medical friends, Elizabeth knew that there was a need for illustrations of the various herbs used in medicines, and she set about producing a book of over five hundred engravings. She accomplished the work normally undertaken by three separate male artisans – a sketcher, an engraver and a painter – entirely unaided. She also had the advantage of good connections, receiving encouragement from Sir Hans Sloane and Isaac Rand, who was then the director of the Chelsea Physic Garden, both of whom recognised her talent, and the renowned hor-ticulturalist Philip Miller provided her with plant material for the illustrations. The book, *A curious herbal: containing five hundred cuts, of the most useful plants, which are now used in the practice of physick*, took her nearly two years to complete, during which time she contended with the death of her infant son and the continued incarceration of her husband. This would be an impressive story in any era, but the fact that this took place in the early eighteenth century is astounding. The quality of her work may not have been the highest but her determination was undeniable.

Having been rescued by his talented and diligent wife, Alexander

Foeniculum vulgare, delicately drawn by Elizabeth Blackwell (bap. 1707, d. 1758) in her attempt to earn money to help her husband out of debt.

Blackwell got involved with another scam from which she could not extricate him. As a result he left for Sweden in the year that Elizabeth gave birth to a second son and, according to Carl von Linné (Linnaeus, the world-famous botanist), even more intrigue followed. Linnaeus later wrote in *Nemesis Divina* that Blackwell became over-friendly with the wife of a broker in whose house he was staying in Stockholm, and the broker died shortly after Blackwell had treated him for colic. He was suspected of murder, and he was also involved in a hare-brained scheme to persuade the King of Sweden to repudiate his heir and appoint a British prince as his successor. This was his final undoing and on 29 July 1747 Alexander Blackwell was executed in Stockholm for treason. Throughout all this, Elizabeth remained devoted to her ne'er-do-well husband but on his death she gave up her work and died alone eleven years later.

What Elizabeth Blackwell had exposed was the need for accurate representations of medicinal plants. Illustrations in popular gardening books were basic to say the least – woodcuts that could not capture any botanical detail. Mary, Duchess of Beaufort, an avid plant collector, often struggled to identify seeds sent to her from the Far East. She wrote exasperatedly to her fellow collector Sir Hans Sloane, wishing there had been a painter on hand 'that would have better exprest this plant'.[2] Until the advent of accurate colour photography, horticulturalists had to rely on botanical illustrations produced by those with a skill far greater than the average drawing-room accomplishment.

The royal family, in particular under George III, led the way in not just enjoying flower painting but showing great talent as well. Queen Charlotte was given art lessons by Francis Bauer, who astutely dedicated *Delineation of Exotick Plants* to his patron in 1796. Some ten years later, Robert Thornton's *Temple of Flora* was also inscribed to Queen Charlotte, lauding the royal women by declaring, 'there is not a plant in the gardens of Kew ... but has either been drawn by her gracious Majesty, or some of the Princesses, with a grace and skill that reflects on these personages the highest honour'.[3]

It was not long before the princesses fulfilled their duty and were married off to various members of European royalty. The Princess Royal took her talent with her to Württemberg on her marriage to the duke, later writing to her father to reassure him that she was not homesick after her arrival at her new home in Louisbourg. 'I amuse myself in watching the progress of the Spring in the little Garden onto which my Room opens, and in drawing the Flowers which blow there.'[4]

George Brookshaw's *A New Treatise on Flower Painting, or, Every Lady Her Own Drawing Master*
(1816) gave women step-by-step guidance on plant drawing and colouring.

Even with royal involvement, not everyone thought such works truly worthy of the name 'art'. In 1818 the floral artist George Brookshaw acknowledged that 'there are men of abilities, who think it beneath them to paint flowers, and affect to treat that branch of the art with contempt',[5] and that is partly the reason why the world of botanical illustration is so often an anonymous one, though nonetheless one that was dominated by men. The artists were also much in demand among the top families in the country, who saw the art of botanical illustration as a genteel accomplishment for their daughters. Georg Ehret taught the daughters of three dukes, several lords and one earl in addition to two duchesses and two countesses. Not surprisingly, he said exhaustedly, 'if I could have divided myself into twenty parts . . . I could have had my hands full'.[6]

With such aristocratic approval, botanical painting was one of the few talents a middle-class woman was encouraged to develop and one that could be in demand if done well. It became highly fashionable to sketch domestic flora, and many women rarely left home without a small sketchbook and a miniature watercolour palette close to hand. These sketchbooks were not worked with publication in mind, but purely for the artist's and her family's own pleasure. By the end of the eighteenth century, no self-respecting young lady could consider herself accomplished if she was unable to turn her hand to producing passable paintings of the flowers and plants in her garden.

Books such as James Sowerby's *A Botanical Drawing Book; or, An Easy Introduction to Drawing Flowers according to Nature*, first published in 1788, and George Brookshaw's *A New Treatise on Flower Painting, or, Every Lady Her Own Drawing Master*, which appeared in 1818, were enormously popular among amateur artists. They were predominantly aimed at female painters, as George Brookshaw's comments in his introduction to *Flower Painting* make clear. 'The general inclination of ladies for flower painting, added to the great progress they may have made in attaining the art, is a convincing proof that the taste, or genius, for this pleasing amusement, is not confined to the male sex; on the contrary, I am much inclined to think, that ladies would sooner arrive at perfection than men, were they at first taught its proper rudiments.'[7]

Unfortunately, the combination of the words 'amateur', 'female' and 'flowers' was enough to strike terror into the heart of any male artist of the establishment and is key to our understanding of why the few women who did rise above the drawing-room accomplishment level were rarely credited for the work they did. True botanical illustration done for a professional market requires painstaking care and dedication, and Brookshaw could see no reason why female artists 'should not bear away the palm of flower painting from the other sex'.[8] But the reality was that hardly any women were to get fair recognition for their work until the early twentieth century. Nevertheless, they all shared a passionate perfectionism in capturing plant material on paper.

Whereas names such as Ehret and Redouté are well known even today, the names of British women have been barely mentioned in bibliographical works on botanical artists and flower painters of the eighteenth and nineteenth centuries. During their own lifetimes their work was ignored or denigrated and many also had a very low opinion of their own skill.

A handful of women artists did achieve varying degrees of success. In the 1790s Queen Charlotte commissioned the flower painter Mary Moser to decorate a room at Frogmore, for which she reputedly received the enormous sum of £900. The room remains a testament to her talent and can still be seen on the rare occasions that Queen Charlotte's favourite place of relaxation is open to the public. Poor Mary Moser was described as being 'so near-sighted, that her nose, when she was painting, was within an inch of the canvas; and it is astonishing, with such an infirmity . . . that she could display such harmony in her performances'.[9]

Moser's paintings now seem rather 'flowery', a trifle Dutch, particularly her pieces depicting overflowing vases of seasonal flowers, but they were all extremely well executed. Her father was George Moser, the first keeper, or head teacher, of the Royal Academy, and Mary was later appointed Flower Painter to the Queen, but neither these antecedents nor her talent saved her from the humiliation in later life of being proposed as president of the Royal Academy, receiving one vote from Fuseli, a former admirer, and then having her name scratched out of the minutes since it was 'evidently intended as a joke'.[10]

Clara Maria Pope (1768–1838), flower artist and artist's model.
This charmingly unabashed study was by her husband-to-be,
artist Francis Wheatley, who made Clara his third wife.

Moser's contemporaries, Clara Maria Pope and Margaret Meen, also made names for themselves in the world of botanical illustration. Meen was a young painter from Bungay in Suffolk who came up to London to make a living from teaching flower and insect painting. The botanist Thomas Jenkinson Woodward, who lived near her in Suffolk, gave her an introduction to William Curtis of *Curtis's Botanical Magazine*, and her flower paintings were accepted by the Royal Academy for ten years between 1775 and 1785. She was also a regular visitor to Kew, where she painted many of the new exotic arrivals and had plans to publish a series called *Exotic Plants from the Royal Gardens at Kew*, but only two issues appeared. Clara Maria Pope turned from miniatures to Dutch-style flower paintings to botanical art, and it was this last style which brought her lasting recognition as the botanical illustrations in

Curtis's 1819 publication, *Monograph of the Genus Camellia*, were all Pope's work.

Mary Lawrance made no claims to paint with the accuracy of a botanical artist, but brought in extra money from lessons in 'drawing Botany at H a guinea a lesson & a guinea entrance' from her home in Queen Anne Street East.[11] Having successfully exhibited a flower piece at the Royal Academy in 1794, Lawrance produced a series of monographs on roses, passion flowers and others from nature which have remained of interest to horticultural historians. Subscribers to her *A Collection of Roses*, for example, were promised 'every approved Species now in cultivation in England ... Price to Subscribers is Ten Shillings and Sixpence'.[12] Her good friend the famed horticulturalist Robert Sweet named *Rosa lawranceana* for her in 1805. It was later rather charmingly renamed *R.* 'Caprice des Dames', since it was an upright miniature rose and hardier than its delicate looks suggested.

Close family connections did little to improve women's chances of recognition. The men of the Sowerby family are particularly well known, especially James, whose *Botanical Drawing Book* was another favourite among young ladies. George Edward Sowerby published the *Repository Magazine*, a botanical periodical, while George Brettingham Sowerby was a shell artist. Unsurprisingly, two of George Edward's daughters, Charlotte and Ellen, were talented botanical artists, and although Charlotte has been called one of the three most important members of the Sowerby family, Blunt's *Art of Botanical Illustration* managed not to mention her at all.

Other well-connected daughters fared little better. In the 1820s and '30s Benjamin Maund was a successful publisher of two periodicals, *The Botanic Garden* and *The Botanist*. The success of Maund's publications rested largely on the outstanding quality of the illustrations, many of which were done by women, including his two daughters, Miss Maund, the eldest, and Miss S. Maund. Yet again, nothing is known about the lives of the two women, except that they did not marry, too busy, no doubt, supporting their father in his publishing business.

PAINTING AND PUBLISHING

When Mrs Henrietta Moriarty published *Fifty Greenhouse Plants* in 1803, the plates were originally dismissed as 'too good to be done by the hand of a woman'. The female artists of the nineteenth century fall into one of two categories: those women who were financially secure enough to have a battery of servants giving them the time to paint, and the less fortunate who used their artistic skills to earn a living to support their families. While the majority of the women were undoubtedly paid for their work, very few received the credit they deserved for their skill. Only a handful joined the professional associations that would have put them into a more public arena, although it may well have been their choice to eschew such membership. As a result, almost without exception the male publisher claimed the credit and fame for the botanical plates. Mrs Moriarty was one such woman who struggled for recognition, and even a hundred years later she was erroneously accused of having plagiarised illustrations by Samuel Curtis from the renowned *Curtis's Botanical Magazine*.

Mrs Moriarty was also unusual in including some gardening advice alongside her illustrations: she had chosen, she told her readers, 'a select number of such plants, as are remarkable for their beauty, their odour, or some peculiarity in their economy; and I have added to each the Linnean name, and a short account of the most approved mode of cultivating it'.[1] However, Mrs Moriarty had a distinctly superior attitude towards the botanical family system, adding that 'I have taken as little notice as possible of the system of the immortal Linneus, and of all the illustrations and comments on it; nay, I have not once named the fanciful Doctor Darwin.'[2]

Curtis's Botanical Magazine has been published continuously since 1787, making it the longest running illustrated botanical journal in the world. Each four-part volume contained twenty-four plant portraits reproduced from watercolour originals by botanical artists, a fair proportion of whom would have been women. The four granddaughters of its founder, William Curtis, were all accomplished botanical artists, and at least one of them supplied plates to the world-famous magazine.

One reason why women were reluctant to push themselves forward in the world of nineteenth-century botanical illustration was because when they did, they were frequently criticised. Priscilla Bury is a case in point. She was a professional artist who did not need to work. Born into a wealthy family near Liverpool in 1799, Priscilla grew up surrounded by hothouse plants and her skill in painting lilies and amaryllis was brought to the attention of William Swainson, a zoologist, and William Roscoe, a Liverpudlian botanist, both of whom encouraged Bury to publish. However, her evident talent was barely acknowledged when she produced *A Selection of Hexandrian Plants* between 1831 and 1834. She had used Robert Havell, well known for his work on the plates of the bird illustrations of Audubon, for the engravings and colouring of the plates and it was he who got most of the praise. To add insult to injury, a reviewer commented, 'Probably her marriage in 1830 to a wealthy engineer meant she could afford the best, and copperplate was done instead of lithography.'

When we do know something about the patterns of these women's lives, however, it can tell us a great deal. The nineteenth century has been traditionally seen as a time when middle-class women in particular were tied to their homes and families with few opportunities for life-enhancing or financially rewarding careers, but modern research discredits the idea of 'separate spheres' and shows that many Victorian women led fulfilling lives through a variety of occupations, especially in philanthropic work. For a handful of women, botanical art was a way in which they were able to reach out into the world of professional publishing without compromising their familial positions in society.

Elizabeth Twining of the eponymous tea family was able to combine the two occupations of philanthropic work and botanical talents. In addition to establishing the Twining Hospital for the Poor near her home in Twickenham and being connected to two newly opened establishments for girls' education, Bedford College and Queen's College, she published fourteen books, including *Ten Years in a Ragged School*. In 1849, then in her mid-forties, she published the second volume of her work *Illustrations of the Natural Order of Plants*, which comprised extremely accurate drawings of plants at the Royal Botanic Gardens at Kew. The 'natural order', however, was not the accepted botanical order of Linnaeus but that of Alphonse de Candolle, who emphasised the mature appearance of plants. This system was popular for a while, but unfortunately for Elizabeth Twining it fell from favour and the botanical world eventually opted for the Linnean order.

Jane Loudon combined illustration with the written word and certainly made a living from her self-illustrated gardening books after her husband's death. *The Ladies' Flower-Garden* series, *Ornamental Annuals*, *Ornamental Bulbous Plants*, *Ornamental Perennials* and *Ornamental Green House*

An illustration of *Agapetes setigera*, brought from the Himalayas in 1838, from Jane Loudon's publication, *The Ladies' Magazine of Gardening* (1852).

Plants, which all appeared in the 1840s, contain lithographic plates that were taken from her own drawings. There is some doubt as to whether these are all her own work as there are so many and Mrs Earle, the late Victorian garden writer, is unusually dismissive of them. She described them as 'artistically bad as flower-paintings, and inferior to those published now in the weekly gardening papers' but grudgingly admitted that 'they resemble the flowers enough to be recognisable'.[3]

Augusta Withers made a good marriage in 1825 when she was in her mid-thirties, which at the time would have been considered quite late in life. Her husband, Theodore Withers, was an accountant and older than Augusta, and as time passed circumstances forced her to find ways of earning money from her talents as an artist. By August 1830 her artistic reputation had led to her appointment as Flower Painter in Ordinary to Queen Adelaide, consort of the last Hanoverian King of England, William IV. It was a position which gave her prestige without any financial support, but she also produced plates for the entire edition of the *Pomological Magazine* during its three-year run from 1828 to 1830, and her work appeared regularly in *Curtis's Botanical Magazine* and in Benjamin Maund's *The Botanist*.

Withers's best work was probably the plates that she produced for James Bateman's massive tome on the orchids of Mexico and Guatemala. Weighing in at a staggering 17½ kilos, it has been described by Wilfred Blunt as 'probably the finest and certainly the largest botanical book ever produced with lithographic plates'. She also found time to submit to and be accepted by the Royal Academy, but when she

Datura rosei, the Thorn Apple flower from Ecuador, illustrated by prolific nineteenth-century botanical artist Augusta Withers (1792–1876).

190

applied for the post of Botanical Flower Painter at the Royal Botanical Gardens its director, Sir Joseph Dalton Hooker, rejected her, shocked that a mere woman should be presumptive enough to apply in the first place, despite the fact that she was undoubtedly qualified for the position.

Mrs Withers's fortunes plummeted after the death of her patron, Queen Adelaide, in 1849, and after her husband lost his sight she was forced to sell her work to a pawnshop to raise funds. She was reputedly too proud to apply to the Artists' Benevolent Fund, though after her experience with Hooker and Kew one can imagine that she expected little sympathy from the male-dominated charitable organisation. Occasionally Queen Victoria bought a small work to help her, and when she was eventually widowed in 1869, she applied to the Privy Purse. 'I am positively pennyless and nearly starving . . . Pray forgive me for troubling you so much with my miserable affairs . . . I am nearly heartbroken.'[4] She was helped once, but turned down a second time and six years later she died penniless.

Augusta Withers's work appeared in Bateman's book alongside that of Sarah Anne Drake. Until quite recently hardly anything was known about Miss Drake other than the marvellous quality of her work, especially her paintings of orchids. The list of the works that she contributed plates to reads like a who's who of the best in botanical publications, not just of the nineteenth century but possibly of any era. They include Bateman's *Orchids of Mexico and Guatemala*, Dr Hamilton's *Plantae Asiaticae rariores*, and other volumes on orchids by John Lindley. Lindley also named a rare genus of the Australian hammer orchid 'Drakaea' for her. These orchids are known for their ability to attract wasps in order to place their pollen correctly. The pinnacle of her work is to be found in Sydenham Edward's *Botanical Register*, to which Miss Drake contributed over one thousand plates, and when she stopped contributing to the *Register* in 1847 it nearly went out of business.

For a long time it was thought that 'the enigmatic Miss S.A. Drake' was perhaps a distant relative of John Lindley,[5] who was the founding father of what was to become the Royal Horticultural Society. This was because she was 'always at Lindley's home'.[6] Alice Coats, the garden historian, believed that Drake must have died in 1847 since there is no evidence of any more of her work after that date; however, new research has provided us with fresh details about her life.

Sarah Drake came from a village in Norfolk close to where John Lindley grew up, and in about 1830, when she was in her late twenties, Lindley invited Sarah to come and live with his family at his home in Turnham Green, west London. Whether this was because he knew of her skill as a botanical artist or whether he merely wanted a reliable nanny for his children isn't clear, but whatever the reason it was a fortuitous choice. She stayed with the family for sixteen years, known as 'Ducky' to the three children and swiftly developing her skills under Lindley's guidance, eventually becoming his 'artist-in-residence' and much in demand. In 1847 she left London and returned to Norfolk, and as she appears never to have painted again, and certainly not to have published any of her work, it was assumed she had died at that time. Perhaps her eyesight was failing or she had become ill from ingesing poison from her painting materials, both common fates which befell her peers. But in November 1853, Lindley's daughter, Sarah, revealed a far happier conclusion: 'We have just received news of a happy wedding in prospect which has made us quite noisy with rejoicing for it is no less than that of our most excellent worthy old friend Ducky who although no relation has all our lives been as dear to us. We had no idea there was such a thing even on the tapis, until we now learn that in about a fortnight's time she is to become Mrs Hastings, the wife of a good and wealthy Norfolk farmer.'[7]

In the event, 'Ducky' Drake had only five years of marriage as the second wife to John Hastings, her 'good and wealthy farmer'. Shortly after her death Hastings took John Lindley's sister, Anne, as his third and last spouse, neatly illustrating the pith in the nursery rhyme that the farmer needs a wife.

It would not have been unusual if Miss Drake had been related to John Lindley, however, for such familial associations were how many female botanical artists came to publish their work. Matilda Smith was second cousin to Sir Joseph Dalton Hooker. Smith was close to him, addressing him in her letters as 'my dear Joseph' and signing herself 'yours affectionately',[8] and he encouraged her to submit her work for publication. When she was only twenty-four, despite having no experience in botanical drawing, she had her first work accepted by *Curtis's Botanical Magazine*. In the next three years she contributed around twenty plates per issue, and within six years she was virtually the only artist working on the magazine, throughout her working career contributing over 2,300 drawings to *Curtis's*. Such was the high standard of her work that she also contributed nearly two thousand illustrations to the *Transactions of the Linnean Society*, the *Transactions of the Royal Society* and *Kew Guild*. By 1910 her value to the herbarium and library at Kew was recognised with an annual salary of £52. By 1915 she had produced over three thousand plates for Hooker's *Icones Plantarum*.

A photograph in later life shows a staunchly conservative but motherly looking woman dressed in heavily braided black bombazine. In a piquant illustration of how such women were viewed by male 'professionals', the art historian Wilfred Blunt, in an article in the *Art of Botanical Illustration* first published in 1950, haughtily dismissed her work, saying that 'Miss Smith . . . remained to the end a rather fumbling draftsman, more remembered for her "great pains" and "untiring efforts" than for her skill', then added patronisingly, 'best of all esteemed for the charm of her personality'.

EN PLEIN AIR

Marianne North is justly famous as an intrepid traveller and floral landscape painter, one of the breed of flower artists who prefer to paint plants in their natural surroundings. There is a danger of losing accuracy because of the necessary rush to get a painting finished before the light goes, but several women have been able to achieve astounding results and, in doing so, capture far more than just the bloom itself.

North began to travel the world after the death of her adored father in 1868 when she was thirty-eight, aiming to cure her grief by 'going to some tropical country to paint its peculiar vegetation in its natural abundant luxuriance'. She never married, so was not constrained by the restrictions of a Victorian family life, and her adventurous journeys and eccentric style are legendary. She admitted she cared little for the social niceties of the time, turning up to a vice-regal ceremony in India wearing an 'old hooped-up serge gown and a shabby hat'.

Among her friends was the fellow traveller and artist Edward Lear, and in August 1877 he provided her with a letter of introduction to Dr Arthur Coke Burnell, an English scholar of Sanskrit based in Madras. 'If this is given to you by Miss North,' wrote Lear, 'please do all you can

Marianne North (1830–90) had the financial independence to travel widely and was
rare among nineteenth-century flower artists in preferring to paint plants *in situ*.

for her as to sights – particularly flowers, etc., etc., as she is a great
draughtswoman and botanist, and is altogetheracriously clever and
delightful.'[1]

Lear's introduction was successful, and she and Burnell became
friends and correspondents, with North often describing her travels to
him. 'I did not enjoy my elephant ride,' she wrote from a hill station in
India in 1878. 'It was like a walking tree, and so slow! So I used my own
feet and two men walked after me with 4 skins of a huge beast on their
backs on which a bamboo seat was fixed and floated and I always came
down the stream homewards on that frail barque – the men resting
their bodies on the skins and paddling with their feet – it was a most
primitive but very efficient means of going.'[2]

A prolific painter, North brought home 240 oils after a visit to

Buitenzorg in Java in 1878. She said she was encouraged to publish them by Sir Joseph Hooker of Kew, especially the paintings of the mangroves which had not been illustrated before, but by that stage North was a little reluctant to continue. 'I do not think it would pay,' she felt. 'After all, few people really care for such things – one half the people who look over my work do it because it is the fashion to do so and would not find out if the things were topsy-turvy!'[3]

However, it was not long before she came up with a scheme to leave her paintings to Kew in a more permanent collection. 'I should like to build a Gallery,' she mused, 'close to the pleasure grounds (or in them) at Kew, hang my pictures and have coffee and tea for all the poor tired visitors – with a cottage for myself to go and sulk and paint in when I want rest and green trees. If Sir Joseph could find me a bit of ground I would build this – and leave it to him and future directors of the gardens, pictures, cups and saucers and all – Do you think my scheme will ever come to pass?'[4]

It proved to be no daydream. Marianne North had the money to finance a gallery and Kew accepted, and while construction work was going on she travelled to Queensland, Sydney, Melbourne, Tasmania and New Zealand, getting to each at their best seasons. She also ensured that the project would be completed if something happened to her during her travels. 'I shall leave the money for the building with the Trustees here, so that even if I am drowned the work will go on, and it will be a great pleasure to think I leave behind something which will be a help and pleasure to others, as the world goes on.'[5] The gallery opened the following year, in 1882, after Miss North had overseen the hanging of over eight hundred of her works, and she lived on another eight years, dying in 1890 at the age of sixty. She has accurately been described as 'a painter who travelled, rather than a traveller who painted'.[6]

In *Visit in the Botanic Garden, Brisbane, Queensland*, Marianne North captured flowers of the Large Water Lily, *Nymphaea gigantea*, peculiar to Australia, as well as Screw Pines, *Pandanus sp.* and an Aralia.

The lesser-known Arabella Roupell was North's contemporary and had a much longer life, dying on the eve of the First World War when she was ninety-seven. Roupell was a clergyman's daughter from Shropshire and, as one of twelve children and the fourth of five daughters, she appeared destined for a traditional Victorian life. She accepted the hand of Thomas Roupell, an official with the East India Company in Madras, while he was on leave in England in 1840. Their first child, a boy, died, but Arabella went on to have five more healthy sons. She also had a significant career as a botanist and botanical artist.

Not long after their arrival in Madras, Arabella was packing again as her husband took leave to visit the Cape Colony of southern Africa. She had begun to paint local flora in India, but in the Cape she was able to increase her knowledge through friendship with Nathaniel Wallich from the Royal Botanic Gardens, Calcutta, who was also visiting the country. On their return to India, such was Roupell's talent that a folio of her work from the Cape was published in England with the support of William Harvey, curator of the herbarium of Trinity College, Dublin, and with Queen Victoria as its first subscriber. The sting in the tail is that the work was published pseudonymously, for reasons either of modesty or of decorum.

The Roupells retired to Reading in Berkshire, where Arabella Roupell lived in astonishing obscurity for the next fifty-five years. Years later, in 1950, the family left her original works from the Cape and India to Jan Smuts.

There was no such obscurity for Margaret Mee, an artist whose talent had shone from childhood. A committed socialist and never conventional, as a young woman Mee had spent much of the 1930s in Germany and France. In 1937 she became the youngest delegate to address the Trades Union Congress on a question of raising the school leaving age, but in this period she produced little painting: 'All I did in those years were some large placard-type cut-outs for the tragic faces of the Hungry 'Thirties which were paraded around Whitestone Pond in Hampstead.'[7]

After the war, with a failed marriage behind her, she was accepted at Camberwell School of Art, then in the late 1940s she met Greville Mee, a commercial artist who was to become her second husband. In 1952, when she was forty-three years old, they heard that Catherine, Margaret's sister, was seriously ill in São Paolo, Brazil. Margaret decided to make the long journey by air to look after her, with Greville to follow on later. 'We thought we would stay for three or four years,' Greville recalled, 'but it [grew] into a lifetime.'[8]

Margaret got a job teaching art at the British School in São Paolo, but was immediately captivated by the flora of the tropics surrounding them. She went on what was to be the first of fifteen expeditions into the Amazon jungle, determined to record the astonishing and flamboyant plants and landscape. Armed with a canvas rucksack, spare clothes, her artist's kit and a revolver, this English woman from Chesham in Buckinghamshire set out to make a systematic study of the region's tropical plants. Bouts of malaria did not stop her from undertaking more and more trips. On one voyage in a boat along the rapids of Rio Marauiá, Mee spotted a *Coryanthes albertinae* orchid dangling from an overhanging tree branch. Her guide made a grab for it and was immediately stung by vicious ants that were nesting in the orchid's root. Undeterred, Mee reached for the plant herself and, with the ants also stinging her, managed to stuff it into a plastic bag. She was later diagnosed with hepatitis, but while recovering in hospital she managed to complete her painting of this rare trophy. The resulting illustration of the orchid was chosen for the front cover of the first volume of *Orchidaceae Brasilienses*, the mammoth work of her friend Guido Pabst, which first appeared in 1975. Mee's work was invaluable for conservationists anxious to show the world what flora the rainforests of Brazil contained, as her exquisite paintings were botanically accurate as well as capturing the feel of the Amazon basin. Tragically and ironically, after all her years of travelling in the Amazon basin, Margaret Mee was killed in a car crash in Leicestershire in 1988 while visiting Britain to promote her third book.

Several female botanical artists have been honoured by the Royal Horticultural Society in the twentieth century, and rightly so. Matilda Smith, the doyenne of Kew, was first in 1926, followed in 1953 by Nellie Roberts, who produced nearly five thousand paintings of all the orchids that had ever received an award of merit or a first-class certificate. Lilian Snelling took over from Smith on *Curtis's Botanical*

Magazine in 1921 and was awarded the Victoria Medal of Honour in 1955. Stella Ross-Craig worked at Kew from 1929, when she was twenty-three, until 1960, quietly producing more than three thousand illustrations, including many for *Curtis's Botanical Magazine*. Her greatest works were the 1,300 scientific pen and ink illustrations for the *Drawings of British Plants*, produced and published between 1949 and 1973. Far from being dry and 'scientific' to look at, these drawings of each plant and its various components are married together on one page in a true work of art, elegant but informative. They were unrivalled, experts agreed, for their show of 'sound botanical knowledge with accurate draughtsmanship'.[9] Such was her precision that she never used a pencil to outline first because, she said with startling honesty, '[I] did not need to as [I] never made mistakes.'[10]

Mary Grierson also joined Kew as a botanical artist for twelve years from 1960 to 1972. In addition she was much sought-after as an illustrator for horticultural writers such Chris Bricknell, Christopher Grey-Wilson and Bryan Mathews. She has been awarded five RHS gold medals for Botanical Illustration, the Veitch Memorial Medal in 1984, and in 1998 their highest honour, the Victoria Medal of Honour. This was the same year as it was awarded to Margaret Stones, who was principal contributing artist to *Curtis's Botanical Magazine* for many years as well as being in demand for illustrations and exhibitions across the world.

Many believe that botanical illustration is still the Cinderella of the painting world, despite the efforts of Shirley Sherwood, who has devoted years to promoting it. The newly opened Shirley Sherwood Gallery at Kew shows that, far from being a dying art, more artists than ever are fascinated by the highly specialised skill of botanical illustration. The majority of students on courses of botanical illustration at the English Gardening School and the Chelsea Physic Garden are women, and while botanical drawings no longer have the scientific significance that they once had, the challenge of capturing the perfection of plants on paper or canvas remains as alluring as it has been for centuries.

FLOWER DECORATION

'Arranging flowers,' the *Gardeners' Magazine* of 1904 concluded, 'is one of those things that every woman in the world thinks nobody can do but herself; she is as much addicted to self-esteem in this direction as a man is over mending the fire; and who does not enjoy the pleasing excitement of setting out the flowers for a dinner party? The very smell of the wet moss, the cool feel of the stalks, the bunches of pliant fern, the baskets ready to be unpacked, every circumstance is in itself a pleasure.'[1]

Until the second half of the nineteenth century the evolution of flower-arranging had progressed at a snail's pace. From Roman mosaics to early paintings, little more had been done with flowers than to place them in a container of water and enjoy them. In the seventeenth century when tulip mania was at its height, exquisite pyramid plant holders of Delft pottery were shown off in the best homes, and while many believe that these were designed to hold bulbs, it is just as likely that they were also used to display individual stems of tulips and hyacinths that had been grown outside. By the eighteenth century, beautifully delicate vases were filled with wet silver sand and moss used to support the flower stems, and there was a boom in domestic porcelain and pottery led by Josiah Wedgwood, who swiftly opened a showroom in London to entice new buyers for the designs emerging from his factory. Coming away after a visit to the shop, Mary Delany declared she was 'quite giddy at looking at so much crockery ware'.[2] Grand homes would fill their fireplaces in the summer with bough or 'bow' pots of cut flowers or branches of flowering shrubs together with pots of *Campanula pyramidalis*.

The fashion for decorating the dinner table arose in part because of changes in people's eating habits. Before the nineteenth century, when tables were laid *à la française*, the food itself was part of the decoration, spread out to cover the table so that guests could help themselves. A variety of individual dishes was placed on the table with the best and most decorative food set in front of the most important guests, but from the early 1800s the Russian fashion of food from the same menu being offered to guests by servants became increasingly popular. However, with this style of service the table suddenly looked bare, so elaborate flower and plant arrangements were brought in to decorate the empty spaces.

Before the invention of Oasis – green blocks of porous foam able to support individual stems – specially designed containers were needed for these arrangements. One such, a green metal cone known as the 'Pyramidal Boquet Stand', was invented by Mr Daniel Stead of Huddersfield and supplied by Messrs Henderson of St John's Wood. The tiny rows of holes were intended to be studded with flower heads in rainbow colours; one suggestion was for a pyramid of scarlet geraniums, asters and pansies or verbenas and chrysanthemums in regular rows of the same colour, or a mass of pansies with a row of white asters around the bottom.

In upper-class homes it was one of the duties of the head gardener to produce elaborate table displays that had to change every day of the week during the social season. Middle-class wives had little choice but to do their own arrangements, and for those less artistically inclined this may well have been a stressful rather than a relaxing chore, but with the rapid expansion of the suburbs and of the publishing industry there was soon no shortage of literature to guide them. In addition to Mrs Beeton, writers such as Miss Maling in the 1860s and Annie Hassard in the 1870s produced helpful books with hints on everything from 'vases for the Breakfast-table' to 'Sprays for the Hair' and 'Button-hole Bouquets and Coat Flowers'.

In the 1867 publication *A Handbook for Ladies on in-Door Plants, Flowers for Ornament and Song Birds* the author, Miss Maling (her first name was never revealed), claimed that her designs were the perfect complement to the London home looking for 'natural' arrangements 'artistically' created. The formal and artificial flower displays she describes were the height of fashion in suburban homes from Barnet to Beckenham, but even she felt the need to justify such stiffness. 'When I say artistically, of course I mean that perfect degree of art in which no art is visible; when everything looks so simple and so natural, that it could hardly be imagined other than what it is.'[3]

As the fashion for flower-arranging took hold it was inevitable that competitions should follow, and when the Royal Horticultural Society celebrated its royal affiliation in 1861 generous prizes were offered for 'groups of Fruit and Flowers' displayed in 'Baskets of any materials, china vases, glass dishes, or epergnes'.[4] The judging was done by a 'Jury of Ladies', two ladies and two countesses to be precise, and two more ladies, Lady Rokeby and Lady Kerrison, came second and third respectively for a 'very elegant display' which included pineapples, and 'a rich display ... of various valuable flowers'. However, the first prize went to a man, Thomas C. March, although it was rumoured that he had been helped by his sisters. What had won him the prize was a completely new way of displaying flowers on a

A prize-winning dinner-table decoration from Annie Hassard's *Floral Decorations for Dwelling Houses* (1876), one of many designs for middle-class wives to copy for their own dining tables.

series of glass stands, allowing the blooms of lilies of the valley, forget-me-nots, pansies and rosebuds to cascade down over Maidenhair Fern with small bunches of grapes 'introduced here and there'. Within weeks the 'March' stand became commercially available; a book, March's *Flower and Fruit Decoration*, followed just a year later, and soon his ideas were 'spreading through the country'.[5]

Other writers recommended the use of the Marchian Vase, including Annie Hassard in her book *Floral Decorations for Dwelling Houses* which appeared in 1875. Hassard lived in Upper Norwood, one of south London's new sprawling suburbs, and although little is known about her she makes it clear that she is well connected in the horticultural publishing world by crediting William Robinson for help with the engraved illustrations, many of which probably came from his magazine *The Garden*. She wrote that her book was 'intended for the use of Ladies and Amateurs', for the wife at home who 'did' her own flowers with florists' materials. By this time the term 'florist' had taken on its modern meaning as someone who sold and often arranged flowers commercially. Her calendar of flower choices suggests that she assumed these women would have had quite deep pockets as well, recommending that for the month of March, for example, her favourite two-tiered Marchian Vase would need to be dressed with the following:

Lower Tazza: Stephanotis, pink Geraniums, double white Primulas, pink Heaths, Sedge (Cyperus alternifolius), and Maiden-hair; round the edge fronds of Pteris serrulata and Pteris cretica albo-lineata Ferns.

Upper Tazza: White Carnations, Pink Azaleas, Lily of the Valley, and Maiden-hair, fronts of the same drooping round the edge.

Trumpet: Lily of the Valley, pink Heaths, and three sprays of the white Polygonatum (Solomon's Seal), a few fronds of Maiden-hair being arranged round the mouth.[6]

This example and the elaborate designs suggested for the breakfast table by John Perkins in 1877 make one wonder where they had room to set out their food. Perkins had been head gardener to the Henniker family at Thornham Hall in Suffolk for twenty-nine years when he published a little book entitled *Floral Designs for the Table; being directions for its ornamentation with leaves, flowers, and fruit.* It was the first book on flower-arranging written by a head gardener.

All his designs are for parties of between eight and one hundred people. The scale of entertaining is clear since Perkins says that many large establishments would need about five designs each week, and 'it will of course be advisable to have them as different in character as possible each night'. No wonder then that he suggested that 'after the company have left the dining-room, the groom of the chambers or the underbutler should place any fern fronds, leaves or anything else worth preserving, into water, whereby many useful pieces may be saved and be made available for other purposes the following day'.

Flowers were also used to create headdresses and corsages, though *The Lady* magazine offered stern caution over the use of gardenias: 'More than *one* gardenia might be overpowering and would savour of ostentation.'[7]

For the middle-class Victorian woman, flower-arranging was about far more than just decorating a dining table or making a corsage; it was also about communication. 'Flower dictionaries' which gave each plant a specific meaning of its own flooded on to the market, making every variety and colour of flower part of a horticultural messaging service. Such was the popularity of floral languages in Britain, and also across Europe and America, that it was quite possible to communicate feelings and emotions through a small posy of flowers. From the A of

The demand for elaborate flower arrangements for the home gave work to skilled young women, changing the meaning of the term 'florists' from specialist amateur growers to professional flower workers.

agrimony ('gratitude') to the Z of zinnia ('thoughts of absent friends'), Victorians would have been able to 'read' far more into a bouquet or a card decorated with pressed flowers or a painting of plants than any prose could have conveyed in the same space. Decoding the messages would have been time-consuming and problematic since there were dozens of different definitions to consider. Great confusion could have been caused by a young woman mixing up a variegated pink ('refusal') with a single pink ('pure love'). By the end of the nineteenth century, such sentimentality had fallen out of fashion, to the relief of Mrs Earle, who drily noted that any misinterpretations were 'always the woman's fault, somehow, in all times'.[8]

The Victorians were not content merely to cram their conservatories and Wardian cases with short-lived exotics, they were equally passionate about creating artificial flowers, in anything from wax to wool. Mrs Emma Peachey was the queen of wax flower-modelling, enjoying royal patronage from Queen Victoria, and examples of wax flowers are still on display in Queen Mary's Room at Frogmore, which may well have been made by Peachey herself.

Like many before her, Mrs Peachey, an army officer's daughter, had turned to promoting her skill as a wax modeller because 'a change of circumstances' had prompted her to make this skill 'a source of profit'. Her book, *The Royal Guide to Wax Flower Modelling*, came out in the year of the Great Exhibition, where she was supposed to have had a display. However, she pulled out, probably wisely, when she saw that her allotted space was just under the glass roof, thus avoiding the humiliation of a slowly melting 'floral' display. Visitors were instead invited to see her wax bouquets in her own home: 'The flowers are so arranged, that they appear to stand in a basket suspended over the surface of a pool of limpid water, in which the *Victoria regia* (*V. amazonica*) and other similar plants are already floating ... The Bouquet comprises specimens of almost every flower known to the botanist, from the simple honey-suckle . . . to the rarest and most valuable exotics of the East.'[9] This was an ambitious claim, but she was an excellent publicist since she must have known that the *Victoria amazonica* had recently been famously on display in Joseph Paxton's greenhouses at Chatsworth, where visitors were able to see Paxton's daughter Annie standing on one of the enormous floating leaves.

Not all arrangements were so formal. Frances Jane Hope, who collected hellebores so assiduously at her home, Wardie Lodge, near Edinburgh, and grew ornamental curly kale in her winter flower beds, filled her house with flowers from her garden. 'Her drawing-room, with its large window overlooking the sea, was adorned each week with fresh combinations of flowers arranged with untold thought and study, and she would mix with perfect taste the humblest leaves and flowers of the field with choice exotics, and rare greenhouse plants and mosses.'[10]

Hope was fastidious but extremely practical in her advice, readily admitting that it was a morning's work to gather, clean and arrange foliage and flowers for the seven to ten glass vases she did every week. She was careful in her choice of flowers because she wanted to make sure that in cool weather the flower water was perfectly clear to the sixth day, and in summer to the third. She always picked her own flowers, and advised others to do the same: 'No gardener can bring you in, the exact quantity, length of stalks, &c., you will soon know you require, and they are all, naturally, very extravagant where buds are concerned.'[11] Frances Jane Hope was in many ways a forerunner of Gertrude Jekyll and Constance Spry in her relaxed use of the plant material from her garden. Even in the matter of strong-smelling flowers in a room, her ideal was to create 'the fresh perfume of an old-fashioned greenhouse'.[12]

Although well connected in the horticultural world, Hope did not move in high society, and it was Queen Alexandra as the Princess of

Wales (which she was for a long time) who broke with the rigid formality of traditional Victorian flower arrangements among the upper classes. Sir Maurice Holzmann, keeper of records for the Duchy of Cornwall, passed on the gossip to Sir William Lawrence, husband of that great gardener Louisa Lawrence, that Her Royal Highness had shocked her guests in the 1860s by using large vases of 'common' beech boughs to decorate the drawing room at Marlborough House.

By the late nineteenth century fussy arrangements with a mixture of flowers, fruit and foliage were frowned upon, and instead fashion dictated that only one type and colour of flower should be used in a vase. While this might appear to have eased the life of the hostess, in reality it was not just a matter of popping some flowers into a handy container. Size would dictate that the new trend could prove an expensive one unless you had your own well-stocked garden; which was the pertinent point, as it was a way of showing off that you had an ample supply on hand, whereas a mix of stems showed up the smallness of your 'picking garden'.

Time was something that many Victorian middle-class housewives had in abundance, but from the turn of the twentieth century domestic life began to change. Staff numbers fell, and the ever-increasing sprawl of surburbia created a class of new homeowners who looked towards modernism for efficient design inspiration. In a revised edition of Mrs C.W. Earle's best-selling *Pot Pourri from a Surrey Garden* her niece, the suffragette Lady Constance Lytton, contributed an appendix on Japanese flower-arranging using only the simplest flowers in the most modest numbers. Gertrude Jekyll also was among the first writers to promote a new style of arranging flowers, far less formal than the fussy, intricate displays so loved by the High Victorians.

Considering the number of women writers on gardens in the late nineteenth and early twentieth centuries, it is rather disappointing

Gertrude Jekyll favoured arrangements of single varieties of flowers
to show one had space for a 'cutting garden'. *Wood and Garden* (1899)

that the first book about the new, more relaxed style of flower-arranging was written by a man, R.P. Brotherston. In the larger households, it was still part of the head gardener's duties to supply and create the many flower arrangements needed when the family were at home and entertaining, and Brotherston had spent fifty years looking after the gardens of the Earl of Haddington, descendant of the countess who had overseen the vast tree planting at Tyninghame in the eighteenth century. He wrote *The Book of Cut Flowers* in 1906 for the woman who could go into her garden to pick and choose the best flowers, including a wide variety of foliage, not for the person who was restricted to buying from markets or shops. Finicky flower arrangements looked out of place as homes became lighter and airier, and simplicity was the watchword, so Brotherston reproduced single varieties of flowers in plain glass vases instead of the more fussy epergne and jardinière styles he would have mastered in the previous decades.

One of the designs of vases in Brotherston's book was called 'Munstead', very plain and practical, designed to hold plenty of water and support the flowers. Munstead Wood was Gertrude Jekyll's house, designed for her by Edwin Lutyens and completed in 1896. It is set in a large wooded garden which she developed over many years and it was there that she wrote *Flower Decoration in the House* eleven years later. In addition to the Munstead vases she had commissioned and sold through a shop near St Paul's, she also advocated using salad bowls and soup tureens from old dinner services, heavy glass fingerbowls and ginger jars, and to support the flowers she recommended wire-netting, 'kept in place by stout wire legs soldered on'. Such devices, she pointed out, 'any handy village blacksmith could make . . . or town ironmonger would have them made to the size required'.[13] She also encouraged the use of wild flowers and seasonal blooms from the garden that she knew so well, and advised her readers not to use blue or purple flowers on the dining table as the evening light drained their colour.

Limited flower-arranging competitions continued well into the twentieth century. Frances Jeanette Roelink was successful just before the First World War, mainly using chrysanthemums grown by her husband. She was known as 'Mrs Yellow and Bronze' after her favourite colour schemes which she arranged skilfully in the still pop-ular glass epergnes. With specially made miniature pliers, she would set individual stems into the tiny glass holders, afterwards using a small syringe to top them up with water so as not to drop any liquid on the damask cloths covering the display tables.

This genteel way of life was about to change with the outbreak of war, and its aftermath was to have an impact on every aspect of domestic life and design, even the way flowers were displayed in the home.

ROOM FOR THE BUTTERFLIES

For anyone who loves flowers, the idea of bringing some of the garden inside is often irresistible, but to others cutting flowers and foliage from the garden, let alone the idea of growing them specifically for that reason, is anathema. The venerable horticulturalist C.E. Lucas Phillips wrote, 'The proper place for flowers is in the garden,' and the Alpine nurseryman Will Ingwersen went further, ranting that 'I am driven into frenzies of rage and despair by the raids of demented female flower-arrangers, to whom nothing in the garden is sacred.'[1] But the high priestess of gardening herself, Gertrude Jekyll, insisted that 'flower decoration in rooms is . . . a branch of gardening', and one that in 1907 she felt 'has made the most rapid and effective progress'.[2]

In the first half of the twentieth century every wife was expected not only to do her own flowers but also to take pleasure and pride in doing so. When Anne Lamplugh wrote *Flower and Vase* in 1937, she calculated that the average British housewife might arrange four to five hundred vases a year. This was based on having three vases on the go in the winter, and six in the summer with a midweek change of water. Her book is in the time-honoured format of a monthly calendar, discussing how to display available flowers. Each month ends with two

In the Medieval period, weeding women were the lowliest of all
horticultural workers – and the most poorly paid

Mary, Duchess of Beaufort (1630–1715) commissioned artist Everhardus
Kychicus to paint many of the 'exotic' plants she grew. Here he combined
Datura stramonium with a rare double snowdrop, *Galanthus nivalis*, and
various sedums

Princess Elizabeth (1770–1840), third daughter of George III and Queen Charlotte, was a talented flower painter and decorated the Cross Gallery at Frogmore with flower garlands

By the start of the nineteenth century, women not only gathered plants and flowers to decorate their homes but also for the more serious and increasingly popular purpose of scientific botanical study

Pl.6.

to face page 14

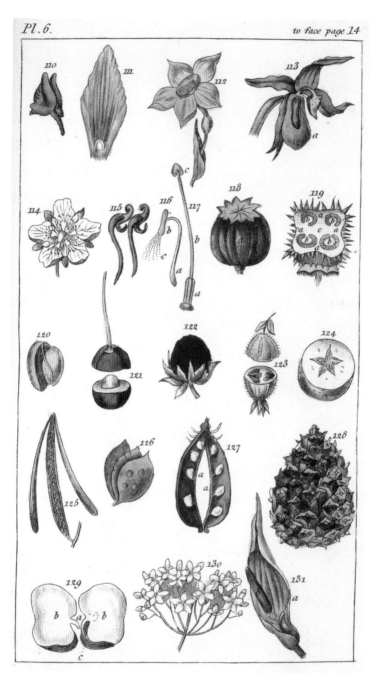

Hand-coloured illustrations from Priscilla Wakefield's *Introduction to Botany* (1823), designed to 'cultivate a taste in young persons for the study of nature'

EVERY LADY HER OWN

FLOWER GARDENER,

BY

LOUISA JOHNSON.

LONDON,

PUBLISHED BY Wᴹ S ORR & Cᵒ PATERNOSTER ROW.

MDCCCLI.

1851

Frontispiece to Louisa Johnson's *Every Lady Her Own Flower Gardener* (1851), one of several horticultural books aimed at women in the mid-nineteenth century

Beatrix Havergal (1901–80), the formidable head of the Waterperry School of Horticulture, near Oxford, surrounded by a sea of Horrockses prints, addressing students and visitors on a summer graduation day

Coryanthes albertinae —
Rio Marauia, Amazonas — 1967

A working drawing of the Amazonian orchid *Coryanthes albertinae* by
Margaret Mee (1909–88), showing the detailed stages leading to her
exquisitely accurate final portrait of this plant

lists, one 'For Gardeners – Flowers from Greenhouse, Garden and Lane' and another, much shorter, 'For Non-Gardeners – Flowers from the Shops'. Things might have moved on slightly from the snobbery of the Edwardian era, but the implication still remained that if you were not able to pick flowers from your own garden, you were something of a failure as a housewife.

Society remained obsessed with keeping up appearances and this influenced everything from the way you spoke to not leaving the house without hat and gloves, and the home was a demonstration of status. It says much of the new century that it was in 1908 that the Ideal Home Exhibition was founded, exploiting those who knew that presentation was vital, even if only seen by the occasional neighbour. However, it wasn't until the 1930s that one woman, Constance Spry, wielded her influence over flower-arranging and floristry, using loose open arrangements in unusual containers. This style led a theatrical designer friend to ask her to decorate the windows of a scent shop in Old Bond Street, and resulted in 1934 in the publication of her book *Flower Decoration*, an instant bestseller that remained in print for many years. A divorced mother and teacher from a relatively humble background, Spry was soon moving among high society, and the title of her book was part of the snobbish vocabulary of the time – *floristry* was something done for money, *flower-arranging* by suburban women, *flower decoration* by upper-middle-class women with country homes.

Spry's path to her position as arbiter of the nation's flower-arranging taste was not as one might expect. Her father was a railway clerk who studied at university extension classes to improve himself. Her early life was spent in Ireland, to which the family moved from Derby, and there she trained in bacteriology and sanitary inspection, becoming involved in medical and welfare counselling by the time of her first marriage. She left her husband in 1916, taking her young son with her, and found a job at the Inland Revenue in London where she met her second husband, Henry 'Shav' Spry. By the early 1920s she was principal of a continuing education day school in one of the poorest parts of east London, and it was to cheer up the school and the girls studying there that she started to bring in flowers from her own garden. In late 1926 the couple had moved to the Old Rectory at Abinger in Surrey, which meant a long journey to work for both of them. The house was very run down, but offered a large overgrown garden for Spry to restore and plant with her favourite old roses.

Her arrangements of her garden flowers brought requests from friends to do the same for them, and when these turned into commissions she was able to give up teaching and open a shop in the West End of London in 1928. Within six years she was employing seventy people and had a royal and aristocratic client list. Spry and her assistant, Val Pirie, were among the party of just twenty people who attended the wedding of the Duke of Windsor and Mrs Simpson (a long-standing client) in France, having done the flowers for the chapel at the Chateau de Candé. For the ceremony Spry was dressed, according to Cecil Beaton, 'robin-like in a picture hat and overalls'.[3]

Spry was a great gardener but not an astute businesswoman and her company had its share of ups and downs; even so, she continued to influence the art of flower-arranging. One of the key changes she introduced was the focus on the container. Spry designed vases suitable for her new style of arrangements, promoting the use of crumpled wire to hold the stems of the flowers and allow the arrangement to be much looser, more open and to tumble over the edge, leaving, as she famously said, 'room for the butterflies'. She detested the stiff, upright style that professional florists used.

Her containers were totally impractical for the single-variety bunch of flowers which was more usually put – 'arranged' is too strong a word – into the classic cut-glass vase now found in car boot sales. She encouraged the use of objects already in the home – china bowls, wicker baskets, brass coal buckets even – as containers. Sometimes the container was centre stage, though more often than not it was only hinted at, very much secondary to the arrangement, which is how she got away with using her junk-shop finds and baking tins.

As a keen gardener, Spry grew many of the old roses she loved using in her arrangements. The subtitle of one of her books, 'A Millionaire for a Few Pence', came originally from Vita Sackville-West's poem 'The Garden',[4] and was Spry's way of encouraging arrangers to use flowers not just from their own gardens but from hedgerows as well. She was realistic enough to know that few of her clients had access either to old

Constance Spry's (1886–1960) rise to fame as a flower arranger was crowned by her decoration of the Queen's table at the Coronation Banquet in June 1953.

roses or to cow parsley, so she encouraged commercial growers to offer these as well as a variety of unusual foliage such as artichoke leaves. By the time she died in 1960 she had published thirteen books and established a world-famous school of both flower-arranging and cookery, where young ladies from good families went to learn the skills of perfect housewifery.

Spry's style of arranging stirred up an interest in floral design in many women, but it was aimed at those women who either had a large enough garden in which to grow the lovely old roses and flowers she advocated, or the money to buy them. In the 1950s there were many women who became interested in arranging flowers on a more modest scale through the inspiration of Julia Clements. Widowed during the Second World War, Clements began a lecturing career in the late 1940s when Britain was still struggling with extreme shortages, something brought home to her during a fund-raising trip to post-war America. There was 'nothing more intimidating', she remembered, 'than a mink coat when you only have a curtain on'.[5] She was inspired by the fact that flowers could be neither rationed nor restricted. 'We can't buy new clothes,' she told her war-weary audience of Women's Institute members, 'we can't get new curtains, we can't paint our house, we've got nothing . . . except flowers!'[6]

Beverley Nichols said that the distance between Constance Spry and Julia Clements was 'equivalent to the distance between . . . Mayfair and the Albert Hall',[7] and there is no doubt that Julia Clements felt she had a message she wanted to get out to British women in a much more public way. In contrast to Spry, Julia Clements's style was far more formal. She lectured and wrote about the principles of form, size and shape. She also encouraged women to be competitive. 'Musicians and artists give titles to their works, so you make a title for your creation. And then have competitions!'[8]

Flower-arranging became so popular that within eight years, clubs had sprung up across Britain. 'I told them to go for walks in the country and pick things,' remembered Clements. 'It didn't matter what they were as long as they were tall, medium and short . . . [it] caught on like a prairie fire.'[9] In 1949 Mary Pope was also urged to start a flower-arranging group, which she did with the encouragement of Constance Spry herself. Ten years later the groups had grown to such numbers that they had more members than the Royal Horticultural Society. It was the RHS who helped with their running until a separate organisation, the National Association of Flower Arrangement Societies (NAFAS), was founded with the help of Mary Pope and Julia Clements together. Clements was in charge of the rules and regulations of competitive arranging. 'I didn't want anyone to come who wanted to know how to do their cocktail party, that wasn't my role in life. My role was to spread it among the masses – I wanted to lift them up.'[10] Pope meanwhile promoted non-competitive flower-arranging and pioneered the idea of church flower festivals across the country. Although Clements and Pope did not fall out over this difference in emphasis, Clements insisted that 'you only advance if you have competition'.[11]

Constance Spry, in addition to her flower-arranging business, also trained thousands of young people from all over the world to display flowers in her own style. Among her staff was Sheila Macqueen, who was with the organisation for over thirty years and went on to become internationally famous as an arranger in her own right, championing the natural style that Spry loved so much. She had spotted one of the windows that Spry had decorated in Bond Street, saying that 'It looked as if the countryside had been brought to London. Lilac and philadelphus; no-one else was arranging like that.'[12]

When Macqueen and her husband bought two run-down, four-hundred-year-old cottages in Leverstock Green in Hertfordshire in the

1950s she was determined to develop the garden as a flower-arranger's paradise, ensuring that there was never any shortage of plant material. 'The only danger,' confessed Macqueen, 'is that flower arrangers who start growing things sooner or later turn into gardeners. And then, of course, you find you can hardly bear to cut anything.'[13] Nevertheless, Macqueen managed to keep a balance by having a garden that was always packed with an astounding array of flowers, forty varieties of hostas for example, enough for cutting not just for the house but also for her numerous demonstrations. The garden became a magnet for flower arrangers everywhere and on her open days the tiny country lanes surrounding the house were always jammed with visitors' cars.

Another alumna of Constance Spry's training school was Rosamund Gould, who, with the indomitable Lady Pulbrook, started a flower shop in Sloane Street over fifty years ago. Throughout the 1950s and '60s no society wedding was complete without an arrangement featuring Pulbrook & Gould's signature cow parsley – a lesson learned, of course, from Constance Spry: gypsophila was never considered a suitable alternative. This was the time when flowers were used only if they were in season. 'I like hedgerow stuff, not greenhouse stuff,' insisted Lady Pulbrook in 1996, still the *grande dame* at ninety.[14] Orange was a fruit, not a flower colour, and theirs was not a shop which provided chrysanthemums, or dahlias, or even irises.

Fashions in flower-arranging are continually changing and florists have always been at the forefront of those changes. Arrangers such as Jane Packer and Paula Pryke are part of a breed of new young florists who have revolutionised the way flowers are displayed in the home, and designer flower arrangers like these are employed by supermarkets to help rethink how we buy our flowers and our arrangements. The way flowers are now grown and supplied for the mass market means there is always something within reach, whatever the season and whatever the budget. In 2008 the cut flower and indoor plant trade was worth over £1.5 billion a year, giving an average spend per person of £19 per annum, which even five years before would have been an unheard-of sum to expend on flowers.

There are three key differences between the current styles and those of the 1950s, '60s and '70s. Containers are design items in their own right, and the easy availability of simple, stylish holders means that it is virtually impossible for anyone not to make a statement even with just three stems of flowers. The arrival of designers into the world of mass floristry has brought elegant 'tied' bunches onto the supermarket shelves. With the increased pace of life the public have become more demanding and want instant arrangements. High street florists, once used to producing bouquets of chrysanthemums in cellophane or wrapping a bunch of daffodils in thin paper, have had to change their style to satisfy this demand. Even street-corner flower sellers offer tied bunches ready to be dropped into a waiting vase, and all the purchaser has to do is add water.

Amid all this commercialism, it is good to be reminded of the links between flower-arranging and gardening. It was a demonstration of flower-arrranging which gave Beth Chatto her very first experience of public speaking and, more importantly for gardeners, made her realise that there was a demand for the 'unusual plants' she was growing in her own garden, the stems of which she used in her demonstrations. Bullied by her friend and neighbour, Mrs Desmond Underwood, into giving a talk to a flower club in Suffolk, the newly married Mrs Chatto set off with a car full of plants. Her debut was so successful that many more invitations followed, and so popular were her green stems of euphorbia and silver-edged hosta leaves that Chatto decided to open her nursery and that in turn led to her showing at Chelsea. The rest is horticultural history.

LITERARY FLOWERINGS

We wish to know how to set about everything *ourselves*, without expense, without being
deluged with Latin words and technical terms,
and without being obliged to pick our way
through multiplied publications, redolent of
descriptions, and not always particularly lucid.

Louisa Johnson,
Every Lady Her Own Flower Gardener (1851)[1]

HISTORY AND HERBALLS

In the shadow of Lambeth Palace in London lies the Garden Museum, housed in the deconsecrated church of St-Mary-at-Lambeth. A small building, St Mary's is packed with display cases narrating the development of gardening in Britain, together with treasures such as Gertrude Jekyll's desk, other gardening ephemera and tools that would fetch good prices in fashionable garden centres across the river in Chelsea. There is always a buzz of enthusiasm about the place, of knowing that one is among friends, like-minded souls who share an enthusiasm and, for those who know its origins, a sense of enormous gratitude for the woman who made it happen.

Rosemary Nicholson appeared to be typical of the image people have of women who garden. She was upper middle class, wore twinsets and pearls, and might have disappeared into the domestic round of married life in Cheltenham after a childhood in the colonies, quietly tending her garden and pruning her roses, had it not been for a pivotal visit to an overgrown Lambeth churchyard in 1976.

Nicholson and her husband, John, had been researching the Tradescants, the famous seventeenth-century father-and-son gardeners, looking for their neglected tomb in the churchyard of the derelict parish church of St-Mary-at-Lambeth, which was to be flattened to make way for a coach park serving Waterloo Station. Nicholson dedicated the rest of her life, first to saving the church from demolition and then to creating the only museum in the country celebrating the history of gardening. From the outset it seemed an impossible task, but those who heard her were convinced by her enthusiasm even when she acknowledged that it would take years – but then patience is one of a gardener's strongest virtues. In 1977 the Tradescant Trust was formed and by 1981, complete with new roof, the museum was ready to open.

Rosemary Nicholson was inspired to found the Museum of Garden History by a book, *The Tradescants*, written by Mea Allan in 1964. Any historical research is both a detective story and a jigsaw puzzle, as one discovered fact leads to another which then leads on and on towards the full picture – or sometimes only a partial picture. Mea Allan's own interest in the Tradescants started not in Lambeth but in Suffolk, a county, she said, which is 'like one vast garden'.[1]

When she began her research into the lives of the father and son John Tradescants, famed for introducing many plants to Britain during the 1600s, Allan was living in Walberswick, on the coast near the most easterly point in England. One of the missing pieces of the jigsaw in her research on the Tradescants was where the family had lived before John Tradescant the Elder suddenly appeared, parents and nationality unknown, in Meopham, Kent, just before his marriage and subsequent move to Lambeth. By pure luck a friend of hers mentioned that there was a Walberswick Street in Lambeth, suggesting a Suffolk connection, and in the old registers of the vestry of Walberswick parish church she came upon Mary, daughter of one Robert Tradescant, in the first half of the seventeenth century. She later discovered that Robert and his family came up to London from Suffolk to visit their relatives' famous nursery garden in Lambeth, returning with 'rootes, seedes and slipes', which seemed to confirm Mea Allan's romantic hunch as to why so many of the gardens in Walberswick were still awash with the great rose daffodil each spring, a Tradescant introduction from Mary's time.

Since Rosemary Nicholson's and Mea Allan's researches, reams have been written about the Tradescants and about plant and garden history in general, but women's contributions to the genre have all too often been overlooked. Even Alicia Amherst, the first person to write a substantial history of gardening in England, which was published in 1896, makes virtually no mention of women although she credits her practical knowledge to her mother, who, she said in a telling statement, had been devoted to gardening long before it was considered a fashionable pastime for women.

A man and woman surveying their well-ordered garden with its raised beds and framed pots in the frontispiece to John Gerard's *The Herball*, first published in 1597.

It might seem extraordinary that women are absent from so many historical records, although gardening and horticulture are far from being the only area of life and industry where this holds true, and it is only in the past few decades that changed social attitudes have enabled this omission to be corrected. One of the best ways to discover what women might have been doing in the garden is to consider what books were available to them for horticultural advice.

Lady Margaret Hoby of Hackness, for example, who stayed longer in her garden than her conscience allowed, may have consulted Master Fitzherbarde's *The Boke of Husbandrie*, which first appeared in 1523. Still wrongly attributed to the judge and legal writer Sir Anthony Fitzherbert, this book was in fact the work of his lesser-known brother, John. Based in Derbyshire, Fitzherbert was the first to spell out a wife's duties in the garden: 'In the begynning of March, or a lytle afore, is tyme for a wyfe to make her garden and to gette as many good sedes and herbes as she can, and specyally such as be good for the pot and to eate.'[2]

Lady Margaret may also have owned Thomas Tusser's work of 1573, *Five Hundred Points of Good Husbandry*. This was aimed at a rural working class, but it was enormously popular and reprinted several times in the eighteenth, nineteenth and twentieth centuries, although the chirpiness of the verses written by a failed farmer from Essex may have been too light-hearted for the devout Lady Margaret.

Wife, unto thy garden and set me a plot
With strawberry roots of the best to be got
Such, growing abroad among thorns in the wood
Well chosen and picked prove excellent food.
In March, May, and Aprill, from morning to night,
In sowing and setting, good huswives delight;

To have in a garden, or other like plot:
To trim up their house and furnish their pot.[3]

The message is clear: women gardened at this time not just to feed their families but also to decorate their homes, and it was no sin to take pleasure from it as well. However, there was great pressure on the housewife to keep her garden visibly neat and tidy as, whatever a woman's status or class, the responsibility lay squarely on her shoulders to be seen to be a 'good huswife'. The importance of the woman's place in the garden was made very clear in Barnabe Googe's 1577 translation of Conrad Heresbach's *Foure Books of Husbandry*: 'Herein were the olde husbandes very careful and used always to judge that where they found the Garden out of order, the wife of the house (for unto her belonged the charge thereof) was no good huswife.'[4]

We can be virtually certain that Lady Margaret knew about William Lawson's *Country Housewife's Garden* because she and her garden were mentioned in it. Its publication in 1617 was significant as it became the

Designs for knot gardens from William Lawson's *The Country Housewife's Garden*, the first book to encourage women to become involved in the design and layout of their gardens.

first recorded book written specifically for women gardeners, its long subtitle giving purchasers a thorough idea of what they would be getting: 'Rules for Herbs and Seeds of common use, with their Times and Seasons when to Set and Sow them *Together with* The Husbandry of Bees Published with Secrets very necessary for every Housewife'.[5] The reference to Lady Margaret appears in a section on ornaments in orchards: 'that honourable Lady at Hackness . . . use to make seats for them [the bees!] in the stone walls of their Orchard, or Garden, which is good, but wood is better'.[6]

The book was immediately successful and went into ten editions, the later ones printed together with Gervase Markham's *A Way to Get Wealth*. The title of one section in this advice manual gives a hint of the exhausting variety of skills that every housewife was expected to excel at: 'Physick, Chirurgery, Extraction of Oyles, Banquets, Cookery, Ordering of Feasts, Preserving of Whine, conceited Secrets, Distillations, Perfumes, Ordering of Wooll, Hemp, Flax, Dying, Use of Dayries, Maulting, Brewing, Baking; and the Profit of Oats'. Small wonder they had little time for the pleasurable growing of flowers in the garden.

With the improvement of printing techniques the general public were increasingly able to acquire gardening books, a few of which occasionally mention women. John Parkinson, a London-based herbalist, botanist and apothecary and correspondent of Thomasin Tunstall in Lancashire, was quite rightly convinced that knowledge was the key to horticultural oneupman- and oneupwoman-ship. His book of 1629, *Paradisi in Sole Paradisus Terrestris*, was aimed at 'many Gentlewomen and others, that would gladly have some fine flowers to furnish their Gardens, but know not what the names of those things are that they desire, nor what are the times of their flowring', adding that 'no lady or gentlewoman of any worth' would not be 'delighted' with tulips, all the rage at that time.[7] It was dedicated to Charles I's queen, Henrietta Maria, and earned him the status of *botanicus Regius Primarius.*

Many literate housewives would have owned a copy of the practical 'receipt' books which were extremely popular, including *The Accomplisht Ladys Delight* written by Hannah Wolley, a seventeenth-century Mrs Beeton, which first appeared in 1675. Wolley had turned to writing in widowhood and was probably the first woman to earn a living, albeit a somewhat precarious one, from her published works. It is packed with practical recipes and beauty treatments, many still usable today, some definitely not. One remedy for removing hair involved stamping on a glow-worm and anointing oneself with its juice; another recipe carried the alarming title of Hedge-Hog Pudding, but turns out to be a concoction of bread, cream and eggs decorated with raisins and blanched almonds for the spines.

What made Hannah Wolley's book different from the others is that later editions include a contribution called 'The Lady's Diversion in Her Garden' written by Thomas Harris, a 'Gard'ner at Stockwel, in Surrey'.[8] It is a short introduction to ornamental gardening aimed at the beginner, in which he lists the usual calendar of horticultural chores but unusually includes ideas on design and content. After recommendations on 'Gardens Form and Situation', Harris turns to plant suggestions and makes a point of keeping it simple. 'I shall only give a Catalogue of the Names of the chiefest of our English Flowers; which may easily be had and sufficient for adorning private Gardens.' There must be roses of course: 'the Damask and Cinnamon Rose, the Rose of the World, the English Red Rose, the blush Belgick Rose, the double Musk Rose, the great Apple Rose'. No *English* garden would be complete, he thought, without 'Tulips, Gilliflowers, Lillies, Primroses & Cowslips, Flower de Luce, Wall Flowers, Sweet Williams, Auriculaes [and] Saffron'.[9]

He follows this with practical advice on making hot beds and protecting plants in winter – the tender 'greens' or evergreens such as orange and lemon trees which were all the rage in wealthy homes for their scent and fruit. 'Stop all Crevices in your Green-Houses,' Harris advised his female readers, 'that no cold may come in.'[10] These tender plants were also the target for thieves, although the penalties could be high, as Thomas Humphrys discovered when he was transported after being caught stealing orange trees and a watering can from Henry Wise's famous Brompton Park Nursery, as well as sixty peach, nectarine and plum trees from another nurseryman.

Harris also gave directions for 'adorning Balconies, Turrets, and Windows with Flowers & Greens all the Year round' but he does not talk down to his female readers. While we must assume that anyone who had turrets or greenhouses would also have had the staff to look after them, this little book was an exciting step forward in acknowledging women's 'green desires'.

BOTANICAL DIALOGUES

In 1745 Eliza Haywood, editor and proprietor of *The Female Spectator*, justified her inclusion in the magazine of an article on gardening. Although she agreed it was 'incongruous' for a 'fine Lady to busy herself about Vegetables . . . why,' she asked, 'should our Gardeners be wiser than ourselves?'[1] So, listed intriguingly between 'Flying Machines, the Impossibility of their Use' and 'Fortitude, a Rare Example of It', she inserted 'Flowers, a Becoming Ornament'. 'Would it not,' she continued, 'furnish agreeable Matter for Conversation, both to inform those less knowing than ourselves, and to be able to argue with those who pretend to greater Skill, on the wonderful Progress of the distinct Sap which feeds every different Flower, proceeding from so many Arms of the same Stem?'[2] It was not just a question of keeping one step ahead of the gardener, but also of absorbing knowledge about an increasingly popular interest. She was particularly fascinated by the art of grafting: 'Methinks it is a most becoming Amusement, to Persons of my Sex, to sit by while the Gardener is performing so curious an Operation, nor in the least beneath the Dignity of the greatest Lady to assist his Work.'[3]

There was no reason why eighteenth-century women could not

have read the general horticultural books that were widely available, and in fact women's names regularly appear on the lists of subscribers to many of the beautifully illustrated and detailed books on plants that were published during the century. Both Richard Bradley's and Stephen Switzer's works were popular, the London nurseryman Thomas Fairchild had written for the new metropolitan class in *The City Gardener* in 1722, and garden designer Batty Langley answered a need for help with the geometry of parterres and the like in *The New Principles of Gardening* in 1728. However, the work of major importance was the vast *Gardener's Dictionary* by Philip Miller, the director of the Chelsea Physic Garden, published in parts throughout the 1730s, which became the horticultural bible of the eighteenth century, running into many editions.

There were, however, few books on gardening written specifically for women, let alone by them. A writer called Sylvia Streatfield is credited with *Sylvia's Flower Garden* in 1735, but it remained an unpublished manuscript and the text itself has disappeared into the mists of time. In 1799 Lady Charlotte Murray published *The British Garden* anonymously. Lady Charlotte was a keen plantswoman and botanist and was credited with discovering the double cranesbill, *Geranium pratense*, in Scotland, but she remained modesty itself when it came to publishing her find, leaving it to be mentioned in Sowerby's *English Botany*, published as a series between 1790 and 1814.

Born in 1754, Lady Charlotte Murray was the daughter of the Duke of Atholl, who established extensive larch woodlands on the family estates of Dunkeld and Blair in Perthshire, and it may be from him that she inherited her love of plants. She never married and lived eventually in Bath. *The British Garden*, which ran to three editions, is her only known publication and was an expensive two-volume catalogue, drawn mainly from botanical works by Withering and Berkenhout, and Erasmus Darwin's translation of Linnaeus. In her introduction to

The British Garden she explained her interest in the native flowers of Britain, which were then at risk of being overshadowed by the new exotic plants arriving from the Americas.

> It is not, however, the intention of the following pages, to enter into the endless and interesting discoveries which have been, and still continue daily to be made in this pleasing science; the Catalogue was undertaken at the request of a Friend, who wished to see those plants which are described in the Hortus Kewensis as adapted to the British climate, in an English dress; this, with the assistance of the Lichfield translation of Linnaeus, and the able and elegant works of Messrs Withering, Berkenhout, and other learned Writers on the subject, has been here attempted; and a few short extracts of the *Linnean System* prefixed, merely sufficient to enable the young Botanist readily to discover the name of any unknown plant, by reducing it first to its *class*, then *order*, then *genera*, finally to its *Species*. And thus, to be considered rather as the Direction-Post, which without any merit of its own, points out to the passenger the road he is desirous to travel, than the Guide who particularly describes the country through which he is to pass, or the various beauties he is likely to meet in his journey.[4]

Following the threads of historical research can lead one to many dead ends, but occasionally one comes across something that makes the heart miss a beat. I felt just such a frisson when looking through *The British Garden* when I realised that the copy I was holding had come from the library of Sir Joseph Banks, that the great man of eighteenth-century horticulture had owned the book. This was doubly satisfying because Sir Joseph, renowned for his plant-hunting voyage to Australia with Captain Cook and later as a long-standing director of

Kew Botanical Gardens, had admitted he owed a debt to women for his early interest in botany. Walking home from Eton aged fourteen, he passed women collecting herbs or 'simples' from the hedgerows which they sold on to the apothecaries, and he paid them sixpence to teach him what they knew about the plants they were harvesting. He also recalled that it was in his mother's dressing room that he first came across *Gerard's Herball*.

Although few children had the enthusiasm of Banks, it was common for young men and women, from the schoolroom upwards, to be encouraged to collect and study local flora. There were detractors of this fascination with the Linnean-led study of plants, including the reactionary poet Richard Polwhele, who railed in 1798, '[If] botanizing girls . . . do not take heed . . . they will soon exchange the blush of modesty for the bronze of impudence.'[5] More typically, however, young women were inspired and sometimes cajoled into an enthusiasm for some systematic study of plants by their fathers and later by their husbands. It was seen as a gentle and appropriate way for women to 'improve their minds' without becoming too taxed by the sciences.

From the mid-eighteenth century, publications aimed at interesting and educating the young in the world of nature were, not surprisingly, written by men. The most popular of these was James Lee's 1760 *Introduction to Botany*, which was a translation by Lee of Linnaeus's *Philosophia Botanica*. It stayed in print for fifty years and made Lee famous. Botanists and plantsmen flocked to his Hammersmith nursery where he stocked the latest exotics grown from seed from South Africa, the Americas and later Australia. The nursery was called 'the Vineyard' simply because it had been built on the site of one, and it survived until the late nineteenth century when it disappeared under building works where the Olympia exhibition hall is now sited.

Nearly forty years later, in 1796, a new book appeared, aimed

The frontispiece to *An Introduction to Botany* by Priscilla Wakefield (1750–1832); in its ninth edition by 1823, it remained in print for another twenty years.

specifically at girls and young women. Although Lee's book had been used to educate girls, Priscilla Wakefield correctly believed that there was a need for a more female-orientated book that explained the Linnean system. By simply adding the indefinite article to the title of Lee's book, Mrs Wakefield's *An Introduction to Botany* was to surpass his success. The book went into eleven editions and remained in print until 1841, later being retitled *Wakefield's Botany*, and was translated into French as well as having three American editions.

Mrs Wakefield's volume, published in the same year as her family moved to their new home in Ship Yard, just off Tottenham High Street in north London, set the tone for the first botanical textbooks by women. It was written in the epistolary style, with 'Felicia' writing to her sister of her botanical finds. 'My fondness for flowers,' Felicia writes, 'has induced my mother to propose Botany, as she thinks it will be beneficial to my health, as well as agreeable, by exciting me to use more air and exercise than I should do, without such a motive . . . You may compare my descriptions with the flowers themselves, and, by thus mutually pursuing the same subject, we may reciprocally improve each other.'[6]

Wakefield hoped that through botany girls would not only see a way to self-improvement, but would also feel part of a network of women with similar interests. 'May [the study of botany],' she wrote, 'become a substitute for some of the trifling, not to say pernicious objects, that too frequently occupy the leisure of young ladies of fashionable manners, and, by employing their faculties rationally, act as an antidote to levity and idleness.'[7]

It is hard for us to know just how many of Wakefield's readers actually got their hands dirty in the garden, but she was successful in encouraging girls out of the drawing room to have a closer look at the nature around them. Mrs Wakefield came from a Quaker family, although she never wore the Quaker style of dress and was known to enjoy the theatre and other outings frowned upon by the Society of Friends. An ardent philanthropic reformer, she was also a champion of early savings or 'frugality' banks, which proved an irony when she was forced to turn to writing in middle age to boost the family finances, a situation caused by her husband's ineptitude and her son's recklessness. In a society where it was extremely rare for a wife to work, this was the all-too-common reason some had to. In addition to her book on botany, Priscilla Wakefield also wrote sixteen books on natural history and travel for young people.

Mrs Wakefield had many imitators, and only a year after *An Introduction to Botany* was published, there appeared *Botanical Dialogues: Between Hortensia and her Four Children* 'by A Lady'. The author was in fact

Maria Jacson, then also in her forties. She never explained why she was reluctant to reveal her identity, but it was by no means uncommon for female writers to publish anonymously when there was a certain shame about women earning a living, particularly those one thought of as gentry. Jacson may well have taken this decision because of the embarrassing financial circumstances she and her sister found themselves in on the death of their father in 1808.

Maria Jacson was yet another daughter of the clergy who never married, but lived with her also unmarried sister and cared for their widowed father. He repaid their filial devotion by leaving the bulk of his estate to his son, providing them with an income equivalent only to that of a curate or artisan labourer. His will allowed them to 'take for their own use such part of the furniture of my house ... of my linnen, plate, and china there, as they shall think necessary for furnishing such house as they hereafter choose to resettle in',[8] but did not settle any such house on them. Although their brother Roger offered them a home with him and his family, his second wife was not so accommodating, forcing Maria and Frances to pack their bags. For the next sixteen months they stayed with their many friends and relatives around Derbyshire, Nottinghamshire and Cheshire.

With any prospects of marriage dimmed by middle age – Maria was fifty-four, Frances fifty-five – it is logical that the two Jacson sisters looked to the world of publishing to supplement their meagre incomes. While Frances wrote novels, Maria made best use of her own interests and connections. She was probably introduced to the botanical world through a cousin, Sir Brooke Boothby of Derbyshire. Sir Brooke was in turn friendly with Erasmus Darwin and Jean-Jacques Rousseau, and was also a member of Darwin's Botanical Society of Lichfield. Jacson may well have met Darwin and he certainly cited her occasionally in his works.

It would have done Maria Jacson no harm that Darwin and Boothby each wrote praising *Botanical Dialogues* for 'so accurately explaining a difficult science in an easy and familiar manner'. After seeing a Venus Fly Trap (*Dionaea muscipula*) at Sir Brooke's home, Darwin also wrote, 'Of this plant I was favored with an elegant colored drawing by Miss Maria Jacson of Tarporly, in Cheshire, a Lady who adds much botanical knowledge to many other elegant acquirements.'[9] *Botanical Dialogues* might not have had the popular success of Mrs Wakefield's *Introduction to Botany*, but it had brought her some recognition.

Twenty years later, in 1816, Jacson published *The Florist's Manual: Hints for the Construction of a Gay Flower-Garden*, a manual written for her 'sister Florists' who needed some help in selecting and growing plants. 'A Flower-Garden is now become a necessary appendage of every fashionable residence, and hence it is more frequently left to the direction of a gardener, than arranged by the guidance of genuine taste in the owner.'[10] These were exciting times in the plant world, with new species being discovered across the globe, but people needed to know how to cultivate all these new exotics. Jacson summed up the potential disappointment that many more adventurous gardeners have felt:

The fashionable novice, who has stored her borders, from the catalogue of some celebrated name, with variety of rare species, who has procured innumerable rose-trees, chiefly consisting of old and common sorts, brought into notice by new nomenclature, who has set apart a portion of ground for American plants, and duly placed them in bog soil, with their names painted on large headed pegs, becomes disappointed when, instead of the brilliant flow of her more humble neighbour's parterre, she finds her own distinguished only by paucity of colour, and fruitless expenditure.[11]

Maria and Frances Jacson were by now living in Somersal Hall in Derbyshire, inherited by their brother from their mother's family. Here the writer Maria Edgeworth visited them. 'We have not yet seen any visitors since we came here and have paid only one visit to the Miss Jacksons. Miss Fanny you know is the author of Rhoda – Miss Maria Jackson the author of Dialogues on botany and a little book of advice about a gay garden. I like the gay garden lady best at first sight but I will suspend my judgment prudently till I see more.'[12]

The Florist's Manual followed what was a trend among women particularly interested in gardening, to eschew the fashion for exotics and for beds of single plants such as hyacinths, primulas, pinks and the like. This may well have been because few women had access to the necessary finance to buy the new arrivals; nor had they the facilities to grow them. The blanket bedding designs, she complained, 'form a blank before [the] species produces its flowers and a mass of decaying leaves when the glow of their petals is no more'.

Jacson's alternative was to encourage a mix of flowers and bulbs, a 'mingled flower garden ... of well-blended quantity', not one based on 'rarity and variety'. She had a particular love of bulbs and kept a record for over twenty years of her seedling crocuses and the development of colchicums and gladioli. She advocated, where space allowed, 'the nicety of placing shaped beds interspersed with turf'. She was well ahead of her time in her approval of creating a bed from a complementary palette, but she cautioned that care was needed 'in arranging the different parts to form a connected glow of colour'.

Maria Jacson was not suggesting these ideas for small, suburban gardens. Of the friends they had stayed with before settling at Somersal, most lived in large houses with substantial grounds, which was where she must have gained much of her gardening experience.

John Loudon's illustration of Lady Broughton's 'Rockwork' at Hoole House, near Chester, reputedly the first example of a rock garden in Britain.

Jacson dedicated *The Florist's Manual* to Lady Broughton, who created a famous rock garden at her home at Hoole House, just outside Chester. J.C. Loudon described it in detail in his publication the *Gardener's Magazine*, noting that Lady Broughton was one of the first in Britain to grow alpines outdoors, and wrote, 'In the case of this rockwork Lady Broughton was her own artist; and the work which she has produced evinces the most exquisite taste for this description of scenery.'[13] Loudon's wife, Jane, was also full of admiration. '[It] consists of an imitation or miniature copy of the Swiss glaciers; with a valley between, into which the mountain scenery projects and retires, forming several beautiful and picturesque openings, which are diversified . . . by mountain trees and shrubs, and other plants.'[14]

Lady Broughton's rock garden has not survived, but Jacson was not in any case generally impressed by 'the unnatural appearance of artificial crags of rock and other stones interspersed with delicate plants'. In deference to her friend, no doubt, she added that this sort of gardening was only acceptable when it was done 'on an extensive scale where we meet with fountains and statuary'.

Like many of us gardening today, Jacson thought the greatest threat to plants were slugs and snails, even more so than caterpillars. While her suggestion of slices of turnip to attract the blighters may be worth a try, she also advocated a swift and humane death from drowning in a bucket of water.

Elizabeth Kent was another gardening author who preferred to remain anonymous when she published her two books, *Flora Domestica, or the Portable Flower-garden* in 1823, and *Sylvan Sketches: or a Companion to the Park and Shrubbery* in 1825. Kent lived near Hampstead Heath with her sister and brother-in-law, the essayist Leigh Hunt, who may well have helped her with the business of publishing. *Flora Domestica* was one of the earliest publications on growing potted plants in towns and in it Kent confesses that she was not very good at keeping her plants alive. Although Hampstead was still some distance from the centre of London and could hardly be considered urban, the Hunts' home was a modest villa and Elizabeth resorted to growing all her plants in pots. Having found there was no advice available for someone attempting 'a portable garden', she 'resolved to obtain and communicate such information' herself.[15] The book ran to several editions with the author determinedly preserving her anonymity; however, such modesty was to disappear as Victorian women found that publishing could be a respectable and, in some cases, profitable outlet for their horticultural knowledge.

GARDENING FOR LADIES

The first experience of horticulture for many women was often through the study of plants as children, and a few women were able to make a career by publishing books on botany that were mainly aimed at children. Anne Pratt was a sickly child and was taught botany by a family friend, Dr Dods. Together with her sister she created a large herbarium, collecting and drying samples of British flora, many of which she also sketched, skills which stood her in good stead in later life. Her first book, *The Field, the Garden, and the Woodland*, published when she was forty in 1846, ran to three editions in less than ten years. The late Victorian gardening writer Theresa Earle still had her copy fifty years later, a Christmas present from an uncle who thought, quite rightly, that she was fond of flowers. Pratt's main work, *The Flowering Plants and Ferns of Great Britain*, published in 1855 in five volumes, became the standard and most popular work of the period for the general reading public.

Anne Pratt's own childhood school, Eastgate House in Rochester, Kent, featured in Charles Dickens's novels *Pickwick Papers* and *Edwin Drood*. However, Anne was never able to explore the surrounding Kent countryside; lame from childhood, she never went far from home and it was her sister who collected plant material for her to study, and to dry and press for her herbarium. Anne's story highlights the great appeal of botanical studies to so many women; the close study of plants was something that could be done in the drawing room, even at the kitchen table, and, for those with no access to a garden, it was a way of getting in touch with nature despite the constraints of Victorian domesticity. It could also be done with the minimum of skills and equipment and was thus an ideal introduction to scientific studies.

Pratt had published her first book without her family's knowledge, probably because she anticipated her mother's disapproval. She may have done so with some outside help, as her publisher was related to her through her sister's marriage. The book was a lengthy but accurate primer for children. The inscription, 'Something to please and something to instruct, E'en from the meanest weed', summed up her aims, which she ably achieved. Over the next thirteen years she published seventeen books, mainly on wild flowers, and they were all, according to contemporary sources, 'marked by more accuracy than is usual in books of the kind'.[1] This was all the more creditable as Pratt was not considered a proper botanist, a mere woman whose name, it was noted, had never appeared in the Royal Society's *Catalogue of Scientific Papers.*

Wild Flowers, illustrated with Pratt's own line drawings, was dedicated with her permission to Queen Victoria, who ordered copies of all Anne Pratt's works for her children. Perhaps because of this she received a small allowance from the Civil List later in life. After the death of her Huguenot mother in 1845, Pratt moved to Dover, where she worked on *The Flowering Plants of Great Britain*, a monumental book of nearly two thousand pages which took her nine years to complete. It was issued in five volumes and also in extremely successful one-shilling parts, and sheets could be purchased for hanging on classroom walls. She had no time for the exotics that were filling Victorian conservatories, but was passionate in trying to get people to look at the plants growing around them. To this end, she used snippets of folklore and poetry to reach her botanically ignorant audience. Her writing was 'sweet, even-tempered, and unpretentious'.[2]

Writing about one of her favourite wild flowers, the cowslip, she quotes an unnamed herbalist who suggests that 'Our city dames know well enough that the distilled water of the cowslip adds beauty, or at least restores it when lost.' Then she describes how children she knew 'ingeniously make the flowers up in balls' by picking clusters of the flower heads when they are 'fully blown, and will search far and wide over the meadows to find the blossoms in perfection'.[3]

A small woman, who was described as having the constant busyness of Miss Mattie in Elizabeth Gaskell's *Cranford*, Pratt was much loved by her family. Finally in her sixties she found love, or more likely companionship, by marrying John Peerless from East Grinstead, whom she had known previously. She was, according to friends, 'much attached to her husband', although his deafness was described by someone who knew them both well, with typical Victorian gentility, as rendering him 'a somewhat trying companion'.

In 1889, when she was in her late eighties, she was interviewed by her nieces for the *Women's Penny Paper*, which was, it claimed, 'The Only Paper Conducted, Written, Printed and Published by Women'. The biographical sketch in this important weekly feminist newspaper confirms that by the end of her life Anne Pratt was a household name, and had 'done more to popularise the study of Botany than any other woman writer'.[4]

Jane Webb, who was to become the most important female horticultural writer of the mid-nineteenth century, had no love of botany as

Mrs Loudon's Gardening for Ladies, first published in 1840, became the mid-nineteenth-century's best-known gardening book for women.

a child. Quite the opposite; she found all the classifications of the Linnean system altogether boring. However, when she married the country's leading horticultural writer, John Claudius Loudon, in 1830 and became his amanuensis, she quickly realised that it would be useful, to say the least, if she had a grounding in plant physiology. She attended public lectures given by John Lindley on de Canolle's natural system of plant classification, studied what she could from her husband's vast botanical library at their home in Porchester Terrace in west London, and rejected the Linnean system because of its sexual allusions. All this laid the ground for her own botanical and horticultural writing and her main book, *Botany for Ladies*, published in 1842, was written as an easy-to-understand introduction to the natural system.

Mrs Loudon was keen that botany should be taught to girls along-side French and music, and later wrote in *British Wild Flowers*: 'I think it more than probable that in another generation it will be so – as, though the Linnean system was unfit for females, there is nothing objectionable in the Natural System, and the prejudice against botan-ical names is every day declining ... I sincerely hope the time may arrive, though probably I shall not live to see it, when a knowledge of botany will be considered indispensable to every well-educated person.'[5]

In her work Loudon rejected the traditional epistolary form and instead addressed her readers directly. She also avoided any domestic asides and stuck strictly to imparting information. Lindley's *Ladies' Botany*, she stated, had not told her 'half' what she wanted to know, 'though it contained a great deal I could not understand'.[6] Lindley, she felt, had raised the bar so high that most basic books on botany might as well have been written in Latin, they were so confusing for the beginner.

Things were very different fifty years later. While the habit of pub-lishing anonymously carried on intermittently, the middle of the nineteenth century saw a boom in horticultural books, particularly those written by women. By then Jane Loudon, now widowed, was making a living through her publications, albeit a meagre one. Many women wrote books on everything from botany to indoor plants and flower-arranging. Mostly they were not very good – flowery in the worst possible sense – and have long been forgotten, and it was not until the end of the nineteenth century that the work of any woman was to have a significant influence on garden design.

Jane Loudon became a practical gardener and horticultural author by default on marrying J.C. Loudon within seven months of meeting him, when she was twenty-three. She had spent her early years in

Birmingham, where her mother died in 1819 when Jane was twelve. Financial problems forced the sale of the family home, but her father, Thomas Webb, was able to buy a small but comfortable replacement in Worcestershire. She spent a year travelling in Europe with her father, an experience that must have been a marvellous substitute for a formal education for a young teenager, and one which stood her in good stead when Thomas Webb died when she was seventeen, having given her enough independent spirit to try to make a living for herself as an author rather than take the traditional route of becoming a governess.

Perhaps in tune with her atypical teenage years, Jane made the curious choice of writing a novel set in the twenty-second century, which was published in 1827 when she was just twenty. *The Mummy!*, which even Jane later admitted was 'strange and wild',[7] shows remarkable foresight, predicting among other things the wide use of steam-power in agriculture, in particular for milking cows and ploughing fields. In one of those quirks of fate it was read by John Claudius Loudon, who was twenty-four years Jane's senior and already had an established career as an authority on horticultural and agricultural practices. Loudon was excited by the vision that the book painted, reviewed it well, and became determined to meet the young author, J. Webb, whom he assumed to be male. Two years later the meeting happened and they 'formed an attachment', which resulted in what must have been the most successful horticultural partnership and marriage of the nineteenth century.

Jane's practical determination to educate herself in her new husband's speciality so that she would no longer be 'heartily ashamed of my ignorance' is only one example of her strength of character, and she needed every ounce of her feistiness. Loudon had lost his right arm after a botched bone-setting operation before he met Jane, and could

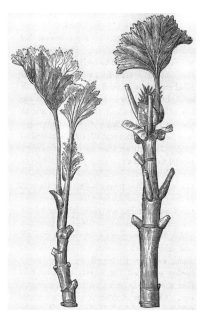

Books by Jane Loudon (1807–58) were packed with practical tips such as the correct way to prepare a pelargonium cutting. More commonly known as geraniums, these were a stable requisite for High Victorian bedding plans.

no longer write with his left hand because of rheumatism, so the rest of his life was dogged by illness and pain.

However, they were both perfectionists and Jane took on the job of transcribing Loudon's *Encyclopaedia of Cottage, Farm and Villa Architecture*, writing rapidly with a quill pen made from a crow's feather, while both drank strong coffee and made do with just four hours' sleep a night. When it was published, it ran to over a thousand pages of small print. In addition to the writing, there was the garden to be looked after. Loudon's alpine house displayed over six hundred species in small pots and the garden over two thousand different species, not including individual varieties, all of which required regular care. Luckily, they shared a passion for tidiness inside and outside the home. 'Some ladies who pretend to admire flowers,' Loudon warned his wife, 'will suffer decayed roses, dead leaves, and withered seed-pods to remain on plants under their drawing-room windows. That is not good gardening, my dear.'[8]

From the outside, their home in Porchester Terrace — which Loudon had designed himself — appeared to be one grand house, but it was actually two dwellings and Loudon's mother and sisters lived in the other part next door. We do not know how Jane got on with her in-laws, but it must have been helpful to have them on hand, especially when their daughter, Agnes, arrived two years after their marriage. The Loudons were still travelling extensively to Scotland and to Paris despite J.C.'s failing health. His two sisters took lessons in wood-engraving so that they could help defray some of the enormous expenses that Loudon built up during his massive project *Arboretum Britannicum*.

The couple had been together for eight years before Jane Loudon felt that she had the knowledge to start writing about horticulture herself. The project, a series called *The Ladies' Flower-Garden*, was to cover hardy annuals, hardy biennials, hardy bulbs, corms and tubers, herbaceous perennials, garden roses, hardy shrubs, greenhouse plants and hothouse plants. The implication in Loudon's announcement of the series, which was initially published in monthly parts for 2s 6d each, was that the sumptuous illustrations, sketched onto zinc, were Jane's own work, 'the production of a member of our family'. One wonders how she had the time to produce these as well as the text, and wait on Loudon hand and foot.

The series gradually appeared over several years, during which time Jane was also writing horticultural manuals for women, the first being *Gardening for Ladies* published in 1840, followed by her book on botany. Almost every year for the next fifteen years, Jane Loudon produced books not just on gardening but on nature, domestic pets and wild flowers, as well as briefly editing *The Ladies' Companion.* Although she thought of herself as a female garden journalist, she firmly believed that no woman would come to enjoy gardening if she left it to someone else to do. To learn you had to get your hands dirty, and with more families than ever moving into the developing suburbs, with their husbands away at work, it was left to the wives to do more practical jobs outside. 'Suburban gardens generally give more pleasure to their possessors than gardens of more importance; principally, perhaps, because they are seldom, if ever, under the control of a master gardener; but are managed by the lady of the house; and thus a suburban garden becomes a kind of domestic pet, for we always love things that are partly of our own creation.'[9]

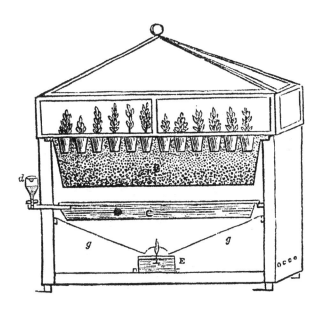

While Jane Loudon assumed that a jobbing gardener would be on hand to deal with routine tasks, she encouraged women to understand the complexities of greenhouse management.

During 1842 Jane Loudon published a monthly journal, *The Ladies' Magazine of Gardening*. Much of the material and many of the illustrations were simply reproduced from the various books that the couple were publishing elsewhere, which is perhaps why it did not last longer than a year, but it did give her an opportunity to voice her strong opinions on horticultural matters in answer to her readers' letters. She was no fan of the fashion for growing plants in Wardian glass cases. 'They have a confined unhealthy look through the dingy glass, which is repugnant to all my ideas of floral beauty. This, however, is entirely a matter of taste; as many persons much more competent to judge than I am think otherwise.'[10]

In contrast to the short-lived magazine series, her book *Ladies' Companion to the Flower Garden* stayed in print for over thirty years. This was partly because it was an extremely useful book and partly because no one else, certainly no other female writer, published anything of her standard aimed at women. There was little competition for Jane Loudon when she was writing; just one example, J.B. Whiting's *Manual of Flower Gardening for Ladies*, published in 1849, was practical if uninspiring.

We know little about Louisa Johnson, author of *Every Lady Her Own Flower Gardener*, published in 1839, but she felt she had something to offer young female amateur gardeners. She pulled no punches in describing what she believed they wanted, writing of their desire for 'a work in a small compass, which will enable us to become our own gardeners: we wish to know how to set about everything *ourselves*, without expense, without being deluged with Latin words and technical terms, and without being obliged to pick our way through multiplied publications, redolent of descriptions, and not always particularly lucid.' This may have been a dig at Mrs Loudon, although there is no way of knowing despite their being in direct competition with each other. However, as useful and compact as Johnson's little books were (she was to write a similar one on greenhouse gardening twelve years later), it was Jane Loudon's that triumphed in terms of sales.

POT POURRI

With the death of Jane Loudon in 1858, no one stepped forward to fill her shoes in writing for women interested in gardening. Due to her late husband's position within the horticultural establishment, she maintained a rare position of authority, and it was a long time before another woman achieved that. Until then, men tried to reach the female market. Samuel Beeton produced three gardening books, including the *Dictionary of Every-Day Gardening* to partner his wife's *Dictionary of Everyday Cooking*. While not specifically directed at women, it was aiming for the same audience as Mrs Beeton, insisting that 'a knowledge of garden management is as essential to every possessor of a garden as a knowledge of domestic management to every mistress of a house',[1] but the book never had the success of the cookery volumes. Similarly *The Ladies' Multum-in-Parvo Flower Garden* by gardening writer Samuel Wood in 1881, with instructions on how to make 'The Ladies' Miniature Nursery Ground' and 'The Miniature Rosery', made little impact.

In general, however, the publishing market was strong. Out of forty-three gardening magazines that appeared in the mid- to late nineteenth century, only Jane Loudon's short-lived *Ladies' Magazine* was aimed at women. However, there was a flood of general horticultural magazines and literature widely available; in addition to Beeton and Wood's works, William Robinson's *The Garden* was first published in 1871 and (James) Shirley Hibberd's *Amateur Gardening* and many other publications appeared around the same time.

Books on the home had also become extremely popular. Mary Haweis had great success in the early 1880s with several series, including *The Art of Decoration*. Although the name of Mary Haweis is barely known now, when she died her family received hundreds of letters and messages including one from Queen Victoria, mourning the passing of 'a unique woman, brilliant, fascinating with the intellect of half a dozen men'. Her skill with interior decoration in particular led to a successful publishing career; so successful in fact that it cast a long shadow over her marriage. Everything had been rosy when she was a young woman, marrying a young curate whom she adored. He soon got a good living in central London and she was able to amuse herself doing up both the house and the garden. Her skill as a needlewoman meant that she was often setting the fashion among her wide circle of friends.

Then tragedy struck. Her first child, a boy, died when he was a baby. She had turned to writing for consolation and all seemed to be going well as her books on household design became instant bestsellers and as influential in their day as Mrs Beeton's. Behind this success lay a fraught relationship with her only surviving child, a daughter, made worse when she found that her beloved husband preferred their daughter's company to her own.

Her only gardening book was a slim volume now rarely seen, *Rus in Urbe*. Its charming sprigged floral inside cover gives the impression that the contents will be full of flowery words to remind the town gardener of the countryside, but one look at the subtitle shows that

Haweis's talent was in offering extremely practical advice for every situation: *Flowers that Thrive in London Gardens and Smoky Towns.* In the book she claimed that 'the worst enemies of London gardens are not so much caterpillars as cats ... why are we to do without a garden because cats like salad in bloom? . . . Is the world made for cats?'[2] It is a *cri de coeur* with which many gardeners may sympathise. In flower-arranging she was imaginative, carefully placing her arrangements where they would best catch the light, and using bunches of garden parsley and soup tureens as containers well before fancy twentieth-century flower arrangers claimed them.

Theresa Earle, always known as Mrs C.W. Earle, was a contemporary of Gertrude Jekyll, and in 1897, when she was in her sixties, she published what was to become an extremely popular book on her garden, later complimented by Jekyll herself. She had been spurred on by friends admiring her skill in transforming her two-acre plot in Cobham, Surrey, and asking her for advice. Mrs Earle was both well connected and artistic so it did not take much encouragement for her to put together a collection of writings and send them to a publisher. With the improvement in printing techniques throughout the nineteenth century, there began to be a wealth of illustrated material available for both books and magazines. As Mrs Earle astutely commented in 1897, 'it is a natural consequence that those who cannot taste the actual fruition of a garden should take the greater delight in reading about one',[3] an observation as true today as it was over a hundred years ago. When *Pot Pourri from a Surrey Garden* came out in 1897 it was an instant success and went into ten editions within two years. It is a credit to the fluency of Earle's writing that it is still in print.

There is a story, which may be apocryphal, that her husband, Charles, offered her £10 not to publish the book. Tragically, and quite unrelatedly, he was killed in a cycling accident a week after its publication. Although she probably did not need the freedom of wid-owhood to carry on writing she brought out several more books in a similar vein, and while the garden she created at Woodlands in Cobham was never famous, Mrs Earle remains a key figure through her writing. Her style of well-informed 'musings' laid the foundation for a horticultural publishing format that Jekyll herself followed a couple of years later and is still popular today. Mrs Earle was particu-larly scathing about the 'execrable' early Victorian taste. 'Baskets and vases, summer-houses and seats, are all tortured into frightful "rustic" shapes. The planting and layout of grounds are equally bad; they con-stantly recommend both kinds of Laurels, which time has taught us are the most destructive of plants, killing all other shrubs in their neighbourhood with their insolent and devouring roots.'[4] She was enthusiastic about the possibilities of horticulture as a career for women, having been impressed by Swanley in 1897, and later became a patron of Viscountess Wolseley's Glynde College.

In contrast to the copious amount of practical gardening advice avail-able in the latter half of the nineteenth century, little in the way of academic research into garden history was being done, with one excep-tion which had, quite naturally, grown out of a love of plants. Alicia Amherst (only distantly related to the plant-hunting Countess Amherst of Arracan) was the daughter of a Conservative MP and a mother, Margaret, who was a passionate gardener. In 1875, at the age of ten, Alicia had her own semi-circular flower bed to care for. Of no mean size, it was forty feet wide. She bought her first rose bush that year, and by the time she was thirteen family holidays to the French Riviera meant an opportunity to bring back exotic tender plants. As well as being instilled with a love of gardening from an early age, Alicia Amherst grew up surrounded by the rare books and manuscripts collected by her father. When she was twenty-six Alicia met Percy Newberry, who had written some short pieces on garden history for the *Gardener's Chronicle* and was a friend of her father's.

Encouraged by Newberry, Alicia decided to expand on his articles written two years previously. This she did with academic vigilance, working in the British Library, the Public Record Office and in the archives of Trinity College, Cambridge, where she found a work unnoticed for centuries, *The Feate of Gardening* by 'Mayster Ion Gardener'. Alicia's study of this book, the earliest known treatise on gardening in the English language, became a paper read by her father to the Society of Antiquaries in March 1893. Although Alicia was not allowed to present the paper herself, it was well received and subsequently published by the Society of Archeologia. Alicia later wrote that Ion Gardener 'must certainly have been a practical gardener, as the poem is a series of most sensible and reasonable instructions for growing fruits, herbs, and flowers, and his work is singularly free from the superstitious beliefs in astrology, and the extravagant fancies and experiments in grafting and rearing plants, especially fruit trees, so prevalent in the writing of this period'.[5]

This paper was only the start of her writing career and by 1895 Alicia had finished the work that was to make her name, *A History of Gardening in England*. It was an immediate sell-out and a second edition followed quickly, with a third in 1910. She was given an honorary freedom of the Worshipful Company of Gardeners, which was a great honour since this was one of only two City livery companies who admitted women, the other being the Fanmakers' Company, and she was also given the freedom of the City of London in 1896. When she was thirty-three Alicia married Evelyn Cecil, who went on to be a Conservative MP like her father. Three children followed, but they by no means stopped Alicia from pursuing her profession as a writer. *Children's Gardens* followed in 1902, no doubt prompted by memories of her own child-hood patch, and the more heavyweight *London Parks and Gardens* in 1907.

The writer and garden historian Eleanour Sinclair Rohde was an early student of Maud Grieve's small training school at The Whins in Buckinghamshire. Whereas Grieve was essentially a practical grower, Rohde had a formidable intellect and was a keen author. She com-bined her love of gardening and herbs with writing to such an extent that, when she died, *The Times* said that her book of 1934, *Gardens of Delight*, showed 'by its combination of the literary-historical with, for the first time, the practical-illustrative that the mantle of Miss Jekyll had fallen on her'.[6] In addition to her writing, Eleanour Rohde helped Maud Grieve create the first herb garden at the Chelsea Flower Show in 1919, and she continued to design such gardens, remodelling the kitchen garden at Lullingstone Castle in Kent in 1946.

Rohde, like many women of her time, lost not only her brother in the early weeks of the First World War but probably also the chance to marry as a whole generation of young men was wiped out. By 1920 she was living at the family home in Reigate looking after her mother, who lived into her nineties. Rohde had been born in India when her father was commercial agent to the Maharajah of Travancore. Sent home to be educated at Cheltenham Ladies' College, she won a place at St Hilda's, Oxford, in 1900, but for unknown reasons did not stay to complete her course; Oxford did not award degrees to women until 1920 but nevertheless it was unusual not to take the final exam. This did not spoil her relationship with St Hilda's as she returned to take a tem-porary post there as history tutor in 1910. After spells teaching elsewhere, she was drawn to politics and went to work at Kedlestone for Lord Curzon, whose children she had tutored. This must have been something of a baptism of fire and she left stating that politics was 'too quarrelsome'.[7]

From then on Rohde devoted herself to researching and writing about garden history, still a relatively untapped vein. Her articles began to appear in *My Garden*, *The Queen* and *The Sphere* among others, including the sporting magazine *The Field*, which rarely featured female authors. Although she was supposed to be a 'retiring' person, it says a great deal for her standing that she became president of the Society of Women Journalists. She became a member of the British Guild of Herb Growers in about 1918, and *A Garden of Herbs* was published in 1920, to be followed by *Old English Herbals* in 1922, and many other titles including studies of biblical and Oxford college gardens.

Rohde was friends with some of greatest names in gardening, including Gertrude Jekyll and Vita Sackville-West. Her friendship with the Messel family at their home at Nymans (she dedicated *The Scented Garden* to Maud Messel in 1931) gave her access to their encyclopaedic library of gardening books until it was tragically enveloped in the great fire that virtually destroyed the house in 1947.

The garden at her home became a testing ground for new plants, in particular rare herbs and unusual vegetables. From these she started to produce a small seed list for 'connoisseurs', illustrated by her with delightful line drawings of her plans for herb gardens, featuring round cones of beehives and charming old brick paths lined with 'alternate clumps of aubretias and Thymus serpyllum in variety'.

On the outbreak of the Second World War Rohde threw herself into the promotion of herb and vegetable gardening, encouraged by the government's efforts to get everyone to 'dig for victory'. The books that she published during those years, *Hay Box Cookery*, *The Wartime Vegetable Garden* and *Culinary and Salad Herbs*, were invaluable companions to coupon-juggling housewives.

Although the Reigate garden of Eleanour Sinclair Rohde has long been destroyed and built upon, one bush of rosemary remained in 2004.

Legend has it that it came from Wiggie Farm in Redhill, owned by Arthur Trower. He had been given a cutting from the garden in Wimbledon belonging to Mary Ann Cross, better known as the writer George Eliot. She in turn had obtained her slip from Shakespeare's garden in Stratford. Given the little time Shakespeare actually spent in Stratford once his theatrical career took off, it is nice to think that this plant of remembrance was most likely cared for by Mrs Shakespeare, Anne Hathaway, just as many other Tudor and Jacobean women would have tended their own gardens.

Another early member of the Garden History Society, Alice Coats, is little known outside the small gardening fraternity, but her contribution to the history of plants is significant. She did much of her research at the Royal Botanic Gardens, Kew, and the British Museum's natural history library from a wheelchair, since she was crippled with arthritis. When it came out in 1956 her first book, *Flowers and Their Histories*, was the only one of its kind. It is still a valuable source work for anyone interested in the background of the flowers and herbs growing in their garden.

Miss Coats was occasionally coaxed out of the libraries, and made two appearances on the BBC's first television gardening programme, *Gardening Club*, during the 1960s. In her debut broadcast she took part in what must have been the first television discussion on the influence of women in the history of horticulture, and it was seen by the 6.5 million regular fans of this popular programme. Her next appearance coincided with research for her book *The Quest for Plants*, which examined geographically and chronologically the explorers and collectors who introduced plants into European gardens. In these early days of gardening programmes viewers had to make do with Miss Coats sitting in the BBC's studio underneath a fruiting banana tree and next to a model of a China tea clipper while she discussed the importance of

Dr Nathaniel Bagshaw Ward's discovery that shipping plants and cuttings in glass cases allowed them to survive salt and sun in their travels across the world.

A talent for writing as well as gardening has enabled several female gardeners to influence a wide audience through publishing and the press. Margery Fish virtually single-handedly was responsible for the renewed popularity of the 'cottage garden' style of planting in the second half of the twentieth century, and she was always far more interested in individual plants than in their overall effect in the design of a garden. One of plantswoman and photographer Valerie Finnis's best 'gardening portraits' was of her friend Mrs Fish working in her

Margery Fish (1892–1969) disliked having her photograph taken but allowed her friend Valerie Finnis to capture her working in her garden at East Lambrook Manor, which she made famous for its cottage-garden-style planting.

garden at East Lambrook in Somerset. The portrait is all the more special because Margery Fish hated having her photograph taken and so there are very few illustrations of her in existence. She has the look of a Mrs Tiggy-Winkle about her – sensible shoes, floral dress and hair scraped back in a bun – but this belies the reality of a woman who came to gardening late in life after a career working for some of the toughest men in British journalism.

After twenty years working for Associated Newspapers and six editors of the *Daily Mail*, in 1933 Margery Townshend finally married one of them, Walter Fish. By now in her forties, Margery was used to doing battle with strong men on the newsroom floor, but on their 'retirement' to their new home at the manor of East Lambrook a new war broke out – over gardening styles. Husband-and-wife gardening partnerships are not always made in heaven, and once at East Lambrook it became clear that Walter Fish had very different ideas to his wife as to how plants should be grown – and where. Walter wanted traditional, neatly edged lawns and beds of hybrid tea roses and dahlias; Mrs Fish wanted a more informal look. An admitted novice in gardening, she stood firm in her passion for a then unfashionable 'cottage garden' look, allowing self-sown seedlings to pop up in Walter's pristine gravel paths, and smuggling in choice cuttings which had been given to her by an ever-widening circle of horticultural friends.

After Walter's death in 1947, Mrs Fish was able to indulge her passions for hellebores, snowdrops, primroses and epimediums. She also started writing books. Her early career had included freelance journalism so it is little surprise that her books were instantly popular. By 1951 she was writing for *The Field* magazine and later for *Punch*, *Amateur Gardening*, *Popular Gardening* and the RHS's journal among many others. She wrote eight books starting with the story of East Lambrook Manor, *We Made a Garden*, first published in 1956.

Her writing style was refreshingly honest. She wrote not just about the differences of opinion between herself and Walter, but also of the hard work and failures they had endured in establishing a garden at East Lambrook. Single-handedly she had infilled the retaining wall surrounding the property, 'wheeling barrowloads of earth along the road . . . and improving the bank at the other end'. Finally satisfied with the 'clean and self-conscious wall', she planted it and the bank with hundreds of valerian seedlings, grown no doubt by herself. The results were a 'blaze of crimson, white and every shade of pink' for two summers, but to her dismay they then all vanished, perhaps, she pondered, having found the soil she had so lovingly improved too rich.[8]

To all of her writing Margery Fish brought her journalist skills, but like the best horticultural writers she also brought her gardening wisdom. Readers knew that she had grown every plant she wrote about, moved it, fed it, divided it, and occasionally consigned it to the compost heap. Even when discussing such an unromantic but vital subject as the last, she managed to inject warmth and wit into her writing. Following a 'recipe' she had found in an American book that allowed everything to be composted except perennial weeds and ever-green material, she made her three bins into receptacles for kitchen refuse, grass cuttings, 'great mountains of Nepeta, aubrietia, Michaelmas daisies and all the other herbaceous things that are cut down'.

One would think that compost would not be a source of marital strife, but once again Walter Fish had strong opinions. He disapproved of Margery adding eggshells to the heap. 'He disliked them so and contended that it was silly to bother about them when I could get all the lime I wanted for a few pence.' Once more, she stood firm. 'I think my plants enjoy a mixed diet and I would not deny them little tit-bits of shell, but I did see that they were crushed very finely so that they did not intrude too forcibly on my lord's eye.'[9]

The horticultural journalist Frances Perry had had the good fortune to grow up next to E.A. Bowles, whose garden at Myddelton House in what was then the small village of Enfield was a magnet for anyone interested in rare and delicate plants. In the years around the First World War Perry collected wild flowers for him and, with such an inspirational mentor, it is not surprising that she chose horticulture as a career.

In 1930 she married her first husband, Gerald, son of Amos Perry, at whose nursery she had her first job. Although her early life was spent working in horticultural education, she is best remembered for her broadcasting, books and journalism, particularly the column in the *Observer* which she wrote for over twenty years. On television in the 1970s, at a time when gardening was still seen as a rather middle-class hobby for a woman, Perry's slight rural accent cut through any snobbery as she dispensed practical hands-on advice that both the expert and the beginner could understand.

The 1960s brought Frances Perry an MBE and the RHS Veitch Memorial Medal for services to horticulture. It also brought a controversy she had not gone looking for. By the late 1960s, despite the fact that women were now being awarded many of the prestigious RHS medals, there was still no female representation on the society's council. At the Annual General Meeting of the RHS in 1967 a question was raised as to why this was so. Because, came the answer, there had never been ladies on the council and there were none 'at present' who had 'as useful experience as the men available'. Within days the writer famous for *National Velvet* and *The Chalk Garden* had a letter published in *The Times* quoting this and suggesting that Gertrude Jekyll must be rolling in her grave.

Alas Miss Jekyll. Sir, A jewel from the proceedings of the Annual General Meeting of the Royal Horticultural Society (Journal):- 'We have never had ladies on the Council.' Mrs Pankhurst glanced at Miss Gertrude Jekyll in the spheres. I am, Sir, yours faithfully, Enid Bagnold, Rottingdean, Sussex.[10]

Lord Aberconway, president of the RHS and scion of Bodnant, retorted that this was a 'little storm in ladies' teacups' and that he had been misquoted. 'We have nothing against the ladies,' he blustered. 'As soon as a lady comes to our minds or is suggested informally . . . who can contribute in our view as much as to our multifarious activities as any man available, we shall support her appointment.'[11]

A year later a suitable candidate was elected unopposed: Mrs Frances Perry. When asked to join the council, Frances Perry famously replied: 'If you want me because I'm a woman, the answer is no, but if you want me because of anything I have done in horticulture, the answer is yes.' There was no doubt that Perry had 'done' a great deal. From Wye, where she had been trained, Perry worked in a nursery, published a bestselling book on water gardening that is still a standard text decades later, and during the Second World War she was appointed organiser for agricultural and horticultural education for Middlesex County Council. In 1953 she became principal of Norwood Hall Institute and College of Horticulture, in Southall, west London, where she stayed until 1967.

As the president was at pains to point out, Perry arrived as no token woman. 'I must emphasize that she was nominated by Council not because she was a woman, but because she was, in the unanimous view of us all . . . more likely than any others to contribute to the works of Council . . . Indeed, it was only because our invitation was couched in those terms that she accepted the nomination.'[12] With the 'little storm in ladies' teacups' dealt with, Perry went on to make an enormous contribution to the society, being awarded the Victoria Medal of Honour in 1971 and eventually becoming a vice-president.

The best practical garden writers often come from solid horticultural backgrounds and Xenia Field was no exception. She was a distinguished gardening journalist, whose father had been a rhododendron-growing associate of the Rothschilds and an RHS gold medal winner himself. For nearly forty years Field worked for the *Daily Mirror*, which, with a circulation of five million in the 1950s and 60s, gave her a greater readership than any other gardening columnist. She was the author of a succession of small gardening books, some, particularly those on growing bulbs and indoor plants, highly successful, and was awarded an MBE in 1958 and the RHS Veitch Memorial Medal in 1972.

The increased interest in garden and plant history has also meant that mainstream publishers have taken on serious scholarship, much of which is led by female writers. Anna Pavord set a high standard with her monumental work on the tulip, for which, in 2000, she was given the RHS's Veitch Memorial Medal. Since the 1970s books on gardening have become some of the most popular non-fiction titles. From coffee-table books with garden photography to drool over to practical how-to titles, there is now a book for everyone on every horticultural subject and single species, whether your interests be the most delicate varieties of wood anemone, wild topiary designs, 3-D garden planning or simply how to grow beans in buckets.

CULTIVATED LADIES

Gardening taken up as a hobby when all the
laborious work can be done by a man is
delightful, but as a life's work [for a woman],
it is almost an impossible thing.

Sir Joseph Hooker,
letter to Miss Symonds, 20 March 1906[1]

A FOOT ON THE LADDER

Weeding has been the bane of every gardener's life since time began. 'I always think of my sins when I weed,' wrote American gardener Helena Rutherfurd Ely in 1903. 'They grow apace in the same way and are harder still to get rid of.'[1] As one of the earliest recorded gardening jobs noted during the medieval and early modern period, weeding was back-breaking, poorly paid and irregular work, invariably done by women, who have always been the lowliest of paid garden workers. In the early sixteenth century, fifteen women are recorded in the accounts of Hampton Court, three of whom were paid just three pence a day for ridding the gardens of 'charlock, nettles, convolvulus, dodder, thistles, dandelions and groundsel'.[2] In the 1540s Katheryn Sherman managed to earn a little more, though hardly a living wage since she was paid only sixpence intermittently 'for a weekes wages to make the gardeyn'.[3] It was a similar picture at Cardinal's College, Oxford (later Christ Church), in 1530 where two women were paid a total of 16d for three days' work 'rooting up unprofitable herbs in the garden'.[4]

Three other local women, Margaret Hall, Joan Fery and Agnes Stringer, also worked at Cardinal's College 'cleansing the garden',

Women were expected to maintain high standards on small plots near their homes on which they grew medicinal and culinary plants essential for the family household.

and were rewarded not just with their penny wages but also with a meal of herrings and bread, with ale to wash it down.[5] Sometimes this employment led to better things; in the late 1520s a widow known as 'Modor Tubbys' worked as a weeder at Bridge House in the City of London where one John Hewett was taken on as a porter. Within a year they were married and the new Mrs Hewett's wages were increased to 8s a year, which she supplemented by selling seeds.[6]

Ales Brewer and Margaret Rogers earned rather more than that at Hampton Court by supplying plants, thirty-four bushels of 'strowberry roots, primerose and violettes' at a rate of 3d a bushel (about 35 litres), plants they may have cultivated in their own nursery or smallholding. It was a common occurrence for women to take over the running of a family business on the death of the male head, a contribution to horticulture in the early modern period which is not often acknowledged. We know, for example, that Ralph Tuggy ran a successful nursery in Westminster, famed for its pinks, carnations and auriculas and other then-rare plants, and when he died in 1633 it was accepted that his widow should take over the running of the nursery.

Although the wealthier households would have employed full-time gardeners, it was rarely a well-paid position for a man or a woman. In the accounts of Hampton Court in 1696, during the reign of William III, it is shown that while two royal gardeners who oversaw the upkeep of the gardens were paid £70 a year, the main workforce earned on average £10 per annum. Among them were twelve women who usually received 8d a day, which may be comparable as a daily rate, but they were employed as casual workers and would have been called upon only as needed.

In the eighteenth century, women were still restricted to the most menial jobs such as digging up potatoes, collecting scythed cuttings and the inevitable weeding. Jobbing gardeners were always male and any women employed on a casual basis for specific tasks were invariably paid less than them. The Duke of Chandos employed sixteen men and two women to care for his gardens in 1721; the men all received 1s 2d a day while the women – employed yet again as weeders – earned just 8d.

There was no opportunity for women to progress in any form of apprenticeship in horticulture. The bothy, the traditional living quarters for gardeners and their apprentices, was strictly for men only, meaning that women could be employed only on a casual basis and for the simplest tasks. In 1767 the Scottish gardening author John Abercrombie recommended, in his enormously popular book *Every*

Man His Own Gardener, that women and boys were the ones best equipped to deal with pests such as slugs, suggesting that they should water them with a mixture of soapsuds, urine and tobacco-water. 'Every drop of the liquor causes almost instant death,' he gloated.[7]

In other areas of the horticultural world, women were still helping to raise plants in family businesses and to manage nurseries, although they received little credit or money for this work. As the demand for plants grew in the nineteenth century and nurseries expanded, women were often employed in the propagating houses for the most routine jobs like pricking out and potting on, but without qualifications or connections it was hard to progress to more interesting employment.

This situation was not just restricted to working-class women. Until the twentieth century it was virtually impossible for a woman of any class to have anything that might be described as a 'career' in horticulture, though this was not a situation unique to gardening. Few middle-class women worked in the nineteenth century, and with the increased separation between the home and the place of work as towns and cities grew, women became exiled from family businesses at a time when society also considered it a man's job to provide a 'family wage'. However, towards the end of the Victorian age, cracks were beginning to appear and a handful of pioneering women took the first steps towards changing attitudes and indeed their lives.

Although Gertrude Jekyll was supplying garden designs by this time, she never charged for them, so she was not technically a professional. The honour of being the earliest professional female landscape gardener must go to Fanny Rollo Wilkinson, whose early career is certainly unique among middle-class women in the mid-1880s.

Wilkinson's father died in 1878 when she was twenty-three, and wanting, though perhaps not needing, to earn a living she decided to turn a childhood hobby into a career. She may have been spurred on by her brother, Matthew Eason Wilkinson, who also trained in horticultural education. With great difficulty she persuaded the head of the then strictly men-only Crystal Palace School of Landscape Gardening and Practical Horticulture to admit her to their eighteen-month course. Here she learned not only about flowers and plants, but also about hard landscaping, business accounts, ordering from suppliers and dealing with a team of what would have been entirely male gardeners. Within a few months, she was appointed honorary landscape gardener to the Metropolitan Public Gardens, Boulevard and Playground Association, whose function was to develop public land in London. The telltale word is, of course, 'honorary' as Wilkinson did not get paid by the MPGA in the early days, although within a couple of years the accounts show that 'Miss W' did receive a payment of £12 3s 4d in April 1888.

Fanny was responsible for the laying out of over seventy-five gardens for the association, including the Red Cross Garden in Southwark, which was named after the adjacent Red Cross Hall. The idea of developing the garden came from the philanthropist Octavia Hill, who was concerned that the clearing away of local cottages 'with their separate little yards' left the neighbourhood with no open space.[8] The new public garden was a great success and soon became the focus for local flower shows, which, a newspaper reported in 1890, had the effect of improving the window boxes in the surrounding houses.

Wilkinson, who listed herself as a 'Landscape Gardener' in trade directories, was being helped at the time by Emmeline Sieveking, daughter of the royal physician Edward Sieveking, and sister of Albert Sieveking, the garden writer. Her partnership with Wilkinson

Edith Chamberlain was one of a new breed of late-Victorian women
who sought to promote career possibilities for girls in horticulture.

was fruitful in more ways than one as she later married Fanny's
brother, Matthew.

Fanny Wilkinson's achievements as a landscape designer are
astounding considering it is hard to find any middle-class women professionally involved with horticulture in that era. Edith Chamberlain,
who published *The Gentlewoman's Book of Gardening* with Mrs Douglas in
1892, may have run a company providing jobbing gardeners in
London. Chamberlain was a founder member of the Women's
Agricultural and Horticultural International Union and one of its
most ardent supporters. She was also one of the first to promote the
acceptability of upper-class women entering such careers. She had
strong ideas about both tools and clothes for women intent on gardening. 'Be not persuaded into buying little toy sets of "ladies'" tools,'

she insisted, 'rather choose each implement separately.'[9] She was equally adamant about how a woman should look when gardening, and her instructions are also a reminder of the restrictions of 1890s female dress:

> The woman who is to make order lovely in the garden should herself be neat – neat, but most certainly not gaudy . . . The serviceable garden frock may be plain to prudishness, or as daringly picturesque as the wearer chooses, but it must have certain qualifications – the skirt must not be skimpy, nor must it have its anterior fullness tied back with tapes, which will either crack and tear the stuff when the wearer stoops . . . the bodice must be made without bones, the sleeves be tight, and of medium length.[10]

Edith Chamberlain also encouraged the gardener to be as colourful as the flower borders she was creating: 'Reseda beige makes a capital summer gardening dress, and nothing beats serge for winter – grey brown, or navy blue for choice. A crimson flannel blouse would give colour if worn with the latter, and the former may be brightened by a bright tinted apron . . . A "butcher's blue" is delightful with the reseda beige, or a deep red, or even orange for those who can stand it.'[11]

Reseda is the botanical name for mignonette, a plant extremely popular with the Victorians although nothing much to look at, and the insignificant flowers are indeed a darkish beige. Its attraction was its heavenly scent and it was widely used in bedding arrangements and window boxes. Gloves were needed, and Chamberlain warned her readers that if they really did 'mean business' these were the items they would have to replace most frequently. In that respect some things never change, as her recommendation on the usefulness of an apron pocket for 'any small articles, wanted handy for one's work – labels, string, wire, nails, tacks, raffia grass, pins for pegging down plants, and so on'[12] strikes a familiar chord today. But those women who did mean business needed more than just the right clothes and tools; they needed training, and at last the door which could lead to careers in gardening for women was finally creaking open.

SWANLEY MISSES

In 1873 a far-sighted but anonymous young woman wrote in William Robinson's magazine, *The Garden*, of her wish that women, or rather 'ladies', would consider horticulture as a profession. This was written at a time before there was any type of formal training available for women interested in gardening as a career, yet here was the first signal that it might be something that ladies should consider, since it 'could not detract in itself in any way from their social status as gentle-women'. Pointing out that there was already a women's school of horticulture in America, she was astonished that 'in the present dearth of remunerative employment for women of the middle class, no one has as yet thought of making them "gardeners" ... Why should we not have our female Paxtons and Kents?'[1]

The writer was not alone in believing that there should be opportunities for women to train professionally as gardeners and subsequently to follow a career in horticulture, and matters did improve in the subsequent decades.

The first specialist school to accept women, Swanley Horticultural College in Kent, was then in open countryside, and in the perfect position to attract young ladies into the 'new' profession of gardening. The fees were £80 a year – more than a gardener's annual wage – so the school was really only accessible to daughters from the middle classes. Among the earliest intakes at Swanley were three women whose backgrounds were typical of this and who were to become horticultural pioneers – Eleanor Morland, Gertrude Cope and Alice Hutchings.

Eleanor Morland's father was a manufacturer in her home town of Glastonbury in Somerset; Gertrude Cope, whose father was a journalist, came from Chelmsford in Essex; and Alice Hutchings was from the seaside town of Deal in Kent, and may have lost her father. When she was eighteen Alice won a Kent County Council scholarship to fund her time at Swanley and started there on a chilly day in February 1894, signing her name in the register alongside that of another student, Annie Gulvin, who was a year younger. After the hard work

Annie Gulvin was one of the first female students at Swanley,
and later the first girl to sign the work register at Kew.

and fun at Swanley, Alice and Annie's lives were to be intertwined for many years.

Professional training for gardeners had been available to men during the nineteenth century, when qualifying from the Royal Botanic Gardens at Kew was the pinnacle of the profession, and the Royal Horticultural Society introduced public exams in 1865. The test, which by 1893 was known as the General Examination, was taught at several men-only horticultural colleges countrywide, including Swanley, which opened as a single-sex establishment in 1889. This changed in 1891 when the principal, Mr Bond, was persuaded by a Mrs Richmond to start accepting female students. Mrs Richmond, a passionate gardener since childhood, had been given her own greenhouse by her father when she was thirteen. She became gardening editor of *Queen* magazine, and wrote articles for *Lady's Pictorial* and *Amateur Gardening*, campaigning for women to be able to train as professional gardeners. It was through her, she claimed, that a Mrs Watson, the widow of a clergyman, was appointed as lady superintendent of the ladies' branch at Swanley. Mrs Watson had got in touch with her after reading one of her articles and appeared to have exactly the right credentials for the position.

Five women were accepted to the programme, moving into a red-brick terrace house nearby and joining their young male colleagues on the campus. 'The only difference made between the sexes,' confided Mrs Richmond, 'is that lady students are not obliged to do hard manual work, though it is a rule of the College that no necessary work shall be considered by any student as too menial for performance.'[2] Of the first year's intake of five female students, two of them were sisters, Mildred and Jessie Smith. They were both star pupils, taking the course in half the time usually allotted, with Mildred scooping the highest place on the first year's diploma list.

By the time Alice and Annie joined in February 1894 there were thirty girl students and the following year, when Eleanor and Gertrude arrived, there were thirty-four. These numbers were swiftly noticed by that august institution the Royal Botanic Gardens at Kew, and the house journal, the *Kew Guild*, made gentle mockery of their potential rival, noting that at Swanley women would be taught how to manage 'their own estates, colonial gardens, market gardens, or gentleman's private gardens, or to act as practical teachers of horti-culture'.[3] The fees charged at Swanley included 'pleasant drawing and dining rooms in a refined and comfortable home, and with a lady superintendent to see them all into bed by a quarter past ten'. For this they were expected to pay £80 a year, which, the *Kew Guild* pointed out, did not include 'washing and books'. After two years or so of this, head gardeners' places at '24s a week with house and vegetables' might be, and, indeed, had been got by the women (not lady) gardeners.[4]

The *Kew Guild* continued with a suggestion:

Cannot some arrangement be made whereby a Kewite and a Swanley Miss can join their forces and thus be a source of strength to each other? We might then have gardeners offering their services for the outdoor department, wife to take charge of the orchids and fruit, or a woman gardener might undertake to manage a large garden, her husband to act as foreman. Kew and Swanley should certainly have a special attraction for each other. Double-barrelled gardeners would be an advantage, and their offspring would be born gardeners; but alas! gardeners as a rule are forbidden to have off-spring.[5]

To begin with the girls sat at the back of the classroom behind the male students, always chaperoned by Mrs Watson. The girls lived in a house called South Bank and the boys at North Bank, clearly well away from each other. The syllabus at Swanley was comprehensive; in addition to horticulture, applied sciences such as zoology, chemistry and botany were studied. A course on meteorology taught them to learn 'the causes of varied climate, temperature, winds, rain, hail, snow, dew, lightening and thunder'.[6] Book-keeping, surveying and the law relating to horticulture equipped them for running their own gardening businesses, while sessions on dairy work, poultry and bee-keeping gave the girls additional skills that might come in useful if they were to manage their own smallholdings in the future. The most important examination was the Royal Horticultural Society's and all students, even those doing one of the shorter courses on individual topics, needed to get a first-class pass in the RHS test if they were to be awarded their Swanley certificate.

In addition to two written papers that were taken at the RHS's centre in Vincent Square, students spent two full days at Wisley doing practical work. Chrystabel Procter, who took the RHS teachers' honours exam in 1919, remembered how tough they were.

Absolutely nothing was labelled! I was shown into an enormous potting shed with every sort of unnamed compost, peat, sand, chalk, leaf mould etc. under the staging with equally anonymous containers on the top:- flower pots and pans of all sizes plus piles of wooden boxes and plant labels. I was supplied with six anonymous plants and told to pot them up in a 'suitable receptacle' with the right sort of compost, lable them correctly and add a short written statement explaining why I had done what I had done.[7]

The new recruits did not betray Mrs Richmond's belief in the capabilities of women to become gardeners: Annie Gulvin achieved the highest marks for the RHS exam on 1 May 1895, winning the society's silver gilt medal with 260 points out of a possible 300. Alice Hutchings and Madeline Agar were also in the first-class category, both with 215 points, and Madeline carried off the college's own first prize for horticulture. Competition between the girls did not stop with the basic horticultural exams: Alice Hutchings got a first-class pass for agriculture (advanced stage) in the South Kensington Science and Art Examination, and Madeline Agar achieved a first-class pass in advanced botany, beating Alice and Annie, who had to make do with second-class passes. Madeline also obtained a first-class pass in advanced theoretical chemistry, the only student who did.

Life at Swanley was not all studying. Annie and Madeline competed against each other in the College Tennis Singles Championship, which Madeline won, and the two of them also took part in the annual Christmas show, singing 'Hunting Quadrilles' and 'When Love is Kind', which went down so well they were forced to perform an encore. The latter was a favourite drawing-room ballad made popular by the Victorian singer and composer Liza Lehmann, famous already for her composition 'There Are fairies at the Bottom of our Garden'. Alice Hutchings sat out both the singing and the tennis sessions, happy perhaps to leave such matters to her seemingly more energetic friends.

The new century brought changes to the college. Matthew Eason Wilkinson became acting principal for a year, during which the numbers of female students increased. In late 1901 the council at Swanley made the decision to no longer take in male students, which made arrangements for accommodation and the like logistically simpler for the remaining staff and pupils. Many of these pioneering female horticultural students brought their sympathies for the suffragette cause to the college, albeit more typically as suffragists in favour of winning the vote for women through passive means rather than the active demonstrations favoured by suffragettes, and in 1904 Fanny Wilkinson, related by marriage to the suffragist Millicent Fawcett, followed her brother and became head of the college. Swanley's governors were rather nervous, however, when students wanted to march for women's suffrage. 'It was agreed . . .' records show, 'that [students] might walk as women gardeners but it was undesirable that they should use the college name.' This decision was in keeping with the suffragist outlook and does not appear to have caused unrest among the students.

By the 1920s there were nearly twenty small private gardening schools in England, but few had the reputation of Swanley. Although scholarships of £40 were available towards the cost of the fees of diploma students, there was extra expense in meeting the demands of the long uniform list supplied by the college: for winter, students required a tunic of Swanley tweed – round yoke – three pleats back and front, length to touch the ground on kneeling; a coat of Swanley tweed (the tweed was obtained from Messrs Egerton Burnett, Wellington, Somerset, who held the regulation patterns); a blazer with monogram for second-year students; a Boy Scout's belt from Messrs Gamages, the London department store; blouses (shirt blouses of natural tussore with turn-down collars, 27s 6d); a jersey or sweater, white or brown; stockings, extra long, brown; and knickers, short, regulation pattern. One student, Margaret Smieton, wrote to her mother with detailed instructions about the 'regulation' pattern of the knickers: 15 inches from waist to crotch, then 10¼ inches long, 'otherwise just like the pattern I think, though possibly not quite so wide, but as the stuff will be softer it will not matter I think. The length of my tunic from the bottom of the yoke to bottom of hem is about 32″ – I am sure you won't need to order as much as the Weldon's pattern says. Someone has made 2 tunics and 2 pr knickers from 6 yds with a squash.'

The list continued with more gardening-related garments: a

coloured silk handkerchief, three-quarter-yard square, or brown felt hat, to be worn at practical work; two pairs extra strong boots, or shoes, brown; a Mackintosh (amazingly, an optional item); one pair of clogs or gumboots; a blue serge apron which could be ordered on arrival from a local dressmaker; and one pair of strong gardening gloves.

There was another list for the summer months: tunics in green sundour – material from Harrods and pattern by Weldon's with their blouses; a straw hat, plain, shady; and, to cover their legs, 'The Swanley Stocking', a summer-weight stocking from the London Glove Co., Bond Street, extra long, regulation. As well as clothing, each student was required to bring '2 pairs of sheets, 2 pillowcases, 4 towels, and 4 dinner napkins [and] all . . . must be distinctly marked with name in full'.[8]

The house rules were strict. Students had to be in their bedrooms at 10 p.m., and all lights were to be out by 10.30 p.m. They were not to bicycle alone except between the college and their houses, neither were they to be out alone after dusk. There was little free time even at weekends, since all students were required to undertake Sunday watering duties for which a rota was kept. Students were allowed to entertain friends at meals (with certain limitations) at fixed charges.

Margaret Smieton, remembering how she and a friend had worked on an allotment before breakfast, wrote later that she felt that throughout her time at Swanley she did far more practical work in the garden than the students who followed her. She finally graduated from Swanley in July 1923, passing finals in horticulture, chemistry, botany, entomology, book-keeping and dairying. By this stage, the college was being run by Dr Kate Barratt, who had arrived in 1922, twenty years after she had been a student at Swanley. 'I shall regard it as a life work and shall spare no efforts to carry out the duties to the full extent of my powers,' she said when she joined, and that is pretty well what she did, running the school until it was absorbed by Wye College in the early 1950s.

With clearly plenty of life left in her, Barratt retired and married the head of governors, R.J. Tabor, whom she had known for many years. Professor Tabor had been one of the few boys to attend Swanley in its very early days in 1892. Although he later joined Imperial College, Tabor remained devoted to Swanley, first teaching there and then as head of the governing council. Barratt and Tabor's lives intertwined throughout their careers as Kate Barratt also spent time demonstrating at Imperial and she then took his place as a teacher at Swanley in 1910. It was only when they both retired that marriage seemed an option, but they did manage to have eight years together.

Life at the college had not changed much by the early 1930s, as Joan Clark discovered when she was a student from 1932 to 1934. The uniform was a little different; girls now wore green cotton jackets in the summer over natural-coloured shirts with thick, brown three-quarter-length coats in the winter. They all had a leather belt with a knife hanging from one side, and on the other a wooden contraption they called a 'little man', which was made for them in the carpenter's shop and used to scrape the soil off one's spade.[9]

By this time the college had a male head of horticulture, Dr W.E. Shewell-Cooper. He was still there during the war when Swanley lay under the path of the German bombers flying to London and the students were evacuated to Nottingham for two years, and then again to Wye College after Swanley was bombed in March 1944. After the war the college lost its all-girl status and was amalgamated with the South Eastern Agricultural College at Wye. Wye has now been absorbed into Imperial College, London, but it remains one of the country's finest horticultural training centres.

HOCKEY AND HORTICULTURE

Whereas Swanley evolved out of a male college, Studley College was started exclusively for females and opened from scratch in only eight weeks in 1898. The project was initiated by Frances Evelyn, Countess of Warwick, a high society beauty then in her late thirties who was also a deeply committed philanthropist and socialist. She had already founded a school for children, and her next project was to encourage educated, middle-class women to consider horticulture and agriculture as possible careers.

The countess was a passionate gardener, and when away from her hectic social life in London oversaw the work at Easton Lodge, one of her country homes, which was in a rural corner of Essex near Great Dunmow. After a visit to the agricultural department of University College, Nottingham, the countess was inspired to start her own 'agricultural settlement' for women. When Lady Warwick met Edith Bradley, who was also working in women's social reform, it seemed a perfect partnership: the countess would front the campaign while Miss Bradley, now employed as her 'confidential secretary', would be the driving force behind the scenes. The town of Reading was chosen as a potential location because of its proximity to the Dairy Institute.

Garbed in a green cycling suit and brown hat, Edith Bradley valiantly cycled round the area and finally found a suitable site in Bath Road. Partially supported by Essex County Council because of Lady Warwick's connections in Great Dunmow, it was intended as a place where women could learn the necessary horticultural skills.

In September 1898, a prospectus for the school, initially called the 'Lady Warwick Hostel', was advertised in *Country Life*. One of the first recruits to the staff was Alice Hutchings from Swanley, who came highly recommended by Thiselton-Dyer, the director at Kew, where she was currently working. In October the school opened with twelve students and Edith Bradley was appointed as its first warden.

The 'Hostel' was an immediate success, due in no small part to Miss Bradley's hard work. In addition to the practicalities of setting up and running the college, Miss Bradley persuaded the nearby seed merchants, Messrs Sutton's, to give students use of their seed trial grounds. Kelways' peony nursery in Somerset and several other horticultural growers also gave generously, and wealthy local families such as the Huntleys and the Palmers of biscuit fame also contributed to the running costs.

In addition to horticultural studies, and in accordance with the school's commitment to the girls' welfare in broader terms, they were encouraged to play popular team sports. The Lady Warwick Hostel Hockey Club frequently played against local teams such as the Scarlet Runners or Miss Everarde's XI. They even managed to defeat the girls from Swanley once, 33–0.

Such was the success of the school that, by 1903, plans were made to move to somewhere with larger facilities and more accommodation. The Countess of Warwick bought the run-down Studley Castle and its farm, and the school moved to Warwickshire, renaming itself the Lady Warwick College. The physical living conditions were much tougher

Although best known as a society hostess and beauty, Frances 'Daisy', Countess of Warwick (1861–1938), was a passionate philanthropist, determined to make the study of horticulture available to women through her college at Studley.

than at Reading, but still the students came and the success continued, but two years after the move and despite all her hard work in establishing the college, there was a falling-out between Edith Bradley and the countess. After an acrimonious meeting on Founder's Day 1905 Miss Bradley resigned, and the two women did not speak again until 1929. When a board took over the running of the school in 1911 the countess had little direct involvement and did not visit Studley for the next twelve years.

Miss Bradley went on to found Greenaway Court, a modest private gardening school, at Hollingbourne in Kent. One of her successors at Studley, Dr Lillias Hamilton, got in touch with her at the time of her appointment in 1909. They were to develop a long and sympathetic correspondence, but Miss Bradley's first response to Dr Hamilton was full of bitterness: 'You have my very deepest sympathy and profound hopes that you will be able to accomplish the apotheosis of Lady Warwick's College,' replied Miss Bradley. 'I know that your task is beset with difficulties on every side, all the more subtle because your enemies are unseen (at least in my case they were) but all the greater will be the victory if you win, as I devoutly hope that you may.'[1]

The task facing Dr Hamilton was to get the school, renamed for the final time as Studley College, recognised as a 'technical institution' by the Board of Education. She also strove to get RHS recognition as an 'approved institution', which was eventually granted in 1916. However, the ever-cautious RHS refused to allow a member of their council to sit on the council of Studley College 'as it would create an undesirable precedent'.[2] Studley students did well in the RHS examinations, winning the society's gold medal for seven years in a row. Funding was a continuous problem although the college attracted students from as far afield as Switzerland, Poland, Russia and Japan.

Dr Hamilton, as head of Studley, did all she could to impress upon prospective students that their chances of employment after completing the course at Studley, or indeed at any serious horticultural college, were excellent. She asserted that some women gardeners were making the astronomical figure of £1,000 a year, and many others reaping large profits.

The growth of the profession of women gardeners during the year has been remarkable. An employment bureau started recently in Westminster is now a centre of great activity. About fifty members of the Women's Agricultural and Horticultural Union are now established as producers, and more than twice this number have salaried posts. To give one example from each group. A post was provided the other day for a lady gardener in a big country house garden. She is paid £1000 a year with a furnished house and a good many extras and a percentage on superfluous fruit sold . . . Some large profits are made by the few garden designers; but the increase in the profession is due to the remarkable success of several pairs of friends from the colleges who have set up for themselves and managed to make a good steady income without excessive work.[3]

An edition in 1912 of the *Daily Mail* proclaimed in true tabloid style, '£1,000 Gardeners – Where Women Excel', citing a relatively easy job on offer for a woman gardener whose duties would include keeping the conservatory entrance to a house always gay with flowers tastefully arranged. She would also have to decorate the ballroom occasionally and arrange the dinner table every night. The salary was £150 a year plus cottage and allowances, but this plum job was in America. Closer to home, most girls were lucky to to find posts at £50 a year all found.

Students went to a wide variety of jobs: running their own market gardens, teaching and lecturing, dairy managing and running a fruit-bottling business in 'the Colonies'. Two girls became head gardeners, one to a Welsh MP who had 'a large place with a lot of glass'. She had three men and a boy working under her, together with a student placement from Studley, yet still she was working nine-and-a-half-hour days in the summer, and from 'dawn to dark' in the winter. She reported back to Studley that she '[went] in for bulbs . . . planted several thousand last year'.[4]

If the poor pay did not put off prospective pupils, neither did the thought of hard physical labour. In 1910, a Studley student had this to say for any doubters:

To ask, 'Do you dig?' seems to me to be as superfluous as to enquire of a hungry boy if he would like a bun . . . the prospective girl gardener . . . should be prepared to adopt the curriculum laid down for 'first years', although it may include manual tasks which, in a private place, would be relegated to the hired boy. Stacking up a manure heap or ridging a vacant piece of land may make arms and back ache, but the girl gardener has to realise that muscles which have hitherto been inactive require as much training as either eye or hand . . . Taking her all round the girl gardener is a 'jolly good fellow', as ready for a dance when the day's work is over . . . as she is to 'walk the plank' with the wheelbarrow when the day is beginning. She confesses to a weakness for pretty clothes, rejoices in a healthy appetite, a sound body, and a cheerful mind; and admits, quite candidly that the tea bell represents one of the nicest events of the day.[5]

The 'weakness for pretty clothes' is understandable after days spent trudging through the infamous Studley mud; long skirts had to be hemmed with leather to allow the mud to be brushed off more easily, and high-collared blouses often made the girls feel faint when they were working in the fiercely heated stove or melon houses. As long Edwardian skirts gave way to khaki breeches in the 1920s the girls had more physical freedom during their working hours; and in their free time as well there is little doubt that the girls of Studley knew how to enjoy themselves after a hard week's work on the land. Photographs survive of the students posing with hockey sticks, punting on the lake or with a precious wind-up record player far, far away from the dorms and the ears of the staff. A great array of argyle-patterned socks, the highly fashionable unisex item made popular by the handsome Prince of Wales, added a bit of style to the basic breeches. As well as hockey, there were tennis tournaments and cricket matches, and the total collapse of opposing tug-of-war teams added to the mix of fun the girls had.

Despite the increased informality that the Second World War initiated, breeches continued to be worn as a uniform. Jennet Blake, from Oxfordshire, studied at Studley in 1947, and thought the breeches were 'most uncomfortable for work, having no stretch'. To their great relief, students were soon allowed to wear dungarees all the year round, instead of just in the summer. The following year, they were even allowed to wear trousers as long as they wore overalls as well, but other formalities still held sway, with the girls all called by their surnames by staff and sometimes among themselves.

Emily Ekins became acting warden in 1922 and was the principal for twenty-two years from 1924 to 1946. She had the distinction of being, according to Dr Hamilton, 'the most highly-qualified man or woman in England in horticulture'.[6] Ekins had been a student and then on the staff at Studley and held the National Diploma in Horticulture and the college's own B.Sc. in Horticulture, which was awarded by London University. One of the first things she did was to contact Edith Bradley and invite her to visit the college, a clear indication of how badly the staff felt Miss Bradley had been treated.

Financial problems were to prove the school's undoing. By 1948 two thousand female students had been enrolled at Studley and its reputation was solid. The arrival of Elizabeth Hess, who had wide experience at government level with the Ministry of Agriculture and Fisheries, brought many bonuses, and the college exhibited at the Chelsea Flower Show, demonstrating controlled lighting techniques for growing saintpaulias and chrysanthemums. However, dark clouds were gathering over the college's future as the Ministry of Education began to formulate plans to create co-educational establishments. The college was not prepared to make such a change and, despite a two-year waiting list and a strong reputation, its funding was cut, a decision which inevitably led to closure. There was a brief but spirited campaign to keep Studley going, including support from 'Dan and Doris Archer' of the BBC radio serial *The Archers*, but the withdrawal of state funding was irrevocable, and the college closed seventy years after it had opened for women only.

SCHOOL FOR LADY GARDENERS

Of the twenty or so private gardening schools that opened around the turn of the twentieth century, there was one which became better known than most because of the connections of its founder. Born in 1872, Frances Garnet Wolseley was the only child of Viscount Wolseley, Commander-in-Chief of the British Army. After a peripatetic childhood spent in Cyprus, Cairo and various European cities, Frances and her family settled in the beautiful South Downs village of Glynde. Although Frances had been a debutante at nineteen and was familiar with the social whirl of fashionable London, she much preferred living in Sussex where she was able to indulge her love of gardening. It was there that her mother had engaged a female gardener after seeing her plea for work in a local paper, describing herself as 'poverty stricken', and it was this episode which gave Frances Wolseley the idea of starting a training school for such women as a way to help them find work.

She set about her plan in 1902, initially basing it at her home at Glynde, sequestering the dower house garden as a training ground and finding lodgings for the students in the nearby village. In 1913 her father died and Frances Wolseley inherited both the title and the

Lady Frances Wolseley (1872–1936) ran Glynde College with an iron grip, and an emphasis on the practical side of horticulture rather than the scientific.

estate. As part of her campaign to publicise the school she sought the support of high-profile patrons, and this she did with consummate success. Four of the leading lights of early-twentieth-century British gardening, William Robinson, Gertrude Jekyll, Ellen Willmott and Theresa Earle, agreed to be patrons of the new school, their names greatly aiding recruitment. In June 1915 the mother of Chrystabel Procter, a bright girl who had gone to St Paul's Girls' School until she lost her hearing at fifteen, wrote to Gertrude Jekyll after getting her daughter into Glynde, and would no doubt have been relieved to receive the following endorsement: 'Dear Mrs Procter, I am very glad to hear your daughter is at the Glynde College. I am sure she will be both happy and well instructed. I generally have a visit from some of the students during the summer and hope she may be among them.'[1]

Within three years the school had outgrown the viscountess's home and new land was purchased, an estate at Glynde known as Ragged Lands. Chrystabel Procter's memories of the gardens there paint a vivid picture of somewhere that must have been lovely to work in:

Banked up terrace gardens had been created enclosed by trellis work covered by climbing roses, clematis, etc: to make secret gardens; pergolas containing different kinds of flowering plants. [Lady Wolseley] was strongly influenced by Florentine landscape gardening so used Italian terra-cotta tubs and jars a lot, containing formal bay trees which had the look of orange or lemon trees. There were little rock gardens with choice alpines; enclosed rose gardens; wild gardens full of informal drifts of bulbs covered with carpets of forget-me-nots; and two magnificent wide herbaceous borders flanking a wide grass path which ran downhill from the formal house-terrace. These were banked up high at the back towards rose-covered trellis fences, to give extra height to the plants at the back of the borders. These showed the influence of Gertrude Jekyll and Ellen Wilmot both friends of Lady Wolseley and patrons of the college. Soft pinks were arranged next mauves and silver-leaved foliage plants; pure blues, dark and pale next clear yellows and whites. Scarlet flowers well away in another place, were mated with orange and yellow ones.[2]

However, it was not so enchanting in the winter months, particularly during the First World War. There was no help on hand to do the hardest physical jobs and Procter recalls having to go down at night to stoke the greenhouse fires and cover frames after a long day of hard physical work in the gardens, sometimes in bitterly cold weather. 'In the summer there was evening watering on top of a still longer day's gardening, as well as at weekends. Heavy barrow loads of loam and compost had to be wheeled from the stacks at the bottom of our very steep hill to the top of it, where were the frames and greenhouses.'[3]

Unlike the Countess of Warwick, Frances Wolseley wanted to be involved with the teaching, lecturing and general supervision of the girls, even to the tilt of their hats. Keen to get official recognition for the school, she asked the council of the RHS to affiliate her school but this was declined. Some girls did take the RHS examinations but, despite the countess's enthusiasm and the outside support from leading gardeners, they achieved only thirteen passes in eleven years. This was not due to any lack of discipline at the school; there was a strict regime in place which was not unusual for educational establishments, but it did not guarantee a high standard of teaching.

The rules were prefaced with the stark announcement: 'RED LETTER LAW, RAGGED LANDS: Official Instructions must be carried out to the VERY LETTER'. They covered every aspect of the students' behaviour and applied to all elements of the girls' appearance. 'The Regulation Garden Kit must always be worn in the garden unless permission has been obtained. Miss More begs every Student working at Ragged to take real pride in their personal appearance, and not to get slack with regard to their clothes, hair, hands, etc.'[4]

Even worse than breaking rules of appearance was to be found guilty of showing neglect – or worse – towards any plant. 'How often in the early morning after the Captain has done her round of inspection,' wrote Lady Wolseley, 'do I hear the tolling of the great garden bell. I know then that some act of negligence has caused the death of one or more plants, and that the students are being summoned, not to a burial but to attendance, whilst reproof is being administered for this lack of care.'

There follows a description of what the crime might have been:

'perhaps freesia bulbs, placed on a warm shelf to get thoroughly dry have had water spilled on them by mistake and will consequently become rotten, or else melon plants that were to grow into finely developed bearers of good fruit have been allowed to get bone dry, so that Red Spider has shown itself on their leaves'.

The girls knew immediately when the bell was rung that they had to drop what they were doing and 'hurriedly, breathlessly' run to the students' office to face their punishment. If it was a serious loss it could mean that all the girls were fined, regardless of culpability. For, as Lady Wolseley insisted, 'all such acts of indifference or forgetfulness, where they affect the welfare of *plants* [my italics], must be punished, and the only thorough way of so doing is to make each member of the community feel individually affected by the mischief that has been done'.[5]

Rules for uniforms at Glynde College were as strict as those for plant care, all part of producing 'the right kind of women gardeners', as Lady Wolseley labelled this photograph of her young students in 1916.

Chrystabel Procter remained a student at the Glynde School for just over a year. No science was taught, which some students, Procter thought, must have found a handicap. They did have lectures on growing carnations and chrysanthemums, violet culture and mushroom growing from commercial growers, and were carefully taught how to perform all gardening operations properly, but all the training at Glynde was essentially practical. 'Had I not studied advanced chemistry and botany at St Pauls,' noted Procter, 'I could not have gained so much from my time at Glynde as I in fact did.'[6]

After a few years, wanting to devote more time to writing and promoting the cause of women's horticultural education, Frances Wolseley stepped back from her hands-on control of the school and passed the teaching over to a younger woman, Miss Elsa More. However, when Frances received a letter from Sir Henry Trueman Wood, secretary of the Royal Society of Arts, asking her to present a paper to his members on the employment of women in horticulture and agriculture, she politely declined. The reply came from Ragged Lands saying, '[Viscountess Wolseley] is . . . somewhat occupied at present with literary work as she is shortly bringing out two books on the above subject & she fears that, not being in a habit of lecturing, she would find the actual delivery of the paper, before so distinguished an audience, beyond her powers just now.'[7]

The two books referred to were most probably *In a College Garden* and *Women on the Land*, published in 1915 and 1916 respectively. In all, Wolseley wrote seven books, including *Gardening for Women* and *Gardens, Their Form and Design*. This last volume was published in 1919, the year in which the vast, decaying greenhouses at Chatsworth were blown up by the 9th Duke of Devonshire as even this great British landowner had to come to terms with the fact that such labour-intensive, expensive-to-run horticultural structures were things of the past. Slowly, very slowly, the world of gardening was changing and Wolseley's book was a far-sighted look at what was to become the career of landscape architecture, one based on practical design rather than endless wealth.

Despite its well-connected patrons and well-meaning owner, the school closed down with the early death of its head teacher, Elsa More. Unlike the other women-only horticultural colleges, the Glynde did not produce any major gardeners of note with the exception of Chrystabel Procter, who had anyway left after a year to nurse her sister. Later she confided that she had meant to go back to college after her sister had fully recovered, but to Swanley not to Glynde, 'Glynde,' she later wrote intriguingly, 'having almost disintegrated owing to the peculiar discipline there and to the physical and nervous breakdowns of some of the students'.[8] Possibly Frances Wolseley's love of military efficiency, perhaps inherited from her father, was too much for some of the girls.

Most of the private gardening schools for women established between 1899 and 1940 were run by a single woman and received no funding. This was the case with Dorothy Hewer, who ran a small school at her smallholding, The Whins, at Chalfont St Peter in Buckinghamshire. Only a handful had RHS recognition, never mind sending their students for the all-important RHS certificates and diplomas, and by the early 1930s women actually had less choice in where to study gardening than had been the case ten years earlier. The most famous of these establishments and one with greater staying power was the Waterperry Horticultural School, started in 1932 by the 'redoubtable' Beatrix Havergal.[9]

Miss Havergal, or 'Trix' to her family, had had the peripatetic childhood of a clergyman's daughter. From her father's side, she had inherited a strong musical talent, singing beautifully with a rich contralto voice and playing the cello to a high standard. Her other great love was gardening, which presented her with a dilemma when she left school in 1916: should she become a professional musician or choose a less romantic career in horticulture?

Havergal had already worked for the Women's War Agricultural Committee and decided to do some further training at Thatcham Fruit and Flower Farm near Newbury in Berkshire, a choice which cemented her career path. Thatcham was one of the many private gardening schools which were founded in the first years of the twentieth century and, during its sixteen-year existence, it produced nearly 120 passes of the RHS general examination. Miss H., as her students came to know her, achieved the RHS's certificate with first-class honours in 1920, a year which saw six women in the top ten of the RHS's exams, including first and second places.

A spell as head gardener at Downe House boarding school persuaded Miss H. that she also would like to set up a school and teach horticulture. She was encouraged in this ambition by Avice Sanders, who was to become her partner and stalwart supporter. In 1928, with less than £250 capital, Havergal and Sanders managed to rent some land near their cottage at Pusey in Oxfordshire and began to take in pupils – just two to start with, Diana Purcell and a Swiss student, Annelise Reinhart.

Annelise's letters home to her mother not only describe the practical routine of the day, but also the family atmosphere that Miss H. and Miss S. evoked throughout the time the school was open.

> Every single job seems to be an interesting one. We went out to collect leaf mould in the woods. We dug up the tomato plants in the glasshouse for forcing in the spring. We potted Roman hyacinths, narcissus, and tulips. My first Saturday was a gay one, after having

done some cleaning of the marketing shed, storing some apples, clearing two frames and putting the straw away in the pot and box house Miss Havergal announced that we were going out tonight, because she and Miss Sanders were now here for a whole year today. We went to the cinema to see 'The Stolen Bride'.[10]

The marketing shed was needed to make ends meet; crops were grown to be sold in Swindon market and later, after the move to Waterperry, in Oxford's famous Covered Market. Whether in the flower garden or tending the marketable produce, the girls worked alongside Miss H., all wearing what was seen as Miss H.'s trademark outfit, 'green [corduroy] breeches with green knee stockings, masculine type shirts buttoned to the neck with a tie, a green smock overall for good measure and, always, a hat'.[11] In the summer they were allowed cotton breeches but everything else remained the same.

By 1931, it was clear that the school needed more room. The pair looked at various properties, with Miss S. keeping the vendors talking while Miss H. surreptitiously took soil samples. When they heard that Magdalen College was looking for tenants for Waterperry House, near Wheatley, their search was over, and they moved in 1932. It was an imposing house with a ballroom and library, which Miss S. ran while Miss H. was in charge of the garden, but it was always a joint venture and the two consulted each other on all aspects of house and garden. The girls did little more domestic duty than to make their beds, otherwise they were waited on at meals and were expected to dress in long gowns on Saturday evenings, but outside in the garden things were tougher. The training at Waterperry was extremely practical, and although the girls could sit the RHS exams, Miss H. was more concerned about them getting their hands dirty and learning through experience. She was determined that her students would keep to the object of the school, which was 'to provide the theoretical foundation, the practical knowledge of horticulture, and the specialised skill required to make a first-class gardener'.[12]

As with all the women's gardening schools, finances were a constant problem. For students to be able to apply for grant funding to study there, the school had to be formally recognised by the Local Education Authority. It was finally inspected in 1958 and accepted with the suggestion that more emphasis should be placed on the teaching of science in a laboratory or lecture room, which was not at all Miss H.'s style of teaching. At about the same time an anonymous benefactor enabled Miss H. and Miss S. to buy Waterperry, but the enormous costs of upkeep were a constant worry.

The students' days were long, starting at 6.40 a.m. and finishing with the writing up of 'work diaries' before supper at 7.30 p.m. Ruth Collings from Kent remembered it as a very practical training. 'We were working outside all day [and] lectures were as few as possible, preferably on wet days.'[13] Miss H. often wrote as she spoke, using capital letters for emphasis, exclaiming in a careers article in 1939 that 'the only way to learn is to DO the actual work'.[14] Not only that, it had to be done to the highest standard; forty years after the event one student remembered the moment she realised that she had knocked off the top of her cucumber plant as 'one of the most traumatic experiences of her life'.[15]

Although Miss H. was undoubtedly a strict taskmaster, her passion instilled enormous loyalty in her students. In September 1958 an 'old girl' of Waterperry wrote to the head of the school. 'I can well remember chewing my nails in apprehension of coming here first as a student but from the moment I arrived that was forgotten, in the general feeling of happiness, interest and enjoyment . . . I fully realise how lucky I have been to have had the opportunity of looking after the Flower Garden and to have had such a free hand with the planting and arrangement and so on.'[16] The old girl was Pamela Schwerdt, who went on to be joint head gardener at Sissinghurst.

Annual reunions were held at Waterperry for the 'old girls' and they all considered them important occasions. Those who were unable to attend kept in touch by letter, bringing Miss H. up to date with their lives and careers. One became a florist in Scotland, and several worked for a short while before marriage diverted them, all of which Miss H. felt was a waste of a Waterperry training, but they were eventually forgiven.

Barbara Harwood (née Kelling) was one of the forgiven ones. After she left Waterperry House in 1938 she had had a busy gardening career, particularly during the war when she was in charge of a mixed five-acre market garden on a farm in Royston, Hertfordshire, which included looking after ducks, chickens, geese and rabbits. She also assisted elsewhere in replanting and laying out and generally helping people with fruit tree pruning and spraying, tending gardens which had gone to rack and ruin during the war years, and working at a boarding school in Horsham, Sussex. In 1945–6 she worked single-handed in a private garden in Cranley, Surrey, and was justly proud of having supervised and arranged the planting out of the bedding in Bloomsbury and Russell Squares in their first year as public gardens, and of carrying out the watering and care of plants in one section of the Britain Can Take It exhibition. In 1948, ten years after she left Waterperry House, she married and her career as a professional gardener came to a halt.

As well as the respect given to her by her students, Miss H. was also recognised by her peers, although when honours came to Miss H., rather like London buses, they came in pairs. At the same time as she was to be awarded an MBE in February 1960, she was informed by the RHS that they were to bestow the Victoria Medal of Honour on her the very same day. After her early battles with the RHS it must have given her some satisfaction to reply to the committee by saying that 'curiously enough, I have to go to the Palace that morning to receive my Award for the MBE, and as my sister will be coming up from Cornwall specially for the occasion of both presentations, she will be coming with me to the RHS Hall in the afternoon . . . could she have another ticket??'[17]

According to a review of her career, written in a *This Is Your Life* style, Miss Havergal practised curtsying 'for days' before collecting her MBE from the Queen. Given that she was nearly six foot tall and more used to dressing in green breeches, green overalls and a rather battered felt hat, it was understandable that she was nervous, particularly in those more deferential times. Disappointingly, when it came to the day, the Queen was not able to take the investiture herself.

Miss Havergal received many letters of congratulations on her Victoria Medal of Honour, and the one from her friend and fellow plantswoman Margery Fish typifies them all: 'Most sincere congratulations on your new honour. I am so glad all your work in training gardeners has been recognised and I have no doubt you are being swamped with letters of congratulation – Please don't bother to answer this but I had to write.'[18]

Illness finally forced Miss H. to retire in 1971 and sell the Waterperry estate to the School of Economic Science, a London-based educational charity. They were chosen from the various interested buyers because, although they were not able to run a full-time school, they did propose to continue running short educational and vocational courses at Waterperry and to maintain the gardens and the nursery.

When the Women's Farm and Garden Association published a careers guide to gardening for women in 1963, an impressive range of colleges across the country offered one-year courses leading to the

National Certificate in Horticultural Practice. Studley and Waterperry offered the RHS's National Diploma in Horticulture as well as their own diplomas, as did the Essex Institute of Agriculture and the Worcestershire Institute of Horticulture, Pershore. Degrees could be taken at Nottingham, Reading and Wye (which had incorporated Swanley since the end of the war). With a more general move towards mixed-sex institutions throughout the educational establishment, women-only colleges finally disappeared with the closure of Waterperry in 1971, Studley having shut its doors in 1968. During their time, however, they had played a vital role in providing a high standard of horticultural training and thereby increasing the opportunities for women in the working world.

'NOT LADIES IN ANY
SENSE OF THE WORD'

Despite the immediate success of women-only colleges like Swanley, it was evident that little progress had been made in attitudes towards the employment of women as professional gardeners. In *The Gentlewoman's Book of Gardening* Edith Chamberlain complained that 'The papers are full of the distressed gentlewoman, and her only resources so far seem to be "art" needlework ... and "decorative" painting.'[1] Surely ladies who had been brought up in a pleasant country house could 'easily qualify themselves for starting as lady-gardeners, and so continue the pleasant country life they have been accustomed to'.[2]

There was a brick wall of male (and indeed some female) attitudes that was solidly against the idea of women being taken seriously as professional gardeners. Boys were able to become apprentice gardeners in London through the Worshipful Company of Gardeners, but even by 1910 there were only three women within the company, all of whom were related to livery officials. Ursula and Joyce Ebblewhite were daughters of the clerk of the company, and Beatrice Shead's father was the upper warden and master-elect. Prior to that, only one woman appears in their records: Lydia Hinch, the widow of a past master, who in 1657 was allowed to take over three apprentices who had been bound to her late husband, in order to enable them to complete their indentures.

Honorary freedoms were granted to women, the first being the Hon. Alicia Amherst in 1896 for the publication of *A History of Gardening in England*. As the Hon. Mrs Evelyn Cecil she wrote to the Revd William Wilkes, secretary to the Royal Horticultural Society, hoping he could recommend a female head gardener but, even though women were by then allowed to sit the RHS exams, the Revd Wilkes could not bring himself to endorse a woman, as his reply stridently shows: 'I am afraid I cannot help you. I know of no woman gardener who has what you want and all round knowledge so as to be able to direct the foreman of the [different] departments. I do not believe such a person exists. Miss Jekyll herself would not be able to take such a post – she could not direct melon growing or early grape forcing & so on.'[3] It was not a question of a lack of supervisory skills, however, that concerned the cleric, it was the old chestnut of women not being strong enough for 'heavy lifting & clay digging'. In this era of heightened tensions over women's suffrage, it is perhaps not surprising that he underlined his last sentence in red: '. . . to put women to [such work] is to go back a big step in the emancipation of your sex'.[4] However, Edith Chamberlain had been right to suggest that all this could change and the advent of colleges like Swanley started to produce a trickle of girls who were not only equipped with basic horticultural qualifications but also keen to improve on these with paid apprenticeships at the country's most famous botanical garden. When Annie Gulvin and Alice Hutchings started work at the Royal Botanic Gardens of Kew, they would have been well aware of the blow they were striking for women and professional gardening. Until their arrival, the only women on the payroll at Kew were caretakers and a pot-washer in the tropical department.

Even when the two girls started at Swanley, council members from the college were in contact with the garden's director, Sir William Thiselton-Dyer, to try to persuade him to take on a couple of the students as 'improvers'. So when, on 13 January 1896, Annie Gulvin and Alice Hutchings signed the register of employment at the Royal Botanic Gardens, Kew, with Eleanor Morland and Gertrude Cope just behind them, they knew that despite being wildly outnumbered by men they were among friends.

The reaction of the public to women being employed by Kew

Alice Hutchings, Gertrude Cope and Eleanor Morland trained at Swanley together and then, with classmate Annie Gulvin, became the first women to work at Kew.

Gardens was as though a new species of animal were on display at the zoo. The press labelled them 'London's Kewriosities', songs were written about them, and people on passing buses strained to look over the walls of Kew Gardens in the hope of catching a glimpse of them.

> A rumour went forth, and the town was aglow
> From Greenwich to Richmond, from Peckham to Bow —
> And the man-in-the-street made a fine how-de-do,
> When he heard of the ladies who gardened at Kew.
>
> They gardened in bloomers, the newspapers said;
> So to Kew without waiting all Londoners sped:
> From the roofs of the 'buses they had a fine view
> Of the ladies in bloomers who gardened at Kew.
>
> The orchids were slighted, the lilies were scorned,
> The dahlias were flouted, till botanists mourned,
> But the Londoners shouted, 'What ho, there, Go to;
> Who wants to see blooms now you've bloomers at Kew.'
>
> So the botanists held a big meeting and said:-
> 'This won't do, all London has gone off its head;
> This costume we find is too painfully "new",
> It is making a side-show of beautiful Kew.
>
> 'These ladies in bloomers are treated as freaks;
> In future they'd all better garden in breeks.'
> Now they look so like men no one rushes to view,
> And a pastoral quiet has settled on Kew.[5]

Since this was the same time that Beatrix Potter had called Thiselton-Dyer a misogynist, it seemed that the odds were against the project's success. Thiselton-Dyer's predecessor and father-in-law, Sir Joseph Hooker, held very strong views about women at Kew. In reply to a letter from a young woman eager to apply for a position, Sir Joseph stated that he could not possibly recommend any 'lady' to go there. 'She would have to work with labouring men, doing all they have to do, digging, manuring, and all the other disagreeable parts of gardening. Then there is the work in the hot houses; the men, I believe, work simply in their trousers, and how could a lady work with them! The work at Kew is <u>most</u> trying and knocks up even the strong man.' His wife held similar views about future employment prospects. 'Lady Hooker says that nothing would induce her and Sir Joseph to have a lady gardener. She says imagine what their feelings would be to see her trailing about in the rain and the snow, and digging etc. in the broiling heat of summer.'[6]

It appears contrary that Thiselton-Dyer agreed to the experiment, and Annie and Alice were well aware that the reputation of their alma mater rested squarely on their shoulders. The women had all been well trained at Swanley and were ready to cope with the rigours of the best botanical garden in Britain, if not the world, and from the outset they were determined not to disappoint their supporters.

Although Kew was in many ways a continuation of their training, the big difference was that the girls were no longer paying for instruction but earning a wage while honing their horticultural skills. Both started working in the propagation pits – not as gruesome as it sounds, merely the starting point for all new recruits at Kew, where tasks such as striking cuttings and potting on were learned by endless repetition. They were both earning 10s a week – a fact, noted the *Court Journal* at the time, that 'is not likely to encourage gardening among business girls'.[7] Within six months this had risen to 14s a week.

Annie moved to the herb department in November 1896, and Alice was promoted first to the rank of 'Gardener' from 1 March 1897, giving her charge of certain houses and frames and an increase in wages to 21s, and then to the illustrious post of sub-foreman, herb department, on 1 April 1898, with a wage of 24s. Other colleagues from Swanley soon joined them, Eleanor Morland and Gertrude Cope arriving in Kew later in 1896 when they were put to work in the herbaceous department.

The arrival of women caused a stir in the horticultural world, but one of the greatest points of interest was not that they were there at all but what they were told to wear. There was no question of the women wearing trousers, but knickerbockers were seen as a sensible alternative since 'skirts might damage valuable plants in the crowded houses'. The provision of a dressing room for the girls 'lest they should be seen unsuitably attired when going to and from their work' was also the subject of some mirth in the gardening press.[8]

Later on during their time at Kew, Annie Gulvin and Alice Hutchings gave a talk to the Kew Guild's Mutual Improvement Society on 'Horticulture for Women'. Either the topic or the speakers, or a combination of both, brought in an above average audience of forty-six members. The two friends gave a sketch of professional horticulture, stressing the value of a scientific as well as a practical training, 'the really competent gardener,' they emphasised, 'being he who understood something more about his plants than the pots, soils, and temperatures they require'.

They were willing to admit that some of the heavy 'rough' work might be beyond them, but opined that this did not have to be done by someone who had gone through a proper training course 'when it could be done at least as well by the garden labourer'.[9] There was a demand for women who were trained horticulturists, they insisted, and hoped that they would be able to meet it. The evening ended with a heated discussion on the physical disadvantages of women and the worry that many male gardeners had that women would have a depreciative effect on wages.

When she was only twenty years old, Annie Gulvin was the first female to leave Kew for full-time employment as a head gardener. The photograph of her in the *Kew Guild* shows an attractive, feisty young woman, her curly hair pulled back and firmly under control, wearing a dark smocked dress buttoned right up to her chin. This was a confident person who had earned the respect of the men around her. The *Kew Guild* proudly wrote: 'Miss Gulvin has the distinction of being the first woman to take sole charge of a garden on exactly the same terms as a man. Her success has been a source of satisfaction to all who know the nature of her undertaking, and clever though she is, many will be surprised that one of her sex so young should have conquered all the difficulties of a first situation which evidently was not of the apple-pie order.'[10]

The job she went to was as head gardener to J. Brogden, Esq., of Iscoed, Ferryside, in Carmarthen. She stayed a year. The previous gardener had left some months earlier and the garden was in a sorry state, with dilapidated walls, a collapsed conservatory, insect pests, rats, rabbits, mice and birds and poor drainage just some of the problems that Annie had to cope with.

On my arrival I was piloted round the gardens by 'an old hand', who gave me discouraging accounts of my predecessors' troubles. The condition of the place too was disheartening: still I set to work in earnest, and we are gradually getting things ship-shape. My men are all that I could wish, no cause for anxiety in that quarter. We are building new houses and relaying out part of the gardens. From what I have seen of the gardens in our neighbourhood, I do not think we shall have occasion to fear comparison with the best of them. If Kew were only nearer I should feel perfectly happy.'[11]

She quickly set to with the help of an assistant 'lady' gardener and four men. Two of the four old vineries were cleared and replanted, one with peaches, the other made ready for tomatoes. The flower garden was redesigned, new beds cut and filled with roses, yuccas, cannas and pampas grass, all the height of fashion for an end-of-the-century garden. The five-acre kitchen garden provided surplus early vegetables, strawberries and flowers which were sold to local hotels. She won first prize for vegetables at a local show, and her employer gave her a £10-a-year salary increase (we do not know what her starting salary had been but presumably it was pretty low). This formidable young woman was clearly not just a good gardener but a good manager as well. 'My staff is now quite contented to be controlled by one of the "weaker" sex,' she explained to her former colleagues in the *Kew Guild*. 'I think that when men see that our intentions are serious and that we are not afraid to work, they respect our efforts to find employment outside the very restricted boundary within which till recently woman's work was confined.'[12]

Her second and, as it turned out, her last professional job as a gardener was at Burstall near Ipswich in Suffolk, as she got married in the summer of 1900. This was an era when, except for the lowest classes, it was socially unacceptable for women to work after marriage, and the *Kew Guild* noted that while her short career had been a distinguished one she had 'ended it by taking to herself a husband'. With no little smugness, the journal also commented that they had 'always held that there was no fear of the profession being over-crowded by the addition of ladies to its ranks', adding condescendingly, 'we can wish no better finish to a lady-gardener's career than that accepted by Miss Gulvin'.[13]

Annie's friend Alice Hutchings stayed on at Kew and rose through the ranks to become sub-forewoman in the alpine pits. In September 1900, she finally left Kew to take over Annie Gulvin's position in Suffolk, working for Mrs Cranfield at Burstall. Two years later she married William Patterson, confirming Kew's prediction that female gardeners would be in the employment market for such a short time that they would hardly be a threat to the working man. This may have put an end to her professional gardening status but Alice's life became anything but purely domestic. William Patterson was appointed to the Agricultural School at St Vincent in the West Indies and later as government entomologist for the Gold Coast. Alice accompanied him on many of his trekking expeditions, often into 'native districts where no white women had previously travelled'.[14] She returned to Kew during the First World War and was one of twenty-four women who worked there for the duration.

Eleanor Morland joined the staff at Swanley on leaving the Botanic Gardens. Her career also came to an early end, first when she went to look after her father (and his garden) and then when she married in 1906 and settled near Birmingham. There, according to her family, she created a large rock garden which was later destroyed when the property was redeveloped. Another Kew apprentice, Edna Gunnell, also had a pioneering career. First she became principal of a horticultural school in Germany, then on returning to England in 1914 she was appointed horticultural superintendent for the county of Devon, the first woman to hold such a post.

Jessie Newsham's career did not have such a positive ending.

Another graduate of Swanley, Jessie had joined Kew in May 1899 and she stayed for sixteen months, working in the tropical and herbaceous departments. When she left, she had jobs in gardens at Abergavenny in Wales and at Haslemere, but tragedy followed her marriage and departure to British Guiana, as reported in the *Kew Guild* of 1908:

> It is with deep regret that we record the first death among our women members, and that it should be in the same number as contains the announcement of her marriage to another Old Kewite, Robert Ward (joined in June 1886) makes it particularly sad . . . She died on January 6, 1909, aged 29, and has left a son, born a few days previously, behind her . . . many of our readers who may not have known her personally, but who will readily identify her as the little lady with the merry face, will learn of the death of their comrade with very real regret. Her husband is indeed to be condoled with. No doubt the climate of British Guiana was contributory to her untimely death, and thus the first of the handful of women Kewites to go may be said to have laid down her life in the interests of the empire.[15]

In the year that Jessie Newsham died, another young woman joined the workforce at Kew and became a botanist in the hallowed herbarium. Jessie Jane Clark was twenty-eight years old with a first-class B.Sc. from London University, but nevertheless was probably surprised to find herself at the top of the list of applicants for this position, vacant because of the retirement of the previous holder. Five years later, in 1914, she too was dead from an unknown but painful illness. In the short time she was at Kew she was a popular member of the herbarium staff, and had begun to make her mark with several short scientific papers and the diagnoses of new species, particularly of tropical African plants. The stories of these two women's short lives are sharp illustrations of the fragility of life just one hundred years ago.

HARDY PLANTERS

Not all women who graduated from horticultural college went on to Kew. Madeline Agar was a contemporary of Gulvin and Hutchings at Swanley, where she had been a high achiever. When her friends went on to Kew, Madeline took a job at Wycombe Abbey School as head gardener and teacher of practical gardening. She did not stay there long and by 1902 was studying surveying and garden design in the hope of setting up a practice with another ex-Swanley student, Lorrie Dunington. Their plan was that Agar would supplement Dunington's garden knowledge 'with such technical matters as surveying and levelling',[1] but Dunington became ill and the partnership never came about. Instead, Agar made a brief attempt at running a nursery with another friend, Miss Holmes, in Amersham, during which time she won first prize in a garden design competition.

Agar subsequently steered away from practical gardening and concentrated instead on building up a garden landscaping business as well as writing. By 1906 she was landscape gardener to the Metropolitan Public Gardens Association, having taken over from Fanny Wilkinson, who was now head of Swanley College. Like Fanny Wilkinson, Agar relished the opportunity to 'greenscape' public places. She transformed the churchyard of All Saints, Poplar, into a public garden, and oversaw tree-planting schemes in various parts of London. She also laid out the grounds of the Godolphin School, Salisbury. She built up a thriving practice, particularly in the work she was doing for the Metropolitan Public Gardens Association, and published several books on her speciality. In 1909 *A Primer of School Gardening* appeared, followed by *Garden Design in Theory and Practice* in 1911, the first work by a woman on the subject. In the following year she travelled to Cairo to lay out a garden there and, through the connections she had made in Egypt, later co-wrote a book on gardening in the sub-tropics.

A piece in a women's magazine, the *Lady's Pictorial*, in November 1912 gives a flavour of the scope of Agar's work.

A profession that very few women take up seriously is that of garden-designing, but that it is well within their scope is proved by Miss Madeline Agar's success. This lady, who is a member of both the Council and Committee of the Women's Agricultural and Horticultural International Union, exhibited drawings and plans illustrating her work at the Union's show and sale last week. The gardens represented must be exquisite, and there is every variety – for example, a sunk garden for a Tudor house, an arrangement of stonework, grass, brick-path, steps, knots of rosemary, and beds of old-fashioned flowers; while two striking photographs show a piece of land as it was in 1907 – just meadow land, with one or two trees, and the same piece less than a year later, laid out with beds of flowers in terraces, with broad path and steps mounting to a summer-house and garden seats near one of the trees.[2]

By 1918 she was also teaching private students at her home in Amersham, and when Margaret Smieton was looking for training in landscape gardening, it was Madeline Agar whom she was advised to approach. 'Miss Agar is quite at the top of the tree . . . and her training is thoroughly to be recommended.'[3] Unfortunately for Smieton, Agar had just accepted a post at her old college, Swanley, to teach garden design, and in any case she correctly pointed out that Smieton first needed to be qualified in gardening before she could benefit from a course in garden design.

Lorrie Dunington, who had hoped to work with Agar before falling ill, did eventually become a garden designer. Dunington, who had also attended Swanley, had never gained her diploma, but this did not seem to hold her back. On leaving college in 1896 she got a job in a private garden in Ireland and by 1900 she was working as a garden designer. Mr Selfe Leonard of Guildford Hardy Plant Nursery employed her as a garden designer and she lectured to the Architectural Association on garden design. In 1906 she was permanent garden adviser to the National Society for the Employment of Epileptics at Chalfont St Peter. She also laid out the grounds for a new school at Kingswood, Surrey, and gave a course of lectures at the Working Women's College in Fitzroy Street, London.

Miss Dunington did her best to promote 'the profession of garden design' and in January 1909 wrote an article for the society magazine *The Queen*.[4] The accompanying photograph shows a very glamorous and confident young woman, with no hint of soil under her fingernails or mud on her shoes. In 1911 she married Howard Grubb, also a landscape designer, and they moved to Canada where they set up a successful practice.

Others who bypassed Kew did so with varying degrees of success. As Mrs Ronald Wilkins reminded prospective students in a booklet on training and employment in horticulture in 1927, 'Whether a woman intends to seek a salaried post as gardener or to set up for herself in a

Despite this new-fangled mower being promoted as easy to use by even the most
unsuitably dressed housewife, it was still rare during the interwar years for women
to do any heavy gardening – much less be paid to do so in a professional capacity.

commercial garden, she is entering into competition with men who
have probably served their apprenticeship from the age of 14, and have
had a life-long experience in their profession.'[5]

Chrystabel Procter, after graduating from the Glynde College of
Lady Gardeners, was offered the post of 'gardener's boy' (with gardener's boy pay to match) at the playing fields and orchards of Bute
House, which were used by her old school, St Paul's. Once she had
passed her RHS teachers' honours exam in 1919, she was promoted to
'lady gardener' and teacher at the school, both of which positions she
filled with great success.[6]

When Chrystabel left Glynde, Frances Wolseley had advised her not
to stay too long in one post. 'Gardeners need to work on different soils,

in different climates and on different kinds of crops.'[7] Accordingly Procter moved up to Yorkshire, to Bingley Training College. She was there for seven years, during which time she got used to the soil and crops but never quite accepted the climate, remembering only one real summer – 'it took place on a Wednesday afternoon when [I] was actually able to put on a cotton frock!'[8] An offer from Girton College at Cambridge brought Miss Procter south again, though there she was to be faced with yet another set of problems.

'<u>Don't</u> waste your time trying to grow flowers,' Miss Swindale, Girton's previous gardener, told Chrystabel. 'All the Fellows had the right to pick flowers for themselves for their rooms whenever they wanted to and almost wherever they wanted to [and] even breaking branches off the flowering and other trees was permissible and commonly done by certain Fellows!' Miss Swindale explained that this practice had once been permitted only in certain places, but had gradually spread to almost all parts of the estate except the borders in the front drive. 'I couldn't bear it,' she added, 'and now the Research Fellows are doing it too.'[9]

With her customary common sense, Miss Procter eventually stopped what she considered vandalism by growing flowers especially for room decoration, but it was a hard-fought battle to get the college staff to agree to this compromise. It was also agreed that 'scissors must be used, as few <u>leaves</u> as possible should be gathered. The Committee would be very grateful if Fellows would abstain from picking from any <u>tree, shrub or shrubby creeper</u>.' These rules applied throughout the year, so there was no time when Miss Procter's horticultural domain was not under attack from lurking flower arrangers.

Procter was initially paid £230 a year with a generous six weeks' holiday, but her duties as the college's garden steward were extensive. She was expected

(a) To be responsible for, and to take active part in, the maintenance and care of the garden and grounds of about forty-five acres, including woodlands, lawns, herbaceous borders, glass houses, etc., three hard tennis courts, eight grass tennis courts, one netball court, one hockey ground and one lacrosse ground, and about fourteen acres of vegetables and fruit.

(b) To be responsible for the irrigation ground, and for the care of the pigs which are bred and sold.

(c) To keep accounts, to order seeds, manures, pigs' food, etc., to pay wages, and to supervise the garden staff, which at present consists of seven men (including a groundsman) and one boy.

Clogs were standard kit for professional gardeners of both sexes until the Second World War. The camaraderie of the job was an added bonus

Procter transformed the gardens of Girton between 1933 and 1945, planting eleven thousand crocus corms and creating autumnal displays of Michaelmas daisies, chrysanthemums and red-hot pokers to 'shout a welcome to Freshers on the day they arrive'. Eventually she made a final move to Bryanston boys' school and was not in the least put out by their tradition of nude swimming: 'Stop worrying about my modesty I have none.'[10] Procter never married; the marriage bar was in full force and women teachers who did so were forced to resign.

There were few opportunities for women in municipal gardening during the interwar period, although it was the traditional training route for many young men wanting a practical apprenticeship. In 1943 W.J.C. Lawrence acknowledged in *The Young Gardener*, a careers guidance book for those interested in horticulture, that an increasing number of women were entering the profession but held out little encouragement that they would be able to progress in the public field even if they found a job in the first place. At the top of the ladder were positions as superintendents of public gardens, of which there were four hundred across the country, but, stated Lawrence sternly, 'openings for women . . . do not exist'. In reality, wartime did bring opportunities, albeit short-lived ones, for women gardeners, especially those with any form of training.

'WE MUST "GO TO IT"'

Now Adam was a gardener, and God who made him sees
That half a gardener's proper work is done upon his knees;
But with Adam gone to fight the foe and only home on leave
The proper one to kneel and plant and grow our food is – EVE![1]

The Situations Vacant columns in the *Gardeners' Chronicle* of 1916 might at first glance appear to give hope to the idea that, with the establishment of several high-quality female horticultural colleges, women were finding it relatively easy to get work:

Wanted, experienced Lady Gardener for Glass Department in private gardens;
Good practical Woman Gardener wanted;
Two Women Gardeners, strong, able to dig;
Two strong Women Gardeners, for Fruit Houses chiefly;
Female Under Gardener for Kitchen Gardens and Vineries;
Young Woman for Orchid Houses, some experience preferred (not essential) to work with another young woman;

and, somewhat reluctantly, 'Wanted, Head Gardener ... lady Gardener would be accepted.'[2]

Elsewhere in the magazine Lucy Joshua, writing on women gardeners, noted that the United Horticultural Benefit and Provident Society, a medical insurance company, were considering taking women members since there were now sufficient numbers to make it worth their while. However, this was less the start of an acceptance of professional women gardeners but more a reaction to the dramatic shortage of male gardeners as they were called up for military service. In 1915, when it was hoped that the war would last only months or maybe a year longer, this situation was hard for many to accept. Far better, some thought, to use men who were too old to join up – anything rather than employ women. 'Would [you] break up our homes, turn us out of the garden and the public park into the street to want that our places might be filled by the young woman gardener?'[3]

At Kew there was little choice, and by 1916 staff depletions had such an effect that when Alice Hutchings returned for the duration she joined twenty-one other women on the staff. The *Kew Guild* in fact reported that twenty-four women gardeners were employed on a temporary basis to keep the gardens open, in good condition and contributing to the war effort. In the following year the numbers went up to a peak of thirty-one women, and over the whole period of the war a total of ninety women were taken on to replace the men who had been called up.

Lucy Joshua was one of the women who joined Kew during the First World War, arriving in August 1915 a couple of months after the first women had been hired, all Swanley-trained and old friends. Since graduating, Lucy had been a head gardener in Switzerland and a lecturer at a small gardening school, but to begin with she and the other girls were given menial outside tasks, including edging lawns and cutting the grass with heavy mowers. Lucy also recalled having to suffer the comments from passing 'gushing' ladies, one in particular who 'after watching us laboriously pushing the mowing machine on a hot day, remarked: "What a privilege to work in such lovely gardens and to take the place of the dear boys at the Front."'[4]

Thousands of young girls found themselves sent to work on farms as part of the Women's Land Army, but this type of agricultural work was quite different from horticulture. It was dirty and exhausting, and could be done by 'townies' with the minimum of training.

It was not just in British gardens that the women were needed. In 1917 twenty young women were sent to France as gardeners in military cemeteries. The women who went to tend the graveyards in Belgium were part of either the Women's Army Auxiliary Corps (WAAC) or

The *Illustrated London News* showed women caring for the graves of British soldiers in France – vital for morale in the last months of the First World War.

Queen Mary's Army Auxiliary Corps (QMAAC) and received a brief training at Kew. Drawing on the words of the recently deceased and glorified British poet Rupert Brooke, the *Illustrated London News* praised the women whose job it became to tend the war graves at Abbeville, saying there is 'Some Corner of a Foreign Field that is Forever England'.[5]

There were similar patriotic feelings within the newly established Women's Institute movement. Members were encouraged to ask themselves, 'What is my home, my garden, my farm doing for my Country?' Indeed, the poster for the very first meeting of a Women's Institute group, in the rather inappropriately named village of Singleton, was particularly aimed at 'holders of cottage gardens and village allotments'.[6]

Meanwhile at Kew, as more male gardeners disappeared, the girls were increasingly allowed 'under glass' and worked in all the garden's departments apart from the hallowed Palm House and its collection of precious plants, many of which dated back to the origins of the gardens in the late eighteenth century. The decorative department, run by the genial Mr Coutts, was at one time run entirely by women and became known as 'Coutts' harem'. Coutts and his wife kept an eye on the young women, 'a kindness,' Lucy Joshua remembered, 'which was especially appreciated when one first came to Kew and everything was new and strange'.[7] The hours were long and when Joshua became sub-forewoman of the Temperate House pits, she also had to work alternate weekends and do the stoking of the house's heating boilers.

In an early display of equality, the girls did not form their own Kew Women's Guild but joined with the men to sort out any work problems. This, considered Lucy Joshua, helped the girls form 'some useful concessions'.[8] They were all invited to join Kew's Mutual Improvement Society and contributed to it themselves with talks on

'Women in Horticulture'. In all, nine women presented papers to the society, including Lucy Joshua and Alice Hutchings, and Lucy even won a prize, a copy of the classic work *Trees and Shrubs* by W.J. Bean, who was at that time assistant curator at Kew. Social outings also included invitations to tea with Matilda Smith, artist for the *Botanical Magazine*, who allowed the girls to use her drawing room to sew items for the forces.

By 1919, however, there were only six women left on the staff. One small advance had been made, although it was only for a short time: the gardeners' wages had risen from a pre-war 21s to 24s and women gardeners received the same as men.

At the beginning of the Second World War twenty-seven women gardeners were employed at Kew to work in all departments bar one,

During the Second World War, women were once again brought in to replace male gardeners at Kew, where flowerbeds were turned over to vegetable production.

yet again the mighty Palm House. 'Women gardeners,' reported the *Kew Guild*,

> have come to Kew once more after an interval of nearly a quarter of a century, and though the costume has changed considerably, the fashion in clogs remains the same, as certain well-preserved specimens can testify. These clogs may now be seen and heard in most departments of the Garden ... It is seven months since the first arrivals started their duties, and the KWGG now has twenty members, with more to come in the near future. They are all trained women, and are taking the place of men Students who have been called up for service in the armed forces. They are employed in the Propagating Pits, Decorative Department, Flower and Rock Gardens, and in certain sections of the Tropical Department, where they can each apply their own particular experience, and by endeavouring to set up a high standard of work, disprove the saying for all time that *Nepeta Mussinii* is the only plant a woman can't kill! In fact, the Kew women gardeners are now part of the Kew landscape.[9]

By 1942 there were fifty 'girl gardeners' at Kew looking after fruit, vegetables and 'drug plants'. 'Many of the famous flower beds and hot-houses at Kew Gardens are now under full-swing vegetable cultivation. Hundreds of tons of fruit and vegetables will be produced this year and much of the work is being undertaken by the small army of girl gardeners.'[10] Kew was also producing herbs and drugs that were difficult, if not impossible, to import in wartime; reputedly the only bananas to be seen in Britain during the war were grown at Kew, with hospitals given the first call on any of these successfully grown. The girl gardeners were kept busy growing huge quantities of cauliflowers, cabbages, onions, leeks and potatoes. The 'Kewties', as they were excruciatingly called by the press, were 'doing a great job'.[11]

During the war Betty Cooper wrote about her experience of working at Kew, recording that in addition to British women there were also girls from Australia, Canada and Denmark, all of whom had to cope with a constant barrage of questions from the garden's visitors. Kew was extremely popular during the war as a place of escape, with its peaceful pathways a reminder of more normal times. At weekends in particular there were 'ceaseless streams and large queues waiting outside the west door'.[12] 'The other day,' remarked a colleague, Miss Watts, 'a visitor asked us why we tapped the pots. "Why," we answered, "if they sound hollow they need a drink." Whereupon the visitor tapped his friend on the shoulder and said: "Ah! Come with me – you need a Worthington!"'[13]

The girls looking after the vegetable plots worked particularly long hours, starting at 6.30 in the morning. It was hungry work hoeing the onion patches and 'tantalising to see visitors sitting on a seat and enjoying tea at 3 p.m.'.[14] The women felt that part of their self-imposed task was to make the public more 'vegetable-conscious', including introducing them to exotic items not usually seen on British allotments, such as garlic. One girl commented that she had never seen it grown in England as a field crop. Kew's garlic was to be sold for medicinal purposes or, quite daringly for the English palate, for 'flavouring', the *Guild* suggesting to its readers that 'perhaps you'll taste some . . . if you happen to have supper at the Corner House'.[15]

It also reported in September 1941 that Miss Tarver, who worked in the propagating pits of the decorative department, had been released to take charge of the model allotments in Hyde Park. These came directly under the Ministry of Agriculture and Fisheries, and served as a valuable source of propaganda in the 'Dig for Victory' campaign. The following year when she left to become a lecturer in horticulture at the Midland Agricultural College, an old Studley student, Margaret Lancaster, succeeded her. By 1944 another woman had joined the team, but once peace was declared female recruitment stopped. At Kew there were only six women gardeners left in 1946, and two years later this number had dwindled to four.

During the Second World War, just as had been the case in the previous one, women were in demand among owners of large estates who were struggling to maintain their gardens. In 1941 the Women's Farm & Garden Association reported to the RHS that there were not enough women available to meet the need for trained women gardeners, a demand which continued to increase as the men were called up.

In the 1940s, with most of the men away at war, women were encouraged to cultivate allotments, traditionally seen as a male preserve.

The girls give their services as garden 'boy' in return for board and lodging, and a small allowance as pocket money. Head gardeners are asked to teach them as much as possible about vegetable growing in the course of the work. As soon as they are fitted to do this well, on their own responsibility they will be available where they are most required, under the guidance of the WF and GA; but, unfortunately, gardening cannot be learnt in a day, or even a month.[16]

Viola Williams spent some time at a stately home called Wychwood. Her mistress was an autocratic female who, Viola remembered, insisted on nurturing orchids in the greenhouse when she was trying to grow tomatoes.[17] At Girton College Chrystabel Procter was the victim of her own success, her apples regularly 'scrumped' from the orchard and the tomatoes stolen as well.[18] Nevertheless she managed to send a ton of damsons to canteens for evacuated children in Cambridge. She also increased potato yields from thirteen hundredweight in 1937 to a staggering nineteen tons in 1941–2.

Girls were encouraged to consider a career in gardening as a contribution to the war effort. Beatrix Havergal of Waterperry was a doer rather than a writer, but in an article for *Women's Employment* entitled 'Horticulture for Women Today', about market gardening, she urged her peers that 'we must "GO TO IT" in the branch for which we are most suited, and do our utmost to help the country in her greatest needs'.[19]

Miss H. was as good as her word, later recalling that in the autumn of 1940,

we began real work, turning ourselves into farmers, and proceeded to equip ourselves with three cart horses, carts, etc., and with the aid of the War Agricultural Committee, we managed to get the 29 acres planted with potatoes for the 1941 season. These were very successful, and we literally waded in potatoes all through the Autumn ... In 1942, we embarked on 12 acres of corn – mostly wheat, 8 acres of potatoes and a few acres of vegetables, amongst which was one acre of onions![20]

The National Federation of Women's Institutes similarly encouraged its members to get out and garden, and produced *The Gardener's Guide* in 1939, priced at 6d, and aimed at WI vegetable producers, the majority of whom were cottage gardeners and smallholders. The NFWI was also called upon by Kew to help with the collection and organisation of native medicinal plants.

At the very top of the tree one enterprising young Swanley graduate wrote to the head gardener at Windsor Castle in 1942, asking if there were any vacancies for a 'lady gardener'. She came with excellent references, having worked for the Countess of Lytton at Knebworth and Lady Beit of Tewin Water in Welwyn, although she was then employed by the BBC. The castle already had seven Land Girls to help grow vegetables, but this young woman clearly had more horticultural experience than the others. 'She is tall, strong and looks capable of doing a good days work, she has also good experience and would I think be useful in leading and guiding the other girls,' wrote the head gardener to the deputy financial secretary to the King.[21]

The girl (her name is not revealed) was offered a job at 55s a week – a good wage considering local girls were being paid just 30s a week – with free accommodation in Windsor Castle's Garden Bothy. Bothies were notoriously basic, but arrangements had been made to find space for the girls in a separate section away from the men. After three months her wage was increased to 60s a week, but the job did not work out as well as had been hoped and nine months later she was being encouraged to apply for a post at the Botanic Gardens in Edinburgh. She had asked to be allowed to change her employment 'in order that she may take up more responsible work'; even the cachet of Windsor Castle could not compensate for having to marshal seven Land Girls with no horticultural experience or enthusiasm. There was a suggestion that Windsor should try to get some girls from Waterperry, but nothing seems to have come of that (probably because they were all too busy looking after Miss Havergal's fields of potatoes) and the castle made do with Land Girls throughout the war.

THE NURSERY SLOPES

After graduating, the best students were often asked to stay on and teach at their college, and this is what happened to Pamela Schwerdt and Sibylle Kreutzberger. They had been pupils together at Waterperry in the 1950s, and stayed on at the school as junior members of staff. Schwerdt worked in the flower garden, while Kreutzberger looked after the vegetables.

After a while Sibylle grew restless and took a series of jobs away from Waterperry, first at a private school looking after their vegetable garden, then a similar job with Reading University's botany department, and finally at a small alpine nursery in Oxfordshire not far from Waterperry. When the owner died suddenly, she went back to Waterperry to take charge of the herbaceous nursery. Pam, having spent nine years on the staff of Waterperry, decided to travel around New Zealand, always a magnet for the keen plantsperson.

On Pam's return to England the two friends decided it was time for a change, and drew up a plan to start a nursery together. They began a search for a suitable site with about two acres of land on which to grow their own stock, and put an advertisement in *The Times*, hoping that a large kitchen garden might be available for rent. However, fate stepped in as the newspaper went on strike and the advertisement's appearance was delayed.

In the meantime they wrote to various people they knew, including Vita Sackville-West, who was at this time the *Observer*'s gardening correspondent. When she offered Schwerdt and Kreutzberger a job — initially she had been reluctant to take on two head gardeners, but the girls insisted they went as a pair — it was the start of a perfect partnership between these highly trained professionals and one of the world's most inspirational gardeners. 'The existing gardeners were all men and had been at Sissinghurst for many years. They must have found us being there very difficult. We were half their age and women. Even some of the visitors used to look at us as if we were exotic animals.'[1]

Three years later, in 1962, Vita Sackville-West died, but the two remained in charge for several decades afterwards, during which time visitor numbers rose from six thousand a year to around two hundred thousand. They faced the problem of trying to maintain the garden in the spirit of Sackville-West while coping with these thousands of visitors. 'We had to stake the irises along the main path to avoid what we called "handbag trouble". Visitors would pass through the gate, say "How lovely" to their companions, and the iris heads would be knocked off in an instant.'[2] They also faced criticism when planting plans were changed, but with the garden now open to visitors throughout the summer, interest had to be sustained. Sometimes the weather was the culprit. 'We heard someone say, "Oh look! They have taken it out since Vita died." But the gap was due to nothing more than a wretched winter.'[3]

Schwerdt and Kreutzberger were very much the exception in finding such a plum job. For the majority of women who had qualified at a horticultural college in the 1960s, there was little choice but poorly

Working in a nursery, whether picking or propagating, was frequently back-breaking, poorly paid work, often delegated to women.

paid jobs either with a nursery or as a gardener, or working for oneself, which was more often done for love than for money.

Wendy Bowie had been at Waterperry just before Schwerdt and Kreutzberger, graduating in 1949. She was the younger daughter of Thomas Carlile, who had started Lodden Nurseries (later Carlile's of Twyford) in the 1900s and introduced many well-known herbaceous plants. After Waterperry, Wendy had a job with Blackmore & Langdon's delphinium nursery near Bristol for a year before she returned to Twyford to work with her father. On his death in 1958 she took over the nursery and ran it together with her husband, David Bowie, whom she married in 1961.

Wendy carried on her father's tradition of exhibiting at RHS shows and won many medals, including a gold at the Chelsea Flower Show in 1984. She served on Floral Committee 'A' from 1970 to 2001, and on the

Trials Subcommittee. Her work was recognised in 1987 when the society made her an Associate of Honour. This is the award for professional gardeners, and it is telling how few women have received it. Four years before, when Pamela Schwerdt and Sibylle Kreutzberger of Sissinghurst had been given it, they were amused to see that they were given a man's badge and a certificate with 'his', not 'her', in the wording.

Rene Clayton was one of a group of brave women who decided to open their own nursery. Alongside her husband, Hollis, she opened her business in the village of Hollingbourne in Kent. It was one of the first 'container-grown' plant nurseries, breaking the tradition of the majority of plants being sold 'bare-rooted', which meant they could only be lifted and transported in the dormant winter months.

In 1944, Carola Cochrane had also chosen Kent, 'the Garden of England', in which to set up her market garden, not an easy way to make a living. The site at East Brabourne covered two acres and cost her nearly £3,000 over five years to develop and equip with tools, cloches, Dutch Lights and all the paraphernalia professional gardeners need. In those pre-polytunnel days, the number of cloches alone increased from 150 to 3,000 in less than nine years. Cochrane employed several girls and a male foreman, though she classed the women as 'part-time labour' since they were restricted by their 'home duties'.[4]

As well as the usual salad crops, Cochrane specialised in growing chrysanthemums for the flower market, which involved months of stopping and disbudding to get the blooms ready for the Christmas rush. Spring was taken up with raising rows of bedding plants – antirrhinums, petunia, stocks, lobelia, nemesia, polyanthus and the ever-popular pansies. Although she hated the combination, in 1953 she grew vast quantities of blue lobelia, red salvia and white alyssum to supply demand received 'from all sides' in the Coronation year.[5] Asters were another money-spinner at that time for Cochrane. They had a double value for market gardeners: first they were popular as bedding plants and secondly, as Cochrane explained, 'should you not have sold all your boxes you are no worse off, as asters if planted out in the open will in due course come in handy as cut flowers'.[6]

Running a small market garden is not for the faint-hearted and Cochrane allegedly did the work of two to three people herself. By 1979 the nursery was struggling to cope with ill health, falling sales, few staff, fourteen glasshouses and rampant weeds, but despite these difficulties, she had no regrets. 'I carry on for the very simple reason that I love my job and cannot conceive of life without it.'[7]

Carola Cochrane was a member of the Women's Farm and Garden Association, which since 1899 had supported women keen to get into agriculture and horticulture. Viola Williams was one young woman

Nursery apprenticeships for women were rare but gave opportunities to learn specialist horticultural skills such as the care of topiary.

who was helped by the WFGA. Her desire to go into gardening had been dismissed by her headmistress because it could only result in a poorly paid, dead-end job, but after a year's apprenticeship in the Earl of Pembroke's gardens at Wilton House, Williams was hooked and became the first woman to achieve a first-class diploma in horticulture at Reading University in 1937. She began her working life in a nursery in north London, from which she got the sack after a week for incompetence after being put in the office to deal with the phone. As indoor office work literally frightened her she was not at all unhappy to leave, but with so few job openings for young women Viola turned to her membership of the WFGA to help her to find work.

Her next job came close to fulfilling her headmistress's prophecy. It was with a glasshouse and frame nursery just outside Fordingbridge, known as 'the concentration camp', where she was put to work in the packing shed with about six others, dealing with lilies, gladioli, all the spring bulbs, carnations, chrysanthemums and summer annuals as cut flowers all going straight up to Covent Garden every night by lorry. 'Our best buncher could do one hundred and twenty bunches of daffodils in an hour with twelve daffodils a bunch of green and two ties.' Viola's pay was 30s a week and overtime, for which she had to do Sundays, with one Sunday off a month and Saturday afternoon 'if you were lucky'. Work started at seven in the morning, and she was often there until midnight, her pay docked if she was even just five minutes late.

'There were about one hundred men and one woman and me,' remembered Viola, but she had no problems with the men except for one early episode. 'The other woman used to do the tea and everything for us. She was off so they put me to making tea at breakfast, lunch, etc. I decided this was not my line at all so I boiled the tea for two hours and they didn't ask me to do it any more.'

For her next job the WFGA offered Viola something in a private house just south of London, which again did not last long, and which was followed by spells at schools and colleges including Cheltenham Ladies' College, where she was head gardener. Again it was temporary, but as Viola notes, it 'looked good on the CV'. Being a gardener at a school was definitely seen as the lowliest of jobs, a fact illustrated by one of the teachers saying to her, 'I'm sending Mary Brown out to you ... she's got no brains and will do very well out in the garden.' Viola responded robustly that 'If I sat up all night and swotted up your subject, I could take your class tomorrow and no-one would know any difference but if you came out into the garden tomorrow you wouldn't even know where to begin – they put me on the careers committee after that!'[8]

WHERE ARE THE WOMEN?

In 1963 Elizabeth Hess, then principal at Studley College in Warwickshire, wrote an impassioned plea in the *Gardeners' Chronicle* entitled 'Where Are the Women?' She bemoaned the fact that career officers were not encouraging girls to consider horticulture as a career. 'At Studley,' she claimed, 'we have . . . between 30 and 40 . . . students studying horticulture at any one time, but to fill all the posts that we hear about we could easily have 50 in training.' Despite her claim that there were jobs aplenty to be had in the UK as well as America, Canada and Europe, if one read between the lines it was clear that these were often jobs which, even Hess had to admit, were 'of the type which provides valuable experience rather than high wages'.[1]

The responses in the correspondence pages over the following weeks showed that there were many who did not agree with Hess. Wendy Carlile, writing from her family nursery in Twyford, knew personally 'several quite outstanding girls who, though they have done well in the NDH Examinations, have had difficulty in finding a really interesting, worthwhile, well-paid job'.[2] By this time there was no official marriage bar in horticulture, but in the 1960s young women still wanted to 'finish up as a wife and mother' and 'at 30 years of age' were said to 'find they do not want to do the hard work'.[3] One twenty-five-year-old had been appointed a plant health inspector and would, Elizabeth Hess pointed out, have earned about £1,050 a year 'if she had not decided to get married instead'. It is easy to forget how incompatible a career was with marriage even in the 'Swinging Sixties'. Similarly, young girls were discouraged from certain jobs because of the difficulty of finding one that would provide them with 'appropriate accommodation' or allow them to remain living at home. A young student from Crediton in Devon was turned down for a post because 'as they had an all-male staff [she] was hardly suitable'.[4]

Elizabeth Hess defined eight categories of horticultural employment for women in the 1960s: garden management and maintenance; advisory work; research and experimental work; landscape design;

In the 1950s head gardeners were still invariably male. Skirts and clogs for women remained standard wear in public gardens.

journalism and broadcasting; nursery work and commercial horticulture; foreign employment; and teaching. Most of these categories are self-explanatory, but, as Hess explained, there was a variety of choices available in horticultural advisory work, from being employed by commercial companies making insecticides or fertilisers to being involved with organisations such as the Road Beautifying Assocation.

Women were often the unsung heroines of family businesses, but in the case of Betty Rochford she unusually achieved the same award as her husband. Betty had studied art and architecture before her marriage in May 1946 to Tom Rochford, head of the then Hertfordshire-based indoor plant company. Rochfords had always been a family-run business and Betty's contribution was to get rid of the plain display shelves at the RHS flower shows and introduce a radical new style of exhibit by grouping the exotic houseplants together. The plants were so skilfully arranged that Rochfords won the Chelsea gold and Lawrence medals (for the best exhibits shown to the society during the year) on many occasions from 1954 until the firm closed down in 1984. Betty was also a member of the RHS Floral Committee 'A', and in 1972 the society awarded her the Gold Veitch Memorial Medal, 'for her contribution to the development of horticultural displays', making the Rochfords part of an elite group in which both husband and wife are Veitch medal holders.

By the 1970s there were many women on the endless committees that judged the shows and selected the best varieties grown on the society's trial beds at their main garden at Wisley. Some of them were more popular than others. For many the name Valerie Finnis is synonymous with what a life in gardening should be all about. Finnis went to Waterperry in 1950, aged eighteen, and left twenty-eight years later. In that time, she taught dozens of girls who went on to become serious gardeners themselves. Usually dressed in the summer uniform of pale green dungarees and a short-sleeved white shirt, Valerie was dwarfed, as most were, by the redoubtable Miss Havergal, but she was enormously popular with the students, who, given the choice, 'would plump for working in the little Alpine Nursery tucked behind the house . . . Volatile and amusing with a strong histrionic streak . . . she charmed the students as indeed she charmed Miss H in whose eyes she could do no wrong.'[5]

Finnis had fallen in love with alpines, and became an expert in growing these tricky plants in the greenhouses at Waterperry. She would propagate an astounding fifty thousand plants a year, including seven thousand saxifrages of the most demanding types. Like her mother before her – who is remembered in *Dianthus* 'Constance Finnis' and the *Papaver nudicaule* 'Constance Finnis' group – Valerie was an

Valerie Finnis (1925–2006) in the summer uniform of Waterperry, where she spent most of her professional life combining her passions for plants and photography.

inveterate breeder and not just of alpine plants. Her creation of a cross between an 'orange peel' clematis, *C. orientalis*, and *C. tangutica* she named after Bill MacKenzie, her 'great friend and mentor' W.G. MacKenzie, curator of the Chelsea Physic Garden from 1946 to 1973.[6]

Armed with an old Rolleiflex camera which was given to her by Wilhelm Schacht, curator of the Munich Botanical Garden, Finnis also began a lifetime's affair with photography. Her library of plant portraits reached fifty thousand and she was always in demand as a lecturer and for service on RHS committees. At the age of forty-six she met and married an equally passionate gardener, Sir David Scott. It was a marriage made not in heaven but outside a potting shed. 'She's got *Gillenia trifoliata!*' exclaimed Scott on a visit to Waterperry. 'You're the first person who's ever known that plant!' he cried as Finnis rushed out of her shed.[7] Within an hour of their wedding in 1970, they were on their hands and knees weeding a small rockery bed. A honeymoon came later, in Japan, where Finnis had been invited to lecture. The couple returned with some three hundred plants.

Thereafter came sixteen years of bliss as Finnis (she always used her maiden name) and Sir David worked in the grounds of the Dower House at Boughton House, Northamptonshire, his home for the previous forty years. 'We just gardened,' remembered Finnis on Sir David's death at ninety-nine in 1986, and was determined to do something to perpetuate the memory of her beloved husband. His only child, Merlin, a talented naturalist, had been killed in the Second World War, and Finnis created a legacy in his name, the Merlin Trust, which funds travel and research grants for young horticulturalists. 'Plants have brought so many people to me,' Finnis later wrote. 'For years it used to be plants before people. But it really is only people that matter.'[8]

Valerie Finnis's name is remembered not just through her friendships, but also through many plants, particularly *Artemisia ludoviciana* and *Muscari armeniacum* and, from her years at the Dower House, *Helleborus* × *sternii* 'Boughton Beauty', *Artemisia stelleriana* 'Boughton Silver', and Hebe cupressoides 'Boughton Dome'. After her death in 2006, a charity, the Finnis Scott Foundation for horticultural and artistic causes, was set up in the couple's memory. The sale of their private art collection raised over £4.5 million in 2008 and gave the charity a considerable boost.

NEW SHOOTS

One of the young nursery owners who were inspired by Valerie Finnis was Carol Klein, best known now as a presenter on the BBC's perennial gardening programme, *Gardeners' World*. 'Valerie visited [my] stand at my first Royal Horticultural Society show in 1990 and gave me huge encouragement. I might have left totally daunted, had it not been for her and the fact that she adored the plants.'[1] Quite a few years later, Klein was a little disappointed to get only a silver medal at Chelsea for a quirky garden called '21 Century Street', until later that day when Finnis arrived at the stand with a banana 'on which she had inscribed, "Gold Medal awarded to Glebe Cottage Plants by Valerie Finnis"'.[2]

The first *Gardeners' World* programme went on air in 1967, but viewers had to wait a long time to see any regular female presenters. When they did arrive on screen in the 1980s, they came with impeccable credentials. Pippa Greenwood is a highly qualified botanist who ran the RHS's plant pathology department for eleven years. Anne Swithinbank, a Kew graduate, had been the glasshouse supervisor at Wisley, living above her laboratory with her husband (another old Kewite), their dog, two cats and two parrots. More recently, Alys

Fowler has added a stint at the New York Botanical Gardens to the usual training route via Kew and Wisley.

Other female presenters demonstrate the lure of the garden whatever your career background. Rachel de Thame was a model, Kim Wilde a pop singer and Carol Klein an art teacher before each succumbed to the passion for planting. In Salford-born Carol's case, it was a move to north Devon that began her second career when she started Glebe Cottage Plants, whose Chelsea displays so impressed Valerie Finnis. Sarah Raven was a doctor before establishing Perch Farm in Sussex as a centre for growing flowers for cutting, and the best organic and unusual vegetables for eating. This is a mission that she and her husband, Adam Nicolson, grandson of Vita Sackville-West, have brought to Sissinghurst, where they are the tenant family.

Gardening programmes on television and the radio have changed the way we learn about horticulture, bringing the potting shed into the living room and giving us practical advice previously available only to the professional. During the interwar years, when radio licences leapt from just over 2 million in 1927 to over 9 million in 1939, the best-known radio gardener was C.H. Middleton. He began the first of his fifteen-minute gardening broadcasts in 1934, but he was pre-dated by the prolific gardening writer Marion Cran, who gave a series of talks on the radio in the 1920s.

Gardeners' Question Time, still one of BBC Radio 4's most popular programmes, began broadcasting in 1947 as *How Does Your Garden Grow?*. Very much the child of the wartime 'Dig for Victory' campaign to encourage home produce, the format of the programme has remained basically unchanged since it started dispensing advice from weekly visits to village halls and horticultural societies across the country, even occasionally travelling to near neighbours and fellow gardening enthusiasts in Ireland and France. The panel also remained resolutely male until 1982, when the landscape gardener Daphne Ledward became the panel's first female member, paving the way for others.

One of the regular *GQT* panellists now, and a Chelsea gold-medal-winning garden designer, is Bunny Guinness. She nearly did not go into horticulture, and admits that coming from a gardening family is no guarantee of an early interest in the subject as her mother's fanatical gardening put her off as a child. At Reading University she started an applied science degree but hated having to spend so much time in the laboratory, until a chance meeting with a horticultural student at a party led to a sea change. She took a year out to get some practical gardening experience before swapping degree courses to landscape architecture.

Guinness's uncle is the legendary rose breeder David Austin, and both her mother and her cousin Clare run nurseries. She finds it a great resource having relations with varied horticultural skills since, as with all gardeners, they are continually discovering new methods, plants and ideas. 'When we meet up there is lots to discuss and [we do] have to be careful not to overdo the horticulture aspects or [it] can send less keen members of the family into Zombie mode!'[3]

Guinness continued with landscape architecture in her postgraduate training, despite her mother's initial disapproval as she thought that a talent for design was innate and could not be taught. 'Now she totally disagrees,' says Guinness, adding that in her mother's day, 'it would have been fairly unusual to have a career and horticulture would have more likely been a job, and not really one for middle-class females.' Bunny Guinness believes women garden differently to men. '[Men] seem to have more gutsy, strong designs while female designs seem softer and looser . . . Men do seem to prefer tending the lawns but perhaps this relates back to the days when starting a mower needed a lot of blood, sweat and tears! But pushing or riding a machine seems to appeal to most men more than getting on their hands and knees and weeding, whereas many of us females relish it.'[4]

Guinness thinks that people are warming to the idea of women head gardeners now that there are some higher-profile ones, such as Debs Goodenough, gardener to HRH the Prince of Wales at Highgrove, but she believes that they are still at a big disadvantage: 'the thought of giving maternity leave to younger women is a huge turn-off to many small employers. When we are past that age, then employers worry we do not have [the] strength.' There are, neverthe-less, many female head gardeners across the country, running both private and public gardens. The National Trust has, according to Tina Hammond, the head gardener at Felbrigg Hall in north Norfolk, been 'gender-blind' for many years. Sissinghurst has always been headed by women, but now more of the other gardens are following suit. In 2009 20 per cent of the Trust's 166 gardens had female head gardeners or gardeners-in-charge, in addition to which 30 per cent of the Trust's paid gardeners are women.

Hammond has been head gardener at Felbrigg for nine years. She looks too young to have held this position for nearly a decade, and vis-itors to the National Trust Jacobean property frequently take her for a volunteer or a young trainee. Hammond's rise to this position is not the typical career path of professional gardeners, but then, as she her-self admits, it is hard to define what is typical these days. From the age of thirteen, after the death of her younger sister, Hammond always knew that she would only be interested in a career where the quality of life was more important than what she could earn. She studied phi-losophy, but after graduating had a wish to do a Ph.D. in scientific methodology. Lack of funding and a period of unemployment sent her home to Ickworth in Suffolk, where she helped her aunt with her garden, and it became obvious to her that this was the career she wanted. Such was her enthusiasm that she talked herself on to a highly competitive horticultural course linked to the National Trust. Except for a brief spell working at a nursery specialising in trees, Hammond has worked for the National Trust throughout her career, first at Saltram in Devon and now at Felbrigg.

Attitudes to professional women gardeners have changed even during her time in Norfolk, which she puts down to the 'Charlie Dimmock effect'. Although Hammond has little time for television gardening presenters as a whole, she believes that seeing Dimmock on television getting stuck into heavy gardening work undoubtedly changed people's perceptions. By showing that she could wield a spade as well as any man, together with her unstuffy attitude towards her personal appearance, Dimmock became the first 'working' female gardener on television, sweeping away the more ladylike image of other women presenters, who, it seemed, were forever being banished to the greenhouse for a bit of gentle potting-on.

Hammond has never experienced any overt prejudice either from visitors or from the team of gardeners and volunteers who work for her at Felbrigg. She is full of praise for the National Trust as an employer, particularly in allowing her a free rein to develop the four-acre walled garden at the hall that had been neglected in the past. She is not constrained by any major restoration projects and has been able to create borders from scratch, using many species from the southern hemisphere which relish the East Anglian climate.

Hammond forecasts that in the world's ever-changing economic climate many more women will be examining their lifestyles and looking towards gardening for a fulfilling career away from the rat race, but she adds the warning that such a path is dauntingly competitive. Experience and qualifications are essential and finding placements is not easy; even the volunteers' posts are over-subscribed. No one goes

Just over a hundred years since they first arrived and raised eyebrows, women caring for the Palm House Parterre at Kew no longer cause a stir.

into professional gardening for the money, she believes, but the rewards are enormous.

At the Royal Botanic Gardens at Kew the invisible glass ceiling shielding the Palm House has finally been cracked. By 1982 Kew was employing over forty women in a variety of departments, a third of all garden staff. Jenny Evans became Kew's first female assistant curator in 1994, and in 2001 Emma Fox was appointed as the first female supervisor of the hallowed Palm House, built by Decimus Burton and Richard Turner in 1848 and home to some of the gardens' greatest treasures. What is amazing is that horticulture was Fox's second career, after she decided that life as a primary school teacher was not for her.

The popularity of garden design among women as either a first or second career has led to the growth of high-quality schools such as the English Gardening School based at the Chelsea Physic Garden, started in 1983 by Rosemary Alexander. With a background in landscape architecture, Alexander was the first woman to be elected to the Society of Garden Designers in 1981 and her peers, including Jinny Blom, Sarah Eberle and Arabella Lennox-Boyd, are just a few of the many women who are now regular gold medal winners at the Chelsea Flower Show.

In 1850 Jane Loudon wrote in the revised edition of *Villa Gardener* by her husband, J.C. Loudon, 'We venture to assert that there is not any lady who can design a pattern, and embroider a gown, that might not in a few hours be taught to design flower gardens with as much skill and taste as a professional landscape gardener.'[5] Graduate training in garden design would have been unimaginable to the Loudons, and while few of us today have the skills to embroider, Jane Loudon would surely be satisfied to see the range of horticultural and landscape design education available to all, and to know that there is now no area of gardening in which women cannot excel at the highest professional level.

ACKNOWLEDGEMENTS

It is inevitable that even with such a long look through horticultural history, there will be omissions. We all have our favourite gardeners and gardens that have inspired us and there would never be room to mention every one. So this has been a subjective choice, but one that I hope shows the enormous strides that have been made, and continue to be made, by women in all areas of horticulture.

This book has been a long time in the writing and would not have been possible without an army of supporters along the way. At the beginning of my research, I had the extreme good fortune to be awarded a fellowship at the Yale Center for British Art in New Haven. I am deeply indebted to Amy Myers, director of the Center, for her support and encouragement of this project, together with all the staff and researchers in the Center's library and picture research departments, in particular Alicia Weisberg-Roberts, together with the staff at the Beinecke Rare Book and Manuscript Library of Yale University. During my time at Yale, I can think of no better person to have had working alongside me than Camilla Smith. From our first meeting at Yale, Mark Laird has been exceptionally generous with his valuable time and extensive knowledge of eighteenth-century gardeners and additional information on Lady Elizabeth Lee.

An earlier research trip to the Huntington Library, Art Collections and Botanical Gardens in San Marino, California, had whetted my appetite for their resources and I was delighted to be awarded their Ernestine Richter Avery Fellowship. Unfortunately I was unable to take this fellowship but I am grateful to the library for all the long-distance help they gave me in my research into Mrs Montagu's circle of friends.

Back in the UK, the majority of my research was done at the RHS's Lindley Library and Picture Collection, where staff were unfailingly helpful and ready to retrieve the most obscure titles for me time and again. Particular thanks go to Christopher Hill and Lucy Waitt. The same can be said of everyone at the London Library, which remains a researcher's joy because of the serendipity of its open shelves. Rosie Atkins at the Chelsea Physic Garden, Michele Losse and everyone at the Royal Botanic Gardens, Kew, Jill Kelsey at the Royal Archives at Windsor Castle, Derek Adlam of the Portland Collection at the Harley Gallery, Agnes Kroll of the Red Cross Bankside Open Spaces Trust, Kate Perry at Girton, Trevor Hines of the Worshipful Company of Gardeners and Carole Jones of Kelmarsh Hall were all supremely help-ful and encouraging, as were staff at the Hextable Archive, the National Women's Library, the Imperial War Museum, the British Library, Reading University's Museum of English Rural Life, Nottingham University Library, the Bedford Centre for the History of Women at Royal Holloway, and the various county record offices I vis-ited across the country.

I am grateful to Her Majesty Queen Elizabeth II for permission to make use of material from the Royal Archives.

Along the way, I have received help from a large number of friends and colleagues. I feel honoured to have been able to discuss this project with Penelope Hobhouse, whose wisdom is boundless. In addition, I would like to thank Pippa Potts for her comments on Lady Anne Clifford, and Rebecca Preston, Julia Matheson, Monica Brewis, Ann Meredith and all at the Garden History Seminar at the Institute of Historical Research; Henry Boyd-Carpenter and everyone at East Lambrook Manor Gardens; Roy Lancaster; Tim Richardson for his thoughts on Constance Spry; Bunny Guinness, Penny Snell, Charlotte Gere, Margaret Flanders Derby, Rosemary Baird, Nicola Phillips, Elizabeth Buchan, Carole Taylor, Eleanor Nairne, and Amanda Vickery, whose large quantities of peppermint tea and sage advice were always available despite her having her own *magnum opus* to finish.

My children and grandchildren have a great deal of time owing to them from the past three years. I promise to make it up to them in spades. My partner, Paddy Barwise, despite being a non-gardener, has shown exemplary enthusiasm for this book. I remain in awe of his editing skills, with which, as ever, he has been so generous. He is also always able to calm me down when feelings of guilt about the neglect of my own garden, not to mention life's greater trials, overcome me. For this and everything, he has my love and gratitude.

Finally, I could not have got this far without the support I have received from my agent, Clare Alexander of Aitken Alexander, my editors, Lennie Goodings, Hilary Hale, Vivien Redman, Linda Silverman and Deborah Adams at Virago, and my awesome indexer, Ann Parry. In addition to their supreme editing talents, during the last stages of the book Lennie, Vivien and Hilary have patiently held my hand with the greatest compassion when life overtook work, constantly giving me encouragement and inspiration. I cannot thank them enough.

PICTURE CREDITS

Picture Credits

Page 89: The Royal Collection © 2009, Her Majesty Queen Elizabeth II

Page 92: © The De Morgan Centre, London/The Bridgeman Art Library

Page 100: Photolibrary.com

Page 106: Photolibrary.com

Page 108: *Gardens for Small Country Houses* (1927)/Private collection

Page 114: *Country Life* Picture Library

Page 127: Getty Images

Page 136: © Trish Gant

Page 139: Osterreichische Nationalbibliothek, Vienna, Austria/Alinari/The Bridgeman Art Library

Page 144: Getty Images

Page 157: © Valerie Finnis/RHS

Page 161: The Royal Collection © 2009, Her Majesty Queen Elizabeth II

Page 165: Victoria and Albert Images

Page 170: © The Trustees of the British Museum

Page 178: Photolibrary.com

Page 180: Yale Center for British Art, Paul Mellon Collection, USA/The Bridgeman Art Library

Page 183: Private collection/The Bridgeman Art Library

Page 189: *The Ladies' Magazine of Gardening* (1853)/Private collection

Page 190: Fitzwilliam Museum, University of Cambridge, UK/The Bridgeman Art Library

Page 196: Royal Botanical Gardens, Kew, London, UK/The Bridgeman Art Library

Page 198: Kew Images

Page 206: *Floral Decorations for Dwelling Houses* (1876)/Private collection

Page 208: Mary Evans Picture Library

Page 212: *Wood & Garden* (1899)/Private collection

Page 217: Getty Images

Page 223: British Library

Page 227: Private collection/The Stapleton Collection/The Bridgeman Art Library

Page 229: Private collection/The Stapleton Collection/The Bridgeman Art Library

Page 237: *An Introduction to Botany* (1823)/Private collection

Page 242: *Loudon's Villa Gardener* (1850)/Private collection

Page 247: *Mrs Loudon's Gardening for Ladies* (1846)/Private collection

Picture Credits

Page 250: *Mrs Loudon's Gardening for Ladies* (1846)/Private collection

Page 252: *The Ladies Companion to the Flower Garden* (1846)/Private collection

Page 263: © Valerie Finnis/RHS

Page 269: Private collection

Page 272: British Library

Page 276: *The Gentlewoman's Book of Gardening* (1892)/Private collection

Page 280: Kew Images

Page 290: Worcester Art Museum, Massachusetts, USA/The Bridgeman Art Library

Page 297: *In a College Garden* (1916)/Private collection

Page 300: *In a College Garden* (1916)/Private collection

Page 311: Kew Images

Page 323: Getty Images

Page 325: Kew Images

Page 329: Getty Images

Page 331: Kew Images

Page 334: Getty Images

Page 340: Getty Images

Page 342: Getty Images

Page 346: *Woman's Illustrated*

Page 348: RHS

Page 356: Kew Images

Photo insert

Page 1: British Library, London, UK/© British Library Board. All Rights Reserved/The Bridgeman Art Library

Page 2: Badminton Estate

Page 3: Peter Edward Stroehling. The Royal Collection © 2009, Her Majesty Queen Elizabeth II

Page 4: Yale Center for British Art, Paul Mellon Collection, USA/The Bridgeman Art Library

Page 5: Private Collection

Page 6: Private Collection

Page 7: © Valerie Finnis/RHS

Page 8: RHS

APPENDIX I:
GARDENS BY WOMEN

The following gardens have all been influenced by women at some point, through design or planting. Many of these women have been discussed in the book. In the case of designers with large portfolios such as Gertrude Jekyll and Norah Lindsay, a selection of accessible gardens has been included.

Those run by the National Trust (NT), English Heritage (EH), Perennial and the Royal Horticultural Society (RHS) are open seasonally, some throughout the year. Others have occasional openings to the public and it is best to check on the internet or by direct contact to confirm opening dates and times.

In addition, many private gardens designed and maintained by women in England and Wales open for charity through the National Gardens Scheme. Details may be found in the NGS's *Yellow Book*, published annually in the early spring and widely available from bookshops and newsagents. Gardens in Scotland and Northern Ireland open through their own NGSs.

ENGLAND

Bedfordshire
Wrest Park, Silsoe (EH)   Jemima Grey

Appendix I: Gardens by Women

Berkshire

Folly Farm, Sulhampstead Abbots	Gertrude Jekyll
Frogmore, Windsor	Queen Charlotte, Mary Moser

Buckinghamshire

Cliveden (NT)	Norah Lindsay

Derbyshire

Hardwick Hall (NT)	Elizabeth Talbot, 'Bess', Countess of Shrewsbury

Devon

Castle Drogo (NT)	Gertrude Jekyll
Knightshayes (NT)	Joyce Heathcoat-Amory
Rosemoor (RHS)	Lady Anne Berry (previously Palmer)

Dorset

Abbotsbury	Elizabeth Strangways

Essex

The Beth Chatto Gardens	Beth Chatto
Easton Lodge	Frances, Countess of Warwick
Hyde Hall (RHS)	Helen Robinson
Warley Place Nature Reserve	Ellen Willmott

Gloucestershire

Hidcote Manor (NT)	Norah Lindsay
Kiftsgate Court	Heather Muir

Hampshire

Mottisfont, near Romsey (NT)	Norah Lindsay
Queen Eleanor's Garden, Winchester	Queen Eleanor of Aquitaine

Appendix I: Gardens by Women

Hertfordshire

Crossing House Garden, Royston	Margaret Fuller
Hatfield House	Marchioness of Salisbury
Trent Park	Norah Lindsay

Kent

Lullingstone Castle, Eynsford	Eleanour Sinclair Rohde
Sissinghurst, near Cranbrook (NT)	Vita Sackville-West

London

Chelsea Physic Garden	Duchess of Beaufort
Garden Museum, Lambeth	Rosemary Nicholson

Middlesex

Hampton Court Palace	Queen Mary II

Norfolk

Blickling Hall (NT)	Norah Lindsay
Felbrigg Hall (NT)	Norah Lindsay
Raveningham Gardens	Lady Bacon

Northamptonshire

Kelmarsh Hall	Norah Lindsay

Northumberland

Alnwick Gardens	Duchess of Northumberland

Oxfordshire

Waterperry Gardens	Beatrix Havergal

Somerset

Barrington Court (NT)	Gertrude Jekyll
Hestercombe, Taunton	Gertrude Jekyll

East Lambrook Manor, South Petherton	Margery Fish
Tintinhull, near Yeovil (NT)	Phyllis Reiss, Penelope Hobhouse

Staffordshire

Biddulph Grange (NT)	Maria Bateman

Suffolk

Helmingham Hall	Lady Xa Tollemache
Ickworth (NT)	Mary Lepel, Lady Hervey

Surrey

Chilworth Manor (NGS)	Sarah, Duchess of Marlborough, Lady Daphne Heald
Ham House (NT)	Elizabeth, Countess of Dysart and Duchess of Lauderdale
Hatchlands, East Clandon, Guildford (NT)	Gertrude Jekyll
Kew Gardens	Various
Munstead Wood, Busbridge, Godalming	Gertrude Jekyll
Vann, Hambledon, Godalming	Gertrude Jekyll

Warwickshire

Ryton Organic Gardens	Jacqueline Gear

Wiltshire

Broadleas Gardens, Devizes	Anne Cowdrey
Heale House, Salisbury	Anne Rasch

Yorkshire

Harlow Carr (RHS)	Phillipa Rakusen
Helmsley Castle, N. Yorks. (EH)	Alison Ticehurst
York Gate (Perennial)	Sybil Spencer

Appendix I: Gardens by Women

Carmarthenshire

Aberglasney Gardens,   Penelope Hobhouse
   Llangathen

Gwynedd

Bodnant, Tal-y-Cafn,   Lady Aberconway
   Colwyn Bay (NT)

SCOTLAND

Argyll & Bute

Achamore Gardens, Island   Kitty Lloyd Jones
   of Gigha

Mount Stuart, Isle of Bute   Rosemary Verey

East Lothian

Tyninghame, Dunbar   Helen Hope, Countess of
                       Haddington

Perth

Branklyn Garden (NTS)   Dorothy Renton

NORTHERN IRELAND

County Down

Rowallane Garden (NT)   Lady O'Neill of the Maine

APPENDIX II:
RHS MEDAL WINNERS

Honorary Fellows of the Royal Horticultural Society

Lady Anne Berry, VMH

Mrs Jacqueline Gear

Dr Valerie Payne

Mary Margaret Rochford

Mary Shirville, VMH

Joyce Stewart, VMH

Mavis Sweetingham, MBE

Victoria Medal of Honour in Horticulture

The Victoria Medal of Honour (VMH) was instituted in 1897 to honour the Diamond Jubilee of Queen Victoria. Initially sixty medals were awarded. The number was later raised to sixty-three to correspond to the total number of years of her reign. Significant similar family awards are included.

1897	Gertrude Jekyll
1897	Ellen Willmott
1901	Eleanor Ormerod
1931	Laura McLaren, Lady Aberconway
[1934]	[2nd Baron Aberconway]

[1961]	[3rd Baron Aberconway]
[1929]	[Sir William Lawrence]
1942	Lady Iris Lawrence
1946	Vera Higgins
1955	Lilian Snelling
1961	HM Queen Elizabeth, the Queen Mother
1964	Gwendolyn Anley
1965	Beatrix Havergal
[1935]	[Amos Perry]
[1970]	[Roy Hay]
1971	Frances Perry
1973	Julia Clements
1975	Valerie Finnis
[1967]	[Sir Giles Loder]
1975	Lady Loder
1977	Mrs Desmond Underwood
1980	Sheila Macqueen
[1966]	[Sir John Heathcoat-Amory]
1981	Lady Heathcoat-Amory
1984	Kath Dryden
1986	Lady Anne Palmer (later Berry)
1987	Beth Chatto
1989	Carolyn Hardy
1990	Sylvia Crowe
1993	Mary Shirville (Newnes)
1995	Helen Robinson
[1897]	[Lord Rothschild]
[1929]	[Lionel de Rothschild]
1995	Miriam Rothschild
[2005]	[Edmond de Rothschild]
1996	Penelope Hobhouse
1997	Mary Grierson
1998	Joyce Stewart
1998	Rosemary Verey

2006	Sybille Kreutzberger
2006	Pamela Schwerdt
2009	Lady Skelmersdale

RHS Veitch Memorial Medals

The Veitch Memorial Trust was established in 1869 to honour the memory of James Veitch, the famous nurseryman. Early medals were given as prizes at horticultural shows. In 1922, the RHS took over the Trust. Show medals were phased out. Since then, over five hundred medals (VMM) have been awarded. It is the only RHS medal that may be awarded to non-British subjects.

1926 (Silver)	Matilda Smith	Botanical artist
1928	Gertrude Jekyll	Gardener and author
1929 (Silver)	Miss Wingfield	Kurume azalea exhibit at Truro Show
1939 (Silver)	Kate Barratt	Principal, Swanley College
1941 (Silver)	Mrs R. Malby	Plant photographer
1953 (Silver)	Nellie Roberts	RHS orchid artist
1954 (Silver)	Mrs W.G. Knox-Finlay	Keillour
1954 (Silver)	Dorothy Renton	Branklyn
1955	Vita Sackville-West	Sissinghurst
1960 (Silver)	Mrs C.B. Saunders	Cyclamen breeder
1963 (Silver)	Margery Fish	East Lambrook
1964	Frances Perry	Horticultural writer
1964 (Silver)	Mrs M. Wreford	Compiler, Addendum to Sander's list of orchid hybrids
1967	Elizabeth Hess	Principal, Studley College
1970	Mary Pope	Founder, National Association of Flower Arranging Societies
1971	Helen Richardson	Daffodil breeder
1972	Xenia Field	Horticultural journalist
1972	Mrs T. Rochford	Horticultural exhibitor
1973	Lady Haddington	Tyninghame

1975	Alice Coats	Plant historian
1976	Iris Bannochie	Plant collector and exhibitor
1976	Blanche Henrey	Author, *British Botanical and Horticultural Literature before 1800*
1976 (Silver)	Margaret Stones	Botanical artist
1976 (Silver)	Miss E. Weise	Administrative assistant, RHS
1977	Alic W. Gray	Promoter of electricity in horticulture
1978	Miss B.M. Fry	Research, Rosewarne Experimental Horticulture Station, Camborne
1979	Stella Coe	Promoter of ikebana
1980 (Silver)	Miss S.J. Orr	Trials recorder, Wisley
1983	Rachel Crawshay	Organising sec., National Gardens Scheme
1984	Mary Grierson	Botanical artist
1984 (Silver)	Mildred Hobbs	Press officer, RHS
1985	Margaret Stones	Botanical artist
1985	Mavis Batey	Sec., Garden History Society
1987	Rachel Mellon	Botanical artist
1987	Princesse Greta Sturdza	Le Vasterival, near Dieppe
1988	Elspeth Napier	Editor, *Journal of the RHS*
1989	Helen Robinson	Developed garden at Hyde Hall, Essex
1989	Elizabeth Scholtz	Director Emeritus, Brooklyn Botanical Garden
1990	Mrs Martyn Simmons	Chairman, RHS Lily Group
1991	Philippa Rakusen	Director, Northern Horticultural Society Garden, Harlow Carr
1992	Olive Hilliard	Botanist
1992	Joy Larkcom	Promoter of unusual vegetables

1993	Brenda Hyatt	Nurseryman, reviver of auriculas
1993	Joyce Stewart	Work with orchids
1994	Anne Kenrick	President, Friends of Birmingham Botanical Gardens
1995	Rosemary Nicholson	Founder, Tradescant Trust and Museum of Garden History (now Garden Museum)
1995	Jane Pepper	President, Pennsylvania Horticultural Society
1999	Helen Dillon	Irish gardener and author
2000	Dr Elizabeth McClintock	US horticulturalist
2000	Lady O'Neill	Chairman, National Trust Gardens Committee
2000	Anna Pavord	Horticultural journalist and author of *The Tulip*
2000	Daphne Vince-Prue	Plant physiologist
2001	Stella Ross-Craig	Botanical artist
2002	Lady Emma Tennant	Chairman, Gardens Advisory Panel, National Trust
2003	Shirley Sherwood	Promoter of botanical art
2005	Anne-Marie Evans	Botanical artist
2009	Joan Morgan	Fruit tree specialist and author of *The Book of Apples*

RHS Associate of Honour

The Associate of Honour (AM) medal was established in 1930 for those who have given distinguished service to horticulture during their employment. It is limited to one hundred recipients at a time.

| 1934 | Mary Burton | Gardener, New Saughton Hall, Edinburgh (private mental institution) |

1960	Mary Page	Horticulturist, Wye College
1968	Joan Stokes	Instructor, Waterperry College
1975	Mrs P. Simmons	Propagator, Ingwersens
1980	Sybille Kreutzberger	Gardener, Sissinghurst
1980	Pamela Schwerdt	Gardener, Sissinghurst
1982	Miss H.M. Hughes	Regional fruit specialist, W. Midlands Region, ADAS
1987	Wendy Bowie	Manager, Thomas Carlile Ltd
1988	Hazel Key	Nurseryman, Fibrex Nurseries
1992	Elizabeth Strangman	Director, Washfield Nurseries
1994	Audrey Brooks	Horticultural adviser, RHS Wisley
1999	Jennifer Adams	Superintendent, Royal Parks
2000	Susan Smith	Manager, Bournemouth Parks
2006	Diana Miller	Keeper of the herbarium, RHS Wisley
2008	Lynette Randall	Savill Gardens, Windsor
2008	Mary Spiller	Waterperry College

For more information, please go to www.gardeningwomen.com

BIBLIOGRAPHY

To make it easier for the reader, the bibliography has been divided into sections. If you are interested in getting a general overview of garden and plant history, and women and gardening, start with the general section.

There follow three chronological sections. Each section covers not just the published works cited but also other books on each of the periods that may have been published later and have been useful. In the later sections, there are also selected texts by women on gardening. Finally, there is a section of selected books on the history of botanical illustration, flower-arranging and embroidery. Place, date and publisher are given where known. Archival sources are listed in the notes.

GENERAL

Amherst, Alicia, *The History of Gardening in England*. London: Bernard Quaritch, 1896

Bennett, Jennifer, *Lilies of the Hearth: The Historical Relationship between Women and Plants*. Camden East, Ontario: Camden House, 1991

Bennett, Sue, *Five Centuries of Women and Gardens*. London: National Portrait Gallery, 2001

Brown, Jane, *The Pursuit of Paradise: A Social History of Gardens and Gardening*. London: HarperCollins, 1999

Campbell-Culver, Maggie, *The Origins of Plants: The People and Plants that Have Shaped Britain's Garden History since the Year 1000*. London: Headline, 2001

Bibliography

Coats, Alice M., *Flowers and Their Histories*. London: A. & C. Black, 1968

——, *The Treasury of Flowers*. London: Phaidon, 1975

Cuthbertson, Yvonne, *Women Gardeners: A History*. Denver: Arden Press, 1998

Desmond, Ray, *Dictionary of British and Irish Botanists and Horticulturists: Including Plant Collectors and Botanical Artists*. London: Taylor & Francis, 1977

Elliott, Brent, *The Royal Horticultural Society: A History, 1804–2004*. Chichester: Phillimore & Co. Ltd, 2004

Fletcher, H.R., *The Story of the Royal Horticultural Society*. Oxford: Oxford University Press/Royal Horticultural Society, 1969

——, *The Glory of the Garden*. London: Sotheby's, 1987

Hadfield, Miles, *A History of British Gardening*. London: Penguin, 1985

——, *Pioneers in Gardening*. London: Bloomsbury, 1996

Hadfield, Miles, Robert Harling and Leonie Highton, *British Gardeners: A Biographical Dictionary*. London: Zwemmer in association with Condé Nast, 1980

Harris, Dianne, 'Women as Gardeners'. *Encyclopedia of Gardens: History and Design*. Ed. C.A. Shoemaker. Chicago: Fitzroy Dearborn, 2001

[Higgins, Vera], V.H., 'Notable Women Gardeners', *Journal of the Royal Horticultural Society*, vol. 66 (February 1943)

Hobhouse, Penelope, *Plants in Garden History*. London: Pavilion Books, 1997

Hollingsworth, Buckner, *Her Garden Was Her Delight*. New York: Macmillan, 1962

Horwood, Catherine, *Potted History: The Story of Plants in the Home*. London: Frances Lincoln, 2007

Hoyles, Martin, *The Story of Gardening*. London: Journeyman Press, 1991

Kellaway, Deborah (ed.), *The Virago Book of Women Gardeners*. London: Virago, 1996

King, Peter, *Women Rule the Plot: The Story of the 100 Year Fight to Establish Women's Place in Farm and Garden*. London: Duckworth, 1999

MacLeod, Dawn, *Down-to-Earth Women*. Edinburgh: Blackwood & Sons, 1982

Massingham, Betty, *A Century of Gardeners*. London: Faber and Faber, 1982

Pankhurst, Alex, *Who Does Your Garden Grow?*. Dedham: Earl's Eye Publishing, 1992

Penn, Helen, *An Englishwoman's Garden*. London: BBC, 1993

Perényi, Eleanor, *Green Thoughts: A Writer in the Garden*. London: Allen Lane, 1982

Quest-Ritson, Charles, *The English Garden: A Social History*. London: Viking, 2001

Uglow, Jenny, *A Little History of British Gardening*. London: Chatto & Windus, 2004

Bibliography

Way, Twigs, *Virgins, Weeders and Queens: A History of Women in the Garden*. Stroud: Sutton, 2006

Wulf, Andrea, and Emma Gieben-Gamal, *This Other Eden: Seven Great Gardens and Three Hundred Years of English History*. London: Little, Brown, 2005

UP TO 1720

Allan, Mea, *The Tradescants: Their Plants, Gardens and Museum, 1570–1662*. London: Michael Joseph, 1964

Amherst, The Hon. Amelia, 'On a Fifteenth Century Treatise on Gardening By "Mayster" Ion Gardener', *Society of Archeologia*, vol. LIV (1895)

Chambers, Douglas, '"Storys of Plants": The Assembling of Mary Capel Somerset's Botanical Collection at Badminton', *Journal of the History of Collecting*, vol. 9, no. 1 (1997)

Christianson, C. Paul, 'Herbwomen in London 1660–1836', *The London Gardener*, vol. 6 (2000)

——, 'The London Gardener: A Tudor-Age Profile', *The London Gardener*, vol. 8 (2002)

Coles, William, *The Art of Simpling, or, An Introduction to the Knowledge and Gathering of Herbs*. 1656

Cornwallis, Jane Lady afterwards Lady Bacon, and Richard Baron Braybrooke Griffin, *The Private Correspondence of Jane Lady Cornwallis, 1613–1644*. London: S. & J. Bentley, Wilson & Fley, 1842

Cottesloe, Gloria, and Doris Hunt, *The Duchess of Beaufort's Flowers*. Exeter: Webb & Bower, 1983

Duthie, Ruth, 'The Planting Plans of Some Seventeenth-Century Flower Gardens', *Garden History*, vol. 18, no. 2 (1990)

Edwards, Arthur Charles, *English History from Essex Sources, 1550–1750*. Chelmsford: Essex County Council, 1952

Evelyn, Charles, *The Ladies' Recreation*. London: J. Roberts, 1717

[Fitzherbert, Anthony], *Here Begynneth a Newe Tracte or Treatyse Moost Profytable for All Husbandemen: And Very Frutefull for All Other Persons to Rede*. R. Pynson, 1523

Gerard, John, *General Historie of Plants*. 1597

Green, David Brontë, *Gardener to Queen Anne: Henry Wise (1653–1738) and the Formal Garden*. Oxford: Oxford University Press, 1956

Bibliography

Harvey, John, *Early Gardening Catalogues*. London: Phillimore, 1972

——, *Early Nurserymen*. London: Phillimore, 1974

Henderson, Paula, *The Tudor House and Garden: Architecture and Landscape in the Sixteenth and Early Seventeenth Centuries*. New Haven and London: Published for the Paul Mellon Centre for Studies in British Art by Yale University Press, 2005

Henrey, Blanche, *British Botanical and Horticultural Literature before 1800*. Oxford: Oxford University Press, 1975

Heresbach, Conrad (trans. Barnabe Googe), *Foure Books of Husbandry*. London: Richard Watkins, 1577

Hoby, Lady Margaret, and D.M. Meads, *Diary of Lady Margaret Hoby*. London: Routledge, 1930

Hoby, Lady Margaret, and Joanna Moody, *The Private Life of an Elizabethan Lady: The Diary of Lady Margaret Hoby, 1599–1605*. Stroud: Sutton, 1998

Landsberg, Sylvia, *The Medieval Garden*. London: British Museum, [n.d.]

Laurence, Anne, *Women in England 1500–1760: A Social History*. London: Weidenfeld & Nicholson, 1995

Lawson, William, *The Country Housewife's Garden* [1617]. London: Breslich & Foss, 1983

——, *A New Orchard and Garden; with, the Country Housewife's Garden* [1618]. Totnes: Prospect, 2003

McClain, Molly, *Beaufort: The Duke and His Duchess 1657–1715*. New Haven and London: Yale University Press, 2001

Mendelson, Sara, and Patricia Crawford, *Women in Early Modern England 1550–1720*. Oxford: Oxford University Press, 1998

Munroe, Jennifer, *Gender and the Garden in Early Modern Literature*. Aldershot: Ashgate, 2008

Munroe, Jennifer, Betty Travitsky and Anne Lake Prescott, *Making Gardens of Their Own: Advice for Women, 1500–1750*. Aldershot: Ashgate, 2007

O'Neill, Jean, 'The Stove House and the Duchess', *Country Life*, 20 January 1983, pp. 142–3

Parkinson, John, and A. Switzer, *Paradisi in Sole Paradisus Terrestris*. Humfrey Lownes and Robert Young, 1629

Pavord, Anna, *The Tulip*. London: Bloomsbury, 1999

——, *The Naming of Names: The Search for Order in the World of Plants*. London: Bloomsbury, 2005

Pollock, Linda, *With Faith and Physic: The Life of a Tudor Gentlewoman, Lady Grace Mildmay 1552–1620*. London: Collins & Brown, 1993

Potts, Philippa, 'Lady Anne Clifford: Revealing the Gardener', *Grand Gardens and Green Spaces*. Ed. Janet Waymark. London: Birkbeck Garden History Group, 2006

Switzer, Stephen, *The Nobleman, Gentleman, and Gardener's Recreation*. London: B. Barker and C. King, 1715

Taboroff, June, '"Wife, Unto Thy Garden", The First Gardening Books for Women', *Garden History*, vol. 11, no. 1 (1983)

Temple, Sir William, *Upon the Gardens of Epicurus*. London: Chatto & Windus, 1908

Tusser, Thomas, *[Five Hundreth Points of Good Husbandry]*. London: Rychard Tottell, 1573

[Wolley, Hannah], *The Accomplisht Ladys Delight*. London: Benjamin Harris, 1675

1720 TO 1870

Abbot, Charles, *Flora Bedfordiensis, comprehending such plants as grow wild in the county of Bedford, arranged according to the system of Linnaeus*. Bedford: [s.n.], 1798

Abercrombie, John, and Thomas Mawe, *Every Man His Own Gardener*. London: W. Griffin, 1767

Allan, Mea, *The Hookers of Kew, 1785–1911*. London: Michael Joseph, 1967

Allen, David Elliston, 'The Women Members of the Botancial Society of London, 1836–1856', *The British Journal for the History of Science*, vol. 13, no. 45 (1980)

Baird, Rosemary, *Mistress of the House: Great Ladies and Grand Houses, 1670–1830*. London: Phoenix, 2004

Barker, Hannah, and Elaine Chalus (eds.), *Gender in Eighteenth-century England: Roles, Representations and Responsibilities*. London: Longman, 1997

Barnard, Lady Anne Lindsay, *South Africa a Century Ago: Letters Written from the Cape of Good Hope 1797–1801*. Ed. W.H. Wilkins. London: Smith, Elder & Co., 1925

———, *The Cape Diaries of Lady Anne Lindsay Barnard*. Cape Town: Van Riebeeck Society, 1999

Bartell, Edmund, *Hints for Picturesque Improvements in Ornamental Cottages*. London: J. Taylor, 1804

Bell, Susan Groag, 'Women Create Gardens in Male Landscapes: A Revisionist

Approach to Eighteenth-Century English Garden History', *Feminist Studies*, vol. 16, no. 3 (1990)

Bending, Stephen, 'Mrs Montague's Contemplative Bench: Bluestocking Gardens and Female Retirement', *Huntington Library Quarterly*, vol. 69, no. 4 (Winter 2006)

Bilston, Sarah, 'Queens of the Garden: Victorian Woman Gardeners and the Rise of the Gardening Advice Text', *Victorian Literature and Culture*, vol. 36, no. 1 (2008)

Blackwell, Elizabeth, *A Curious Herbal: Containing Five Hundred Cuts, of the Most Useful Plants Which Are Now Used in the Practice of Physick*, 2 vols. London: Samuel Harding, 1737–9

Blunt, Wilfrid, *The Complete Naturalist: A Life of Linnaeus*. London: Collins, 1984

Bond, Elizabeth, 'Louisa Lawrence: A Victorian Gardener', *Country Life*, 30 August 1973, p. 580

Boniface, Patricia (ed.), *In Search of English Gardens: The Travels of John Claudius Loudon and His Wife Jane*. Wheathampstead: Lennard Publishing, 1987

Brown, Jane, *My Darling Heriott: Henrietta Luxborough, Poetic Gardener and Irrepressible Exile*. London: HarperPress, 2006

Carter, Elizabeth, and Montagu Pennington, *A Series of Letters between Mrs. Elizabeth Carter and Miss Catherine Talbot from the Year 1741 to 1770*. London: F.C. & J. Rivington, 1808

Coke, Mary Lady, *The Letters and Journals of Lady Mary Coke*. Ed. J. A. Home. Bath: [Kingsmead Bookshops], 1970

Colvin, Christina, and Charles Nelson, '"Building Castles of Flowers": Maria Edgeworth as Gardener', *Garden History*, vol. 16, no. 1 (1988)

Daniels, Stephen, *Humphry Repton: The Red Books of Brandsbury and Glemham Hall*. Harvard: Harvard University Press for Dumbarton Oaks, 1994

Darley, Gillian, *John Evelyn: Living for Ingenuity*. New Haven and London: Yale University Press, 2006

Darwin, Erasmus, *The Botanic Garden: A Poem, in Two Parts*. London: J. Moore, 1790

Delany, Mary, *et al.*, *The Autobiography and Correspondence of Mary Granville, Mrs. Delany*. London: Richard Bentley, 1861

Desmond, Ray, *The European Discovery of the Indian Flora*. Oxford: Royal Botanic Gardens Kew with Oxford University Press, 1992

Duthie, Ruth, 'A Cast of Auriculas', *Country Life*, 27 December 1990, pp. 36–8

Festing, Sally, 'Rare Flowers and Fantastic Breeds: The 2nd Duchess of Portland and Her Circle – I', *Country Life*, 12 June 1986, pp. 1684–6

——, 'Grace Without Triviality: The 2nd Duchess of Portland and Her Circle – II', *Country Life*, 19 June 1986, pp. 1772–4

——, 'The Second Duchess of Portland and Her Rose', *Garden History*, vol. 14, no. 2 (1986)

Fiennes, Celia, *Through England on a Side Saddle*. Field & Tuer, The Leadenhall Press, 1888

Ford, Lisa, 'A Progress in Plants: Mrs Delany's Botanical Sources', in *Mrs Delany and Her Circle*. Eds M. Laird and A. Weisberg-Roberts. New Haven and London: Yale Center for British Art, Sir John Soane's Museum in association with Yale University Press, 2009

Fraser, Flora, *Princesses: The Six Daughters of George III*. London: John Murray, 2005

——, *Frogmore House and the Royal Mausoleum*. Royal Collection Enterprises, 2005

Hayden, Ruth, *Mrs Delany: Her Life and Her Flowers*. London: British Museum Publications, 1980

[Haywood, Eliza Fowler], *The Female Spectator*. London, 1745

Hervey, Mary Lepel Baroness, and Edmund Morris, *Letters of Mary Lepel, Lady Hervey*. [s.n.], 1821

Howe, Bea, *Lady with Green Fingers: The Life of Jane Loudon*. London: Country Life, 1961

——, *Arbiter of Elegance*. London: Harvill Press, 1967

Hyams, Edward, *Capability Brown and Humphry Repton*. London: Dent, 1971

[Jacson, Maria], *The Florist's Manual, or, Hints for the Construction of a Gay Flower Garden*. London: Henry Colburn, 1816

Johnson, Louisa, *Every Lady Her Own Flower Gardener*. London: William S. Orr, 1851

——, [By a Lady], *Every Lady's Guide to Her Own Greenhouse*. London: n.p., 1851

[Kent, Elizabeth], *Flora Domestica, or, the Portable Flower-garden with Directions for the Treatment of Plants in Pots*. London: Whittaker, Treacher & Co., 1823

——, *Sylvan Sketches*. London: Whittaker, Treacher & Co., 1831

Knight, Henrietta Baroness Luxborough, Eliza Gulston and John Hodgetts, *Letters . . . To W. Shenstone, Esq. Ed. J. Hodgetts*. London: J. Dodsley, 1775

Knox, Tim, 'Lady Mary Coke's Garden at Notting Hill House', *The London Gardener*, vol. 4 (1998–9)

Laird, Mark, and John Harvey, '"Our Equally Favorite Hobby Horse": The Flower

Gardens of Lady Elizabeth Lee at Hartwell and the 2nd Earl Harcourt at Nuneham Countenay', *Garden History*, vol. 18, no. 2 (1990)

——, *The Flowering of the Landscape Garden: English Pleasure Grounds, 1720–1800*. Philadelphia: University of Pennsylvania Press, 1999

——, 'The Culture of Horticulture: Class, Consumption, and Gender in the English Landscape Garden', *Bourgeois and Aristocratic Cultural Encounters in Garden Art, 1550–1850*. Ed. M. Conan, vol. 23, Dumbarton Oaks Research Library and Collection, 2002

——, 'Mrs Delany's Circles of Cuttings & Embroidering in Home & Garden', in *Mrs Delany and Her Circle*. Eds. M. Laird and A. Weisberg-Roberts. New Haven and London: Yale Center for British Art, Sir John Soane's Museum in association with Yale University Press, 2009

le Lièvre, Audrey, 'Herb Strewer to the King', *Country Life*, 12 February 1987, pp. 72–3

Lindley, John, *An Introductory Lecture Delivered in the University of London on Thursday 30 April 1829*. London: John Taylor, 1829

Longstaff-Gowan, Todd, *The London Town Garden 1740–1840*. New Haven and London: Published for the Paul Mellon Centre for Studies in British Art by Yale University Press, 2001

Loudon, J.C., *The Gardener's Magazine and Register of Rural & Domestic Improvement*. London: Longman, Orme, Brown, Green, & Longmans, 1826

——, *The Suburban Gardener and Villa Companion*. London: Longman, Orme, Brown, Green, & Longmans, 1838

Loudon, J.C., and Mrs Loudon, *The Villa Gardener*. 2nd edn, edited by Mrs Loudon. London: W.S. Orr & Co., 1850

Loudon, Jane, *Gardening for Ladies*. London: John Murray, 1840

——, *The Ladies' Companion to the Flower-Garden*. London: William Smith, 1841

——, *The Ladies' Magazine of Gardening*, vol. 1. London: William Smith, 1842

——, *Botany for Ladies, or, a Popular Introduction to the Natural System of Plants According to the Classification of de Candolle*. London: John Murray, 1842

——, *The Ladies' Flower Garden of Ornamental Greenhouse Perennials*. London: William Smith, 1843

——, *The Lady's Country Companion*. London: Longman, Brown, Green, & Longmans, 1845

——, *British Wild Flowers*. 2nd edn. London: William S. Orr, 1846

Bibliography

Martin, Joanna, *Wives and Daughters: Women and Children in the Georgian Country House.* London: Hambledon & London, 2004

Mavor, Elizabeth, *Ladies of Llangollen.* London: Michael Joseph, 1971

Miller, James, *St Baldred of the Bass, a Pictish Legend: The Siege of Berwick.* Edinburgh: Oliver & Boyd, 1824

Murray, Lady Charlotte, *The British Garden: A Descriptive Catalogue of Hardy Plants, Indigenous or Cultivated in the Climate of Great Britain.* Bath: S. Hazard, 1799

Percy, Joan, 'Lady Luxborough (1700?–1756), Farmeress and Her Lost *Ferme Ornée*', *Hortus*, no. 14 (Summer 1990)

——, 'Maria Elizabetha Jacson and Her "Florist's Manual"', *Garden History*, vol. 20, no. 1 (1992)

Phillips, Patricia, *The Scientific Lady: A Social History of Women's Scientific Interests 1520–1918.* London: Weidenfeld & Nicolson, 1990

Powys, Caroline, and Emily J. Climenson, *Passages from the Diaries of Mrs Philip Lybbe Powys.* London: Longmans & Co., 1899

Pratt, Anne, *The Flowering Plants and Ferns of Great Britain.* London: SPCK, 1840

——, *Flowers and Their Associations.* London: Charles Knight & Co., 1840

——, *Wild Flowers.* London: SPCK, 1852

Pye, J. Henrietta, Mrs, *A Peep into the Principal Seats and Gardens at and about Twickenham . . . With a suitable companion for those who wish to visit Windsor or Hampton-Court. To which is added, A History of a little kingdom on the banks of the Thames, and of its present Sovereign, his laws, government, etc.* Ed. J. Bew, London 1775

Richardson, Tim, *The Arcadian Friends.* London: Bantam Press, 2007

Roupell, Arabella, *Specimens of the Flora of South Africa by a Lady.* 1849

Schenker, Heath, 'Women, Gardens, and the English Middle Class in the Early Nineteenth Century', *Bourgeois and Aristocratic Cultural Encounters in Garden Art, 1550–1850.* Ed. M. Conan, vol. 23, Dumbarton Oaks Research Library and Collection, 2002

Shteir, Ann B., 'Botanical Dialogues: Maria Jacson and Women's Popular Science Writing in England', *Eighteenth-Century Studies*, vol. 23, no. 3 (1990)

——, *Cultivating Women, Cultivating Science: Flora's Daughters and Botany in England 1760 to 1860.* Baltimore and London: Johns Hopkins University Press, 1996

Stott, Rebecca, *Duchess of Curiosities: The Life of Margaret, Duchess of Portland.* Welbeck: Harley Gallery, 2006

Taylor, Geoffrey, *Some Nineteenth Century Gardeners*. London: Skeffington, 1951

Vickery, Amanda, *The Gentleman's Daughter: Women's Lives in Georgian England*. New Haven and London: Yale University Press, 1998

——, *Behind Closed Doors: At Home in Georgian England*. New Haven and London: Yale University Press, 2009

Wakefield, Priscilla, *An Introduction to Botany*. 1798

Webber, Ronald, *The Early Horticulturists*. Newton Abbot: David & Charles, 1968

Willson, E.J., and James Lee, *James Lee and the Vineyard Nursery, Hammersmith*. London: Hammersmith Local History Group, 1961

Wulf, Andrea, *The Brother Gardeners: Botany, Empire and the Birth of an Obsession*. London: William Heinemann, 2008

1870 TO 1950

Agar, Madeline, *Garden Design in Theory and Practice*. 2nd edn. London: Sidgwick & Jackson, 1913

Allan, Mea, *Tom's Weeds: The Story of Rochford's and Their House Plants*. London: Faber and Faber, 1970

——, *E.A. Bowles and His Garden at Myddelton House, 1865–1954*. London: Faber and Faber, 1973

Balfour, (Lady) Eve, *The Living Soil*. London: Faber and Faber, 1943

Beeton, Samuel, *Beeton's Dictionary of Every-Day Gardening*. London: Ward Lock, 1874

Berger, Rachel, 'Kitty Lloyd Jones: Lady Gardener and Nurserywoman', *Garden History*, vol. 25, no. 1 (Summer 1997)

Blunden, Margaret, *The Countess of Warwick*. London: Cassell, 1967

Boyle, E.V. [Eleanor Vere], 'E.V.B.', *Days and Hours in a Garden*. London: Elliot Stock, 1884

——, *A Garden of Pleasure*. London: Elliot Stock, 1895

——, *The Peacock's Pleasaunce*. London: John Lane, 1908

Brown, Jane, *Gardens of a Golden Afternoon: The Story of a Partnership: Edwin Lutyens and Gertrude Jekyll*. London: Allen Lane, 1982

——, *Vita's Other World*. London: Viking, 1985

——, *Eminent Gardeners: Some People of Influence and Their Gardens 1880–1980*. London: Viking, 1990

Bibliography

Chamberlain, Edith L., and Fanny Douglas, *The Gentlewoman's Book of Gardening*. London: Henry & Co., 1892

Christie, Ella, *A Long Look at Life by Two Victorians*. London: Seeley, Service, 1940

Clark, Timothy, 'Mrs C.W. Earle (1836–1925), a Reappraisal of Her Work', *Garden History*, vol. 8, no. 2 (1980)

——, 'Flashes from a Mirror: Eleanour Sinclair Rohde and Her Gardening Books', *Country Life*, 21 April 1983, pp. 1045–53

Cran, Marion, *The Garden of Experience*. [s.l.]: Herbert Jenkins, 1921

——, *The Garden of Ignorance: The Experiences of a Woman in a Garden*. [s.l.]: Herbert Jenkins, 1924

——, *The Story of My Ruin*. [s.l.]: Herbert Jenkins, 1924

——, *Garden Talks*. London: Methuen, 1925

——, *The Garden Beyond*. [s.l.]: Herbert Jenkins, 1937

——, *Hogar's Garden*. [s.l.]: Herbert Jenkins, 1941

du Cane, Florence, *The Flowers and Gardens of Japan*. London: A. & C. Black, 1908

——, *The Flowers and Gardens of Madeira*. London: Adam & Charles Black, 1909

Earle, Mrs C.W., *Pot-Pourri from a Surrey Garden*. [1897] Chichester: Summersdale, 2004

——, *More Pot-Pourri from a Surrey Garden*. London: Smith, Elder, 1899

——, *A Third Pot-Pourri*. London: Smith, Elder, 1903

Ely, Helena Rutherfurd, *A Woman's Hardy Garden*. New York: Macmillan, 1903

Festing, Sally, 'Viscountess Wolseley and Her College for Lady Gardeners', *The Garden (Journal Royal Horticultural Society)*, vol. 106 (1981)

——, *Gertrude Jekyll*. London: Penguin Books, 1993

——, *Gertrude Jekyll 1843–1932: A Celebration*. London: Museum of Garden History, 1993

Grieve, Maud, and Hilda Winifred Wauton Leyel, *A Modern Herbal*. London: Jonathan Cape, 1931

Haweis, Mary Eliza, *Rus in Urbe: Or, Flowers That Thrive in London Gardens and Smoky Towns, Etc.* London: Field & Tuer, 1886

Hayward, Allyson, *Norah Lindsay: The Life and Art of a Garden Designer*. London: Frances Lincoln, 2007

Helmreich, Anne, *The English Garden and National Identity: The Competing Styles of Garden Design, 1870–1914*. Cambridge: Cambridge University Press, 2002

Hope, Frances Jane, Miss, and Anne J. Hope Johnstone, *Notes and Thoughts on Gardens and Woodlands*. London: Macmillan, 1881

Jekyll, Gertrude, *Wood and Garden*. London: Longmans, Green, 1899

——, *Home and Garden*. London: Longmans, Green, 1900

——, *Lilies for English Gardens*. London: Newnes/Country Life, 1901

——, *Children and Gardens*. London: Newnes/Country Life, 1908

——, *Colour in the Flower Garden*. London: Newnes/Country Life, 1908

——, 'Women as Gardeners', *Country Life*, 29 April 1916, pp. 541–2

——, *Garden Ornament*. London: Country Life, 1918

Jekyll, Gertrude, and Sir Lawrence Weaver, *Gardens for Small Country Houses*. London: Country Life, 1924

le Lièvre, Audrey, *Miss Willmott of Warley Place: Her Life and Her Gardens*. London: Faber and Faber, 1980

Leyel, Hilda, *The Magic of Herbs: A Modern Book of Secrets*. London: Jonathan Cape, 1926

——, *Herbal Delights*. [s.n.], 1937

——, *Truth about Herbs*. [s.n.], 1943

——, *Compassionate Herbs*. London: Faber and Faber, 1946

——, *Elixirs of Life*. London: Faber and Faber, 1948

Lindsay, Norah, 'Where is Spring?', *Country Life*, 65, 1929, pp. 387–90

——, 'The Garden in July', *Country Life*, 66, 1929, pp. 78–80

——, 'The Manor House – 1. Sutton Courtney, Berks', *Country Life*, 69, 1931, pp. 610–16

Macartney, Lady, *An English Lady in Chinese Turkestan*. London: Ernest Benn, 1931

Meredith, Anne M., 'Horticultural Eduction in England, 1900–40: Middle-Class Women and Private Gardening Schools', *Garden History*, vol. 31, no. 1 (Spring 2003)

Morrell, Ottoline, *Ottoline at Garsington: Memoirs of Lady Ottoline Morrell, 1915–1918*. London: Faber and Faber, 1974

Morris, William, *Hopes and Fears for Art: Five Lectures Delivered in Birmingham, London, and Nottingham, 1878-1881*. London: Ellis and White, 1882

Nevill, Guy, *Exotic Groves: A Portrait of Lady Dorothy Nevill*. Salisbury: Michael Russell, 1984

Ormerod, Eleanor A., and Robert Wallace, *Eleanor Ormerod Ll.D, Economic Entomologist, Autobiography and Correspondence*. London: John Murray, 1904

Bibliography

Rohde, Eleanour Sinclair, *The Old English Herbals*. London: Longmans, 1922

——, *The Old English Gardening Books*. London: M. Hopkinson, 1924

——, *A Garden of Herbs*. London: H. Jenkins, 1926

——, *The Scented Garden*. London: Medici Society, 1932

——, *Herbs and Herb Gardening*. London: Medici Society, 1936

——, *The War-Time Vegetable Garden*. London: Medici Society, 1940

Sanecki, Kay, 'Hard Work in High Society', *Hortus*, no. 2 (Summer 1987)

——, *A Short History of Studley College*. [Studley College Trust], 1990

——, 'The Ladies and the Gentlemen', *Hortus*, no. 32 (Winter 1994)

Seymour, Miranda, *Ottoline Morrell: Life on a Grand Scale*. London: Hodder & Stoughton, 1992

Stearn, William T., 'Mrs Robb and "Mrs Robb's bonnet" (*Euphorbia robbiae*)', *JRHS*, vol. 98 (1973), pp. 306–10

Stewart, Averil, *Alicella: A Memoir of Alice King Stewart and Ella Christie, 1861–1949*. London: John Murray, 1955

Stout, Mary, and Madeline Agar, *A Book of Gardening for the Sub-Tropics, with a Calendar for Cairo, Etc.* [s.l.]: H.F. & G. Witherby, 1921

Trotter, W.R., 'The Glasshouses at Dangstein and their Contents', *Garden History*, vol. 16, no. 1 (1988)

Warwick, Frances Evelyn Maynard Greville, *Life's Ebb and Flow*. London: W. Morrow & Company, 1929

Willmott, Ellen, *The Genus Rosa*, 2 vols. London: John Murray, 1914

——, *Warley Garden in Spring and Summer*. London: Bernard Quaritch, 1909

Willmott, E.A., and Sotheby & Co., England, *Catalogue of Valuable Books and Manuscripts on Botany, Music and General Subjects Selected from the Library at Warley Place, Essex; the Property of Miss E. A. Willmott (Decd.) (Sold by Order of the Executor) . . . Which Will Be Sold by Auction by Messrs. Sotheby & Co . . . 1st April, 1935, and Two Following Days*. Printed by Kitchen & Barratt Ltd, 1935

Wolseley, Frances, Viscountess Wolseley, *Gardening for Women*. London: Cassell, 1908

——, *In a College Garden*. London: John Murray, 1916

——, *Women and the Land*. London: Chatto & Windus, 1916

——, *Gardens: Their Form and Design*. London: Edward Arnold, 1919

Wood, Martin (ed.), *The Unknown Gertrude Jekyll*. London: Frances Lincoln, 2006

Wood, Samuel, *The Ladies' Multum-in-Parvo Flower Garden*. London: Crosby Lockwood & Co., 1881

1950 ONWARDS

Andrews, Maggie, *The Acceptable Face of Feminism: The Women's Institute as a Social Movement*. London: Lawrence & Wishart, 1997

August, Ian, *The Making of the Alnwick Garden*. London: Pavilion, 2006

'Beth Chatto', *Garden Museum Journal*, issue 21 (Winter 2008)

Brownlow, Margaret, *Herbs and the Fragrant Garden*. London: Darton, Longman & Todd, 1957

——, *The Delights of Herb Growing*. [s.l.]: the author in association with Herb Farm Ltd, 1966

Buchan, Ursula, *Garden People: The Photographs of Valerie Finnis*. London: Thames & Hudson, 2007

Chatto, Beth, *The Dry Garden*. London: J.M. Dent, 1978

——, *The Damp Garden*. London: J.M. Dent, 1982

——, 'Mrs Desmond Underwood – the Silver Queen', *Hortus*, no. 5 (Spring 1988)

——, *Beth Chatto's Gravel Garden*. London: Frances Lincoln, 2000

——, *Beth Chatto's Woodland Garden*. London: Cassell Illustrated, 2002

Chivers, Susan, and Suzanne Woloszynska, *The Cottage Garden: Margery Fish at East Lambrook Manor*. London: John Murray, 1990

Cochrane, Carola. *Two Acres Unlimited: A Market Garden Success Story*. London: Crosby Lockwood & Son, 1954

Colborn, Nigel, 'Lady Anne Palmer, Creator of Rosemoor', *Hortus*, no. 4 (Winter 1987)

——, 'Dr Miriam Rothschild', *Hortus*, no. 9 (Spring 1989)

Dillon, Helen, *The Flower Garden*. London: Conran Octopus, 1993

——, *Helen Dillon on Gardening*. Dublin: TownHouse, 2005

——, *Helen Dillon's Garden Book*. London: Frances Lincoln, 2007

Fish, Margery, *We Made a Garden*. London: Collingridge, 1956

——, *An All the Year Garden*. London: Collingridge, 1958

——, *Cottage Garden Flowers*. London: Collingridge, 1961

——, *Ground Cover Plants*. London: Collingridge, 1963

Bibliography

——, *Gardening in the Shade*. London: Collingridge, 1964

——, *Carefree Gardening*. London: Collingridge, 1966

——, *Gardening on Clay and Lime*. Newton Abbot: David & Charles, 1970

——, *A Flower for Every Day*. Newton Abbot: David & Charles, 1973

Hess, Elizabeth, 'Opportunities for Women in Horticulture: Lecture Given on 24th March 1964', *Journal of the Royal Horticultural Society*, vol. 89 (July 1964)

Hobhouse, Penelope, *Colour in Your Garden*. London: Collins, 1985

——, 'Phyllis Reiss at Tintinhull', *Hortus*, no. 1 (Spring 1987)

——, *The Country Gardener*. London: Little, Brown, 1989

——, *Penelope Hobhouse's Gardening through the Ages*. London: Simon & Schuster, 1992

——, *The Gardens of Persia*. London: Cassell Illustrated, 2006

Hunniger, Erica (ed.), *Making Gardens: A Celebration of Gardens and Gardening in England and Wales from the National Gardens Scheme*. London: Cassell & Co., 2001

Hyatt, Brenda, *Auriculas: Their Care and Cultivation*. London: Cassell, 1989

Larkcom, Joy, *Vegetables from Small Gardens*. London: Faber and Faber, 1976

——, *Oriental Vegetables*. London: John Murray, 1991

——, *Salads for Small Gardens*. London: Hamlyn, 1995

Lees-Milne, Alvilde, and Rosemary Verey, *The Englishwoman's Garden*. London: Chatto & Windus, 1980

Maddy, Ursula, *Waterperry: A Dream Fulfilled*. Oxfordshire: Waterperry, 2001

Nicolson, Adam, *Sissinghurst*. Swindon: National Trust, 2008

Perry, Frances, *The Woman Gardener*. London: Hulton Press, 1955

——, *Shrubs and Trees for the Smaller Garden*. London: C. Arthur Pearson, 1961

——, *Flowering Bulbs*. London: Ebury Press, 1966

——, *The Water Garden*. London: Ward Lock, 1981

Sackville-West, V., *In Your Garden*. London: Michael Joseph, 1951

——, *In Your Garden Again*. London: Michael Joseph, 1953

——, *More for Your Garden*. London: Michael Joseph, 1955

——, *Even More for Your Garden*. London: Michael Joseph, 1958

Simpson, Bill, *Gardening for Wives*. London: Corgi, 1967

Stearn, William T., 'Obituary: Miss Alice Margaret Coats (1905–78)', *Garden History*, vol. 6, no. 3 (1978)

Traeger, Tessa, and Patrick Kinmonth, *A Gardener's Labyrinth: Portraits of People, Plants and Places*. London: Booth-Clibborn Editions, 2003

Underwood, Mrs Desmond, *Grey and Silver Plants*. London: Collins, 1971

Verey, Rosemary, *Classic Garden Design: How to Adapt and Recreate Garden Features of the Past*. London: Viking, 1984

———, 'The Making of an English Garden – part one', *Hortus*, no. 8 (Winter 1988)

———, *Rosemary Verey's Garden Plans*. London: Frances Lincoln, 1993

———, *The English Country Garden*. London: BBC Books, 1996

Verey, Rosemary, with Alvilde Lees-Milne, *The Englishwoman's Garden*. London: Chatto & Windus, 1980

———, *The New Englishwoman's Garden*. London: Chatto & Windus, 1987

Wilson, Karen, *Rosemoor*. London: Royal Horticultural Society, 2002

FLORAL ARTS

Beck, Thomasina, *The Embroiderer's Garden*. Newton Abbot: David & Charles, 1988

———, *The Embroiderer's Flowers*. Newton Abbot: David & Charles, 1992

———, *The Embroiderer's Story: Needlework from the Renaissance to the Present Day*. Newton Abbot: David & Charles, 1999

Bermingham, Ann, *Learning to Draw: Studies in the Cultural History of a Polite and Useful Art*. New Haven and London: Published for the Paul Mellon Centre for Studies in British Art by Yale University Press, 2000

Berrall, Julia S., *A History of Flower Arrangement*. London: Thames & Hudson, 1978

Blacker, M.R., *Flora Domestica: A History of Flower Arranging 1500–1930*. London: National Trust, 2000

Blunt, William, and William Stern, *The Art of Botanical Illustration*. Woodbridge: Antique Collectors' Club, 1994

Brookshaw, George, *A New Treatise on Flower Painting, or, Every Lady Her Own Drawing Master*. Longman, Hurst, Rees, Orme, & Brown, 1818

Brotherston, R.P., *The Book of Cut Flowers*. London: T.N. Foulis, 1906

Browne, Clare, 'Mary Delany's Embroidered Court Dress', in *Mrs Delany and Her Circle*. Eds M. Laird and A. Weisberg-Roberts. New Haven and London: Yale Center for British Art, Sir John Soane's Museum in association with Yale University Press, 2009

Clayton, Ellen C., *English Female Artists*. London: Tinsley Brothers, 1876

Bibliography

Clements, Julia, *Fun with Flowers*. London: C. Arthur Pearson, 1950

——, *Flower Arranging*. London: Newnes, 1966

——, *My Life with Flowers*. London: Cassell, 1993

Coxhead, Elizabeth, *Constance Spry: A Biography.* London: Luscombe, 1975

Hassard, Annie, *Floral Decorations for Dwelling Houses*. London: Macmillan, 1875

Hobhouse, Penelope, and Christopher Wood, *Painted Gardens: English Watercolours 1850–1914*. New York: Atheneum, 1988

Jekyll, Gertrude, *Flower Decoration in the House*. [1907] Woodbridge: Antique Collectors' Club, 1982

Laird, Mark, 'Exotics and Botanical Illustration', in *Sir John Vanbrugh and Landscape Architecture in Baroque England, 1690–1730*. Eds C. Ridgway, R. Williams and J. Vanbrugh. Stroud: Sutton in assocation with the National Trust, 2000

Laird, Mark, and Alicia Weisberg-Roberts (eds.), *Mrs Delany and Her Circle*. New Haven and London: Yale Center for British Art, Sir John Soane's Museum in association with Yale University Press, 2009

Lamplugh, Anne, *Flower and Vase*. London: Country Life, 1937

Lawrance, Mary, *A Collection of Roses from Nature*. Published by Miss Lawrance, teacher of botanical drawing, &c. No. 86 Queen Ann street, East, Portland place, 1799

——, *Proposals for Publishing by Subscription: A Collection of Passion-Flowers from Nature*. 1799

le Lièvre, Audrey, 'Flower Painter Extraordinary', *Country Life*, 2 February 1989, pp. 66–9

Macqueen, Sheila, *Flowers for Arrangement*. London: Collingridge, 1962

——, *Sheila Macqueen's Complete Flower Arranging*. London: Papermac, 1986

Maling, E.A., *A Handbook for Ladies on in-Door Plants, Flowers for Ornament and Song Birds*. London: Smith, Elder & Co., 1867

March, T.C., *Flower and Fruit Decoration*. London: Harrison, 1862

Mee, Margaret, and Tony Morrison, *Margaret Mee in Search of Flowers of the Amazon Forests*. Woodbridge: Nonesuch Expeditions, 1988

Mongon, Agnes, 'A Fête of Flowers: Women Artists' Contribution to Botanical Illustration', *Apollo*, no. 119 (April 1984)

Moriarty, Henrietta Maria, *Viridarium: Coloured Plates of Greenhouse Plants*. 2nd edn. London: J. White, 1806

Nichols, Beverley, *The Art of Flower Arrangement*. London: Collins, 1967

Bibliography

North, Marianne, *A Vision of Eden: The Life and Work of Marianne North*. Exeter: Webb & Bower in association with the Royal Botanic Gardens, Kew, 1980

Peachey, Emma, *The Royal Guide to Wax Flower Modelling*. Published and sold by Mrs. Peachey, 1851

Perkins, John, *Floral Designs for the Table, Being Directions for Its Ornamentation with Leaves, Flowers, and Fruit*. London: Wyman, 1877

Pointon, Marcia R., *Strategies for Showing: Women, Possession, and Representation in English Visual Culture, 1665–1800*. Oxford: Oxford University Press, 1997

Saunders, Jill, *Picturing Plants: An Analytical History of Botanical Illustration*. London: University of California Press in association with the Victoria & Albert Museum, 1995

Scrase, David, *Flower Drawings*. Cambridge: Cambridge University Press, 1997

Sherwood, Shirley, *A Passion for Plants*. London: Cassell, 2001

———, *A New Flowering: 1000 Years of Botanical Art*. Oxford: Ashmolean, 2005

Spry, Constance, *Flower Decoration*. London: J.M. Dent, 1934

———, *Flowers in House and Garden*. London: J.M. Dent, 1937

———, *Constance Spry's Garden Notebook*. London: J.M. Dent, 1940

———, *Summer and Autumn Flowers*. London: J.M. Dent, 1951

———, *Winter and Spring Flowers*. London: J.M. Dent, 1951

———, *Party Flowers*. London: J.M. Dent, 1955

———, *Simple Flowers: 'A Millionaire for a Few Pence'*. London: J.M. Dent, 1957

Stewart, Amy, *Gilding the Lily: Inside the Cut Flower Industry*. London: Portobello, 2009

Tongiorgi Tomasi, Lucia, and Oak Spring Garden Library, *An Oak Spring Flora: Flower Illustration from the Fifteenth Century to the Present Time: A Selection of the Rare Books, Manuscripts, and Works of Art in the Collection of Rachel Lambert Mellon*. Oak Spring Garden Library: distributed by Yale University Press, 1997

Tyas, Robert, *The Sentiment of Flowers, or, Language of Flora*. London: Houlston & Stoneman, 1844

———, *The Language of Flower: Or, Floral Emblems of Thoughts, Feelings, and Sentiments*. London: Routledge, 1869

Vickery, Amanda, 'The Theory & Practice of Female Accomplishment', in *Mrs Delany and Her Circle*. Eds M. Laird and A. Weisberg-Roberts. New Haven and London: Yale Center for British Art, Sir John Soane's Museum in association with Yale University Press, 2009

Bibliography

Walpole, Josephine, *A History and Dictionary of British Flower Painters, 1650–1950.* Woodbridge: Antique Collectors' Club, 2006

Ward, Marilyn, and John Flanagan, 'Portraying Plants: Illustrations Collections at the Royal Botanic Gardens, Kew', *Art Libraries Journal,* 28 February 2003, [n.p.]

NOTES

Introduction

1 Miles Hadfield, *A History of British Gardening* (London: Penguin, 1985), p. 46.
2 Gertrude Jekyll, *Wall and Water Gardens* (London: C. Scribner's Sons, 1901), p. 141.
3 Helen Dillon, *Helen Dillon's Garden Book* (London: Frances Lincoln, 2007), p. 215.
4 Talk given at the Garden Museum, 15 April 2009.

A PASSION FOR PLANTS

1 *Gardeners' Chronicle*, 25 December 1875.

'What Progress She Made . . .'

1 John Parkinson and A. Switzer, *Paradisi in Sole Paradisus Terrestris* (London: Humfrey Lownes and Robert Young, 1629), p. 348.
2 Quoted in Douglas Chambers, '"Storys of Plants": The Assembling of Mary Capel Somerset's Botanical Collection at Badminton', *Journal of the History of Collecting*, vol. 9, no. 1 (1997), p. 49.
3 Quoted in Molly McClain, *Beaufort: The Duke and His Duchess 1657–1715* (New Haven and London: Yale University Press, 2001), p. 118.
4 Chambers, '"Storys of Plants"', p. 50.
5 Stephen Switzer, *The Nobleman, Gentleman, and Gardener's Recreation* (London: B. Barker and C. King, 1715), p. 54.
6 Chambers, '"Storys of Plants"', p. 49.
7 David Brontë Green, *Gardener to Queen Anne: Henry Wise (1653–1738) and the Formal Garden* (Oxford: Oxford University Press, 1956), p. 32.

8 British Library, Sloane MS 4063, fol. 44.

9 Chambers, '"Storys of Plants"', p. 50.

10 Ruth Duthie, 'The Planting Plans of Some Seventeenth Century Flower Gardens', *Garden History*, vol. 18, no. 2 (1990), p. 88.

11 Switzer, *Nobleman*, p. 54.

12 *Curtis's Botanical Magazine*, vol. 42 (1815), plate 1733.

13 Quoted in Sally Festing, 'Grace without Triviality: The 2nd Duchess of Portland and her Circle – II', *Country Life*, 19 June 1986, p. 1773.

14 Caroline Powys and Emily J. Climenson, *Passages from the Diaries of Mrs Philip Lybbe Powys* (London: Longmans & Co., 1899), p. 121.

15 Papers of Margaret Bentinck, Duchess of Portland (1717–1785) in the Portland (Welbeck) Collection, University of Nottingham (PMB), PwE 22.

16 PMB, PwE 18.

17 Charles Abbot, *Flora Bedfordiensis, comprehending such plants as grow wild in the county of Bedford, arranged according to the system of Linnæus* (Bedford: [s.n.], 1798), pp. iii-iv.

Home and Abroad

1 Mary Delany et al., *The Autobiography and Correspondence of Mary Granville, Mrs Delany* (London: Richard Bentley, 1861), p. 559.

2 John Lindley, *An Introductory Lecture Delivered in the University of London on Thursday 30 April 1829* (London: John Taylor, 1829), p. 17.

3 *Curtis's Botanical Magazine* (1806), plate 977.

4 Ray Desmond, *Dictionary of British and Irish Botanists and Horticulturists: Including Plant Collectors and Botanical Artists* (London: Taylor & Francis, 1977), p. 10.

5 Ray Desmond, *The European Discovery of the Indian Flora* (Oxford: Royal Botanic Gardens, Kew, with Oxford University Press, 1992), p. 86.

6 Ibid., p. 272.

7 J.C. Loudon, *The Gardener's Magazine and Register of Rural & Domestic Improvement* (1826), p. 254.

8 Lady Macartney, *An English Lady in Chinese Turkestan* (London: Ernest Benn, 1931), p. 119.

9 Ibid., pp. 119–20.

10 Parliamentary Archives: HL/PO/PB/1/1757/30G2n82 Private Act, 30 George II, c.42.

11 'Clas Alströmer to Carl Linnaeus, 10 July 1764', *The Linnaean correspondence*, http://linnaeus.c18.net, letter L3427 (consulted 26 May 2009).

12 Wilfrid Blunt, *The Compleat Naturalist: A Life of Linnaeus* (London: Collins, 1984), p. 224.

13 E.J. Willson and James Lee, *James Lee and the Vineyard Nursery, Hammersmith* (London: Hammersmith Local History Group, 1961), p. 32.

14 Ibid., p. 40.

15 Ibid.

16 Lady Anne Lindsay Barnard, *South Africa a Century Ago: Letters Written from the Cape of Good Hope 1797–1801* (London: Smith, Elder & Co., 1925), p. 45.

17 Lady Anne Lindsay Barnard, *The Cape Diaries of Lady Anne Lindsay Barnard* (Cape Town: Van Riebeeck Society, 1999), p. 131.

Behind the Microscope

1 Ann B. Shteir, *Cultivating Women, Cultivating Science: Flora's Daughters and Botany in England 1760 to 1860* (Baltimore and London: Johns Hopkins University Press, 1996), p. 169.

2 David Elliston Allen, 'The Women Members of the Botanical Society of London, 1836–1856', *The British Journal for the History of Science*, vol. 13, no. 45 (1980), p. 240.

3 Eleanor A. Ormerod and Robert Wallace, *Eleanor Ormerod Ll.D Economic Entomologist, Autobiography and Correspondence* (London: John Murray, 1904), p. 54.

4 Ibid., p. 83.

5 Ibid., p. 86.

6 Archives of Royal Holloway, University of London (RHUL), PP26/1/9.

7 RHUL, PP26/12.

Stoves and Society

1 *Gardener's Magazine* (1834), p. 337.

2 Ibid., pp. 340–1.

3 Ibid., p. 337.

4 Jane Loudon, *The Ladies' Magazine of Gardening*, vol. 1 (London: William Smith, 1842), p. 223.

5 *Gardener's Magazine* (1838), p. 310.

6 Archive of the Royal Botanic Gardens, Kew (RBGK), Letters of Sir William Hooker, no. 326.

7 W.R. Trotter, 'The Glasshouses at Dangstein and Their Contents', *Garden History*, vol. 16, no. 1 (1988), p. 85.

8 Guy Nevill, *Exotic Groves: A Portrait of Lady Dorothy Nevill* (Salisbury: Michael Russell, 1984), p. 113.

From Seed to Show

1 *Gardeners' Chronicle*, 8 May 1880, p. 585.

2 Frances Jane Hope, *Notes and Thoughts on Gardens and Woodlands* (London: Macmillan, 1881), p. xv.

3 Mrs C.W. Earle, *Pot Pourri from a Surrey Garden* [1897] (Chichester: Summersdale, 2004), p. 254.

4 *Gardeners' Chronicle*, 25 December 1875.

5 William Stearn, 'Mrs Robb and "Mrs Robb's bonnet" (*Euphorbia robbiae*)', *Journal of the Royal Horticultural Society*, vol. 98, 1973, pp. 306–7.

6 Ibid., p. 309.

7 Betty Massingham, *A Century of Gardeners* (London: Faber and Faber, 1982), p. 133.

8 Ibid., p. 132.

9 Audrey le Lièvre, *Miss Willmott of Warley Place* (London: Faber and Faber, 1980), p. 121.

Cultivating the New

1 Miles Hadfield, *A History of British Gardening* (London: Penguin, 1985), p. 119.

2 Brenda Hyatt, *Auriculas: Their Care and Cultivation* (London: Cassell, 1989), p. 8.

3 Alvilde Lees-Milne and Rosemary Verey, *The Englishwoman's Garden* (London: Chatto & Windus, 1980), p. 84.

4 *Quarterly Bulletin of the Alpine Garden Society*, vol. 36, no. 2, June 1968, p. 203.

5 *Gardeners' Chronicle*, 20 April 1940, p. 194.

6 Mrs Desmond Underwood, *Grey and Silver Plants* (London: Collins, 1971), p. 9.

7 Beth Chatto, 'Mrs Desmond Underwood – the Silver Queen', *Hortus*, 5 (Spring 1988), p. 62.

8 *Daily Telegraph*, 28 August 1999.

SHAPING THE LANDSCAPE

1 Thomas Harris, 'The Lady's Diversion in Her Garden', in Hannah Wolley, *The Accomplisht Ladys Delight* (London: Benjamin Harris, 1675), p. 161.

The Grand Design

1 Stephen Switzer, *The Nobleman, Gentleman, and Gardener's Recreation* (London: B. Barker and C. King, 1715), p. 55.

2 Charles Evelyn, *The Lady's Recreation* (London: J. Roberts, 1717), p. 1.

3 William Lawson, *The Country Housewife's Garden* [1617] (London: Breslich & Foss, 1983), p. 15.

4 Switzer, *Nobleman*, p. 55.

5 James Miller, *St Baldred of the Bass, a Pictish Legend: The Siege of Berwick* (Edinburgh: Oliver & Boyd, 1824).

6 Rosalind K. Marshall, 'Hope, Helen, Countess of Haddington (*bap.* 1677, *d.* 1768', *Oxford Dictionary of National Biography* (Oxford: Oxford University Press, 2004).

7 Huntington Library (HL), MO 1124, c. 1780, George Simon Harcourt, 2nd Earl of Harcourt, to Elizabeth Montagu.

8 HL, MO 6514, 1778, Elizabeth Montagu to Elizabeth Vesey.

9 HL, MO 6565, 1781, Elizabeth Montagu to Elizabeth Vesey.

10 Quoted in Edward Hyams, *Capability Brown and Humphry Repton* (London: Dent, 1971), p. 105.

11 Quoted in Stephen Bending, 'Mrs Montague's Contemplative Bench: Bluestocking gardens and female retirement', *Huntington Library Quarterly*, vol. 68, no. 4 (Winter 2006), p. 577.

12 John Phibbs, 'Brown, Lancelot [Capability Brown] (*bap.* 1716, *d.* 1783)', *Oxford Dictionary of National Biography* (Oxford: Oxford University Press, 2004).

13 Mark Laird, '"Our Equally Favorite Hobby Horse": The Flower Gardens of Lady Elizabeth Lee at Hartwell and the 2nd Earl Harcourt at Nuneham Courtney', *Garden History*, vol. 18, no. 2 (1990), pp. 141–2, fn. 62.

14 Ibid., p. 106.

15 Ibid.

16 Ibid., pp. 139-140, fn. 12.

17 Ibid., p. 108.

'My Little Paradise'

1 Royal Archives (RA), RA/GEO/Add 9/124, Queen Charlotte to Augustus, Duke of Sussex (6th son of George III), 11 February 1791.

2 RA, RA/GEO/MAIN/55624, RA/GEO/MAIN/55557, RA/GEO/MAIN/ 55545.

3 RA, Queen Charlotte to [Augustus] Duke of Sussex, 13 January 1798. RA/GEO/Add 9/158.

4 RA, RA/GEO/Add 9/124, Queen Charlotte to Augustus, Duke of Sussex, 11 February 1791.

5 Caroline Powys and Emily J. Climenson, *Passages from the Diaries of Mrs Philip Lybbe Powys* (London: Longmans & Co., 1899), p. 158.

For the Love of Gardening

1 Jane Brown, *My Darling Heriott: Henrietta Luxborough, Poetic Gardener and Irrepressible Exile* (London: HarperPress, 2006), p. 82.

2 Joan Percy, 'Lady Luxborough (1700?–1756), Farmeress and Her Lost *Ferme Ornée*', *Hortus*, no. 14 (Summer 1990), p. 90.

3 Brown, *My Darling Heriott*, p. 148.

4 Wrest Park, Family and Estate Papers, Bedfordshire Record Office, L30/9/50/18, quoted in Mark Laird, 'The Culture of Horticulture: Class, Consumption, and Gender in the English Landscape Garden', in *Bourgeois and Aristocratic Cultural Encounters in Garden Art, 1550–1850*, ed. M. Conan, vol. 23, Dumbarton Oaks Research Library and Collection (2002), p. 228.

5 Percy, 'Lady Luxborough', p. 92.

6 Brown, *My Darling Heriott*, p. 227.

7 Lady Mary Coke, *The Letters and Journals of Lady Mary Coke*, ed. J.A. Home (Bath: [Kingsmead Bookshops], 1970), p. 135.

8 Tim Knox, 'Lady Mary Coke's Garden at Notting Hill House', *The London Gardener*, vol. 4 (1998), p. 55.

9 Coke, *Letters and Journals*, p. 245.

10 Ibid., p. 166.

11 Knox, 'Lady Mary Coke's Garden', p. 60.

12 Coke, *Letters and Journals*, p. 249.

13 Knox, 'Lady Mary Coke's Garden', p. 58.

14 Ibid.

15 Coke, *Letters and Journals*, p. 249.

16 Brown, *My Darling Heriott*, p. 227.

17 Mary Lepel, Baroness Hervey, and Edmund Morris, *Letters of Mary Lepel, Lady Hervey* ([s.n.], 1821), p. 106.

18 Ibid.

19 Ibid., p. 97.

20 Elizabeth Carter, *A Series of Letters between Mrs Elizabeth Carter and Miss Catherine Talbot from the Year 1741 to 1770* (London: C. & J. Rivington, 1808), p. 395, 15 July 1751.

21 Ibid., p. 222, 26 October 1747.

22 Ibid., p. 230, 29 October 1747.

23 Stephen Daniels, *Humphry Repton: The Red Books for Brandsbury and Glemham Hall* (Harvard: Harvard University Press for Dumbarton Oaks, 1994), pp. x–xi.

24 Ibid., p. xi.

25 Christina Colvin and Charles Nelson, '"Building Castles of Flower": Maria Edgeworth as Gardener', *Garden History*, vol. 16, no. 1 (1988), p. 61.

26 Ibid., p. 63.

Autumn Flowerings

1 Jane Brown, *Gardens of a Golden Afternoon: The Story of a Partnership: Edwin Lutyens and Gertrude Jekyll* (London: Allen Lane, 1982), p. 24.

2 Gertrude Jekyll, *Home and Garden* (Longmans, Green, and Co., 1900), p. 117.

3 *The Garden*, 120, April 1995, p. 218.

4 Averil Stewart, *Alicella: A Memoir of Alice King Stewart and Ella Christie, 1861–1949* (London: John Murray, 1955), p. 210.

5 Letter, 24 April 1907, Kyoto, in Stewart, *Alicella*, p. 203.

6 Stewart, *Alicella*, p. 210.

7 Ibid., p. 211.

8 Ibid., p. 212.

9 Ibid., p. 214.

10 Ibid., p. 215.

11 Ibid., p. 216.

12 Allyson Hayward, *Norah Lindsay: The Life and Art of a Garden Designer* (London: Frances Lincoln, 2007), p. 50.

13 Norah Lindsay, 'The Manor House – I. Sutton Courtney, Berks', *Country Life*, 23 May 1931, p. 612.

14 Jane Brown, *Eminent Gardeners: Some People of Influence and Their Gardens 1880–1980* (London: Viking, 1990), p. 72.

Breaking New Ground

1 *Landscape Design*, 125 (1979), p. 8.

2 Ibid.

3 Ibid.

4 Ibid.

5 Dawn MacLeod, *Down-to-Earth Women: Those Who Care for the Soil* (London: William Blackwood, 1982), p. 150.

6 *The Times*, 10 July 1997.

A Growing Legacy

1 Mrs J. Henrietta Pye, *A Short View of the Principal Seats and Gardens in and about Twickenham*, (London: J. Bew 1775)

2 Adam Nicolson, *Sissinghurst* (Swindon: National Trust, 2008), p. 18.

3 Vita Sackville-West, *In Your Garden* (London: Michael Joseph, 1951), p. 7.

4 Vita Sackville-West, *More for Your Garden* (London: Michael Joseph, 1955), p. 6.

5 *The Times*, 12 January 1933.

6 *Daily Telegraph*, 9 October 2004.

7 Karen Wilson, *Rosemoor* (London: Royal Horticultural Society, 2002), p. 26.

8 Alvilde Lees-Milne and Rosemary Verey, *The Englishwoman's Garden* (London: Chatto & Windus, 1980), pp. 23–4.

9 British Library, British Library Sound Archive, *Down to Earth: An Oral History of British Horticulture*, ed. Louise Brodie, 'Penelope Hobhouse, 1929–'.

10 Ibid.

11 *Gardens Illustrated*, December 2000.

12 Ibid.

13 *The Times*, 28 August 2004.

14 *Gardens Illustrated*, December 2000.

15 Correspondence with author, June 2009.

MOTHER EARTH

1 Jane Loudon, *The Lady's Country Companion* (London: Longman, Brown, Green & Longmans, 1845), p. 200.

'Here's Al Fine Herbs of Every Sort'

1 Lady Margaret Hoby and D.M. Meads, *Diary of Lady Margaret Hoby* (London: Routledge, 1930), p. x.

2 Lady Margaret Hoby and Joanna Moody, *The Private Life of an Elizabethan Lady: The Diary of Lady Margaret Hoby, 1599–1605* (Stroud: Sutton, 1998), p. 211.

3 Ibid., p. 18.

4 Miles Hadfield, *Pioneers in Gardening* (London: Bloomsbury, 1996), p. 12.

5 William Lawson, *The Country Housewife's Garden* [1617] (London: Breslich & Foss, 1983), p. 22.

6 Ibid., p. 23.

7 William Coles, *The Art of Simpling, or, An Introduction to the Knowledge and Gathering of Herbs* [1656] (Pomeroy, WA: Kessinger Publishing, 2004), p. 112.

8 Ibid.

9 [Anthony Fitzherbert], *Here Begynneth a Newe Tracte or Treatyse Moost Profytable for All Husbandemen: And Very Fruitefull for Al Other Persons to Rede* (R. Pynson, 1523), p. 61.

10 Lawson, *Country Housewife's Garden*, p. 34.

11 C. Paul Christianson, 'Herbwomen in London 1660–1836', *The London Gardener*, vol. 6 (2000), p. 28.

12 Levinus Lemnius, 'Notes on England' [1560], in William Brenchley Rye (ed.), *England as Seen by Foreigners* ([s.l.]: [s.n.], 1865), p. 80.

13 Audrey le Lièvre, 'Herb Strewer to the King', *Country Life*, 12 February 1987, p. 72.

14 Christianson, 'Herbwomen in London', p. 28.

15 Jane Loudon, *The Lady's Country Companion* (London: Longman, Brown, Green, & Longmans, 1845), p. 200.

16 Edith Chamberlain and Fanny Douglas, *The Gentlewoman's Book of Gardening* (London: Henry & Co., 1892), p. 183.

Daughters of Ceres

1 Maud Grieve and Hilda Leyel, *A Modern Herbal* (London: Jonathan Cape, 1931), p. xiv.

2 Hilda Leyel, *Truth About Herbs* ([s.n.], 1943), p. 28.

3 Hilda Leyel, *The Magic of Herbs: A Modern Book of Secrets* (London: Jonathan Cape, 1926), p. 29.

4 Ibid., p. 60.

5 Ibid.

6 Imperial War Museum, 'Women, War & Society, 1914–1918', EMP. 67/88, *The Herb Doctor*, 19 August 1916.

7 Anne Pimlott Baker, 'Grieve, Sophia Emma Magdalene (1858–1941)', *Oxford Dictionary of National Biography* (Oxford: Oxford University Press, 2004).

8 *The Times*, 22 January 2005.

9 *Gardens Illustrated*, May 2003.

10 Ibid.

11 Oxfordshire Record Office (ORO), ORO/06/1/N2/5.

12 *Gardens Illustrated*, May 2003.

13 British Library, British Library Sound Archive, *Down to Earth*, 'Joy Larkcom, 1935–'.

THE FLORAL ARTS

1 Vita Sackville-West, *In Your Garden* (London: Michael Joseph, 1951), p. 149.

'Embroidered So with Flowers'

1 Mary Delany et al., *The Autobiography and Correspondence of Mary Granville, Mrs Delany* (London: Richard Bentley, 1861), p. 465.

2 Thomasina Beck, *The Embroiderer's Story: Needlework from the Renaissance to the Present Day* (Newton Abbott: David & Charles, 1999), p. 17.

3 Huntington Library, MO 5544, 20 Aug 1740, Bulstrode, Elizabeth Robinson later Montagu to her sister Sarah Robinson (after Scott).

4 Mark Laird, *The Flowering of the Landscape Garden: English Pleasure Grounds, 1720–1800* (Philadephia: University of Pennsylvania Press, 1999), p. 17.

5 William Roberts, *Memoirs of the Life and Correspondence of Mrs Hannah More* (1834),

p. 287, quoted in Susan Groag Bell, 'Women Create Gardens in Male Landscapes: A Revisionist Approach to Eighteenth-Century English Garden History', *Feminist Studies*, vol. 16, no. 3 (1990), p. 478.

6 Ann Bermingham, *Learning to Draw: Studies in the Cultural History of a Polite and Useful Art* (New Haven and London: Published for the Paul Mellon Centre for Studies in British Art by Yale University Press, 2000), p. 271.

7 Ruth Hayden, *Mrs Delany: Her Life and Her Flowers* (London: British Museum, 2006), p. 85.

8 Ibid., p. 86.

9 Ellen C. Clayton, *English Female Artists* (London: Tinsley Brothers, 1876), p. 135.

10 Erasmus Darwin, *The Botanic Garden: A Poem, in Two Parts* (London: J. Moore, 1790), p. 88.

11 Ibid., p. 89.

12 Royal Archives, RA/GEO/Add 9/123.

13 Clayton, *English Female Artists*, p. 137.

14 William Morris, *Hopes and Fears for Art: Five Lectures Delivered in Birmingham, London, and Nottingham, 1878–1881* (London: Ellis and White, 1882), pp. 126–7.

15 Ibid., p. 127.

16 Miranda Seymour, *Ottoline Morrell: Life on a Grand Scale* (London: Hodder & Stoughton, 1992), p. 225.

17 Ibid., p. 231.

18 Lady Ottoline Morrell, *Ottoline at Garsington: Memoirs of Lady Ottoline Morrell, 1915–1918* (London: Faber and Faber, 1974), p. 195.

Every Lady Her Own Drawing Master

1 Elizabeth Carter and Montagu Pennington, *A Series of Letters between Mrs. Elizabeth Carter and Miss Catherine Talbot from the Year 1741 to 1770* (London: F.C. and J. Rivington, 1808), p. 395.

2 Douglas Chambers, '"Storys of Plants": The Assembling of Mary Capel Somerset's Botanical Collection at Badminton', *Journal of the History of Collecting*, vol. 9, no. 1 (1997), p. 58.

3 Alice M. Coats, *The Treasury of Flowers* (London: Phaidon, 1975), p. 14.

4 Royal Archives, RA/GEO/MAIN/41432, Princess Royal to King George III, 266 April 1799.

5 George Brookshaw, *A New Treatise on Flower Painting, or, Every Lady Her Own Drawing Master* (London: Longman, Hurst, Rees, Orme, and Brown, 1818), p. 2.

6 Coats, *Treasury of Flowers*, p. 13.

7 Brookshaw, *A New Treatise*, p. 3.

8 Ibid.

9 Ellen C. Clayton, *English Female Artists* (London: Tinsley Brothers, 1876), p. 302.

10 Marcia R. Pointon, *Strategies for Showing: Women, Possession, and Representation in English Visual Culture, 1665–1800* (Oxford: Oxford University Press, 1997), p. 161.

11 Lucia Tongiorgi Tomasi and Oak Spring Garden Library, *An Oak Spring Flora: Flower Illustration from the Fifteenth Century to the Present Time: A Selection of the Rare Books, Manuscripts, and Works of Art in the Collection of Rachel Lambert Mellon* (New Haven: Oak Spring Garden Library distributed by Yale University Press, 1997), p. 298.

12 Mary Lawrance, *A Collection of Roses from Nature* (London: Miss Lawrance, 1799).

Painting and Publishing

1 Henrietta Maria Moriarty, *Viridarium: Coloured Plates of Greenhouse Plants*. 2nd edn (London: J. White, 1807), p. v.

2 Ibid., p. vi.

3 Mrs C.W. Earle, *Pot-Pourri from a Surrey Garden* [1897] (Chichester: Summersdale, 2004), p. 235.

4 Audrey le Lièvre, 'Flower Painter Extraordinary', *Country Life*, 2 February 1989, p. 69.

5 Royal Horticultural Society, Lindley Library (RHS), R.M. Hamilton and Lawrence Duttson, 'A Sketch of the Life of Miss Drake', unpublished MSS, p. xviii.

6 Alice M. Coats, *The Treasury of Flowers* (London: Phaidon, 1975), p. 23.

7 RHS, Hamilton, 'A Sketch', p. xix.

8 Royal Botanic Gardens, Kew, DC 102 English Letters SME-SYM 1855–1900 (f45) MF.

En Plein Air

1 Royal Botanic Gardens, Kew, MN/1/1.

2 Ibid.

3 Ibid.

4 Ibid.

5 Ibid.

6 Dorothy Middleton, 'North, Marianne (1830–1890)', in *Oxford Dictionary of National Biography*, Oxford University Press, 2004.

7 Margaret Mee and Tony Morrison, *Margaret Mee in Search of Flowers of the Amazon Forests* (Woodbridge: Nonesuch Expeditions, 1988), p. 21.

8 Ibid., p. 24.

9 *The Times*, 6 February 2006.

10 Ibid.

Flower Decoration

1 *Gardeners' Magazine* (47), 2 January 1904, p. 35.

2 Mary Delany, *The Autobiography and Corespondence of Mary Granville, Mrs Delany* (London: Richard Bentley, 1861), 7 June 1774.

3 E.A. Maling, *A Handbook for Ladies on In-Door Plants, Flowers for Ornament and Song Birds* (London: Smith, Elder & Co., 1867), p. 2.

4 Brent Elliott, *The Royal Horticultural Society: A History, 1804–2004* (Chichester: Phillimore & Co., 2004), p. 305.

5 Ibid.

6 Annie Hassard, *Floral Decorations for Dwelling Houses* (London: Macmillan, 1875), p. 99.

7 *The Lady*, quoted in Beverley Nichols, *The Art of Flower Arrangement* (London: Collins, 1967), p. 100.

8 Mrs C.W. Earle, *Pot Pourri from a Surrey Garden* (Chichester: Summersdale, 2004: 1897), p. 241.

9 Emma Peachey, *The Royal Guide to Wax Flower Modelling* (London: Mrs Peachey, 1851), p. 61.

10 *Gardeners' Chronicle*, 8 May 1880, p. 586.

11 Frances Jane Hope, *Notes and Thoughts on Gardens and Woodlands* (London: Macmillan, 1881), pp. 219–20.

12 Ibid., p. 243.

13 Gertrude Jekyll, *Flower Decoration in the House* [1907] (Woodbridge: Antique Collectors' Club, 1982), pp. 125–6.

Notes

Room for the Butterflies

1 Brent Elliott, *The Royal Horticultural Society: A History, 1804–2004* (Chichester: Phillimore & Co., 2004), p. 309.

2 Gertrude Jekyll, *Flower Decoration in the House* [1907] (Woodbridge: Antique Collectors' Club, 1982), p. 6.

3 Elizabeth Coxhead, *Constance Spry: A Biography* (London: Luscombe, 1975), p. 106.

4 Constance Spry, *Simple Flowers: 'A Millionaire for a Few Pence'* (London: J.M. Dent, 1957), Vita Sackville-West, *The Garden* (London: Michael Joseph, 1946), p. 69.

5 British Library (BL), British Library Sound Archives (BLSA), *Down to Earth*, 'Julia Clements, 1906–'.

6 *The Garden*, no. 131 (2006), p. 241.

7 Beverley Nichols, *The Art of Flower Arrangement* (London: Collins, 1967), p. 195.

8 *The Garden*, no. 131 (2006), p. 242.

9 BL, BLSA, *Down to Earth*, 'Julia Clements'.

10 Ibid.

11 Ibid.

12 *Daily Telegraph Weekend*, 1 February 1992.

13 Ibid.

14 *Daily Telegraph magazine*, 12 March 1996.

LITERARY FLOWERINGS

1 Louisa Johnson, *Every Lady Her Own Flower Gardener* (London: William S. Orr, 1851).

History and Herballs

1 Mea Allan, *The Tradescants: Their Plants, Gardens and Museum, 1570–1662* (London: Michael Joseph, 1964), p. 15.

2 [Anthony Fitzherbert], *Here Begynneth a Newe Tracte or Treatyse Moost Profytable for All Husbandemen: And Very Frutefull for All Other Persons to Rede* (R. Pynson, 1523), p. 61.

3 Thomas Tusser, *Five Hundreth Points of Good Husbandry* (London: Rychard Tottell, 1573), p. 69.

4 Conrad Heresbach, *Foure Bookes of Husbandry*, trans. Barnabe Googe (London: Richard Watkins, 1577), fol. 48r-v.

5 William Lawson, *The Country Housewife's Garden* [1617] (London: Breslich & Foss, 1983).

6 William Lawson, *A New Orchard and Garden; with, the Country Housewife's Garden* [1618] (Totnes, Prospect, 2003), p. 55.

7 John Parkinson and A. Switzer, *Paradisi in Sole Paradisus Terrestris* (London: Humfrey Lownes and Robert Young, 1629), pp. 8–9.

8 [Hannah Wolley], *The Accomplisht Ladys Delight* (London: Benjamin Harris, 1675).

9 Ibid.

10 Ibid.

Botanical Dialogues

1 [Eliza Fowler Haywood], *The Female Spectator*, vol. 4. (London, 1745), pp. 57–9.

2 Ibid., pp. 58–9.

3 Ibid., p. 59.

4 Charlotte Murray, *The British Garden: A Descriptive Catalogue of Hardy Plants, Indigenous or Cultivated in the Climate of Great Britain* (Bath: S. Hazard, 1799).

5 Ann B. Shteir, 'Botanical Dialogues: Maria Jacson and Women's Popular Science Writing in England', *Eighteenth-Century Studies*, vol. 23, no. 3 (1990), p. 316.

6 Priscilla Wakefield, *An Introduction to Botany* (London: E. Newbury, 1798), p. 2.

7 Ibid., p. v.

8 Shteir, 'Botanical Dialogues', p. 310, fn. 20.

9 Erasmus Darwin, *The Botanic Garden: A Poem, in Two Parts* (London: J. Moore, 1790), p. 190.

10 [Maria Jacson], *The Florist's Manual or, Hints for the Construction of a Gay Flower Garden* (London: Henry Colburn, 1816), p. 5.

11 Ibid., pp. 5–6.

12 Cited in Shteir, 'Botanical Dialogues', p. 307.

13 *Gardener's Magazine*, XIV (1838), p. 359.

14 Jane Loudon, *The Ladies' Magazine of Gardening*, vol. 1 (London: William Smith, 1842), p. 5.

15 [Elizabeth Kent], *Flora Domestica, or the Portable Flower-Garden with Directions for the Treatment of Plants in Pots* (London: Whittaker, Treacher & Co., 1823), p. xiii.

Notes

Gardening for Ladies

1 *Journal of Botany*, no. 32 (1894), p. 205.
2 Ann B. Shteir, *Cultivating Women, Cultivating Science: Flora's Daughters and Botany in England 1760 to 1860* (Baltimore and London: Johns Hopkins University Press, 1996), p. 205.
3 Anne Pratt, *Wild Flowers* (London: SPCK, 1852), pp. 20–1.
4 Shteir, *Cultivating Women*, p. 206.
5 Jane Loudon, *British Wild Flowers* (London: William S. Orr, 1846, 2nd edn), pp. 1–2.
6 Jane Loudon, *Botany for Ladies, or, a Popular Introduction to the Natural System of Plants According to the Classification of de Candolle* (London: John Murray, 1842), p. vi.
7 Geoffrey Taylor, *Some Nineteenth Century Gardeners* (London: Skeffington, 1951), p. 25.
8 Bea Howe, *Lady with Green Fingers: The Life of Jane Loudon* (London, Country Life, 1961), p. 45.
9 Mrs Loudon, *The Ladies' Companion to the Flower-Garden* (London: Bradbury & Evans, 1853), p. 27.
10 Jane Loudon, *The Ladies' Magazine of Gardening*, vol. 1 (London: William Smith, 1842), p. 148.

Pot Pourri

1 Samuel Beeton, *Beeton's Dictionary of Every-Day Gardening* (London: Ward Lock, 1874), preface.
2 Bea Howe, *Arbiter of Elegance* (London: Harvill Press, 1967), p. 183.
3 Mrs C.W. Earle, *Pot-Pourri from a Surrey Garden* [1897] (Chichester: Summersdale, 2004), p. 261.
4 Ibid., p. 235.
5 *Gardeners' Chronicle*, 29 September 1894, p. 363.
6 *The Times*, 24 June 1950.
7 Timothy Clark, 'Flashes from a Mirror: Eleanour Sinclair Rohde and Her Gardening Books', *Country Life*, 21 April 1983, p. 1050.
8 Margery Fish, *We Made a Garden* (London: Collingridge, 1956), pp. 75–6.
9 Ibid., p. 66.
10 *The Times*, 21 April 1967.

11 *Journal of the Royal Horticultural Society*, vol. 92, 1967, p. 328.

12 Ibid., vol. 93, 1968, p. 149.

CULTIVATED LADIES

1 Royal Botanic Gardens, Kew, letters from J.D. Hooker vol. 13 f261 [JDH/2/3/13 f261], Sarah A.M. Brown writing to Miss Symonds on behalf of Sir Joseph Hooker, 20 March 1906.

A Foot on the Ladder

1 Helena Rutherfurd Ely, *A Woman's Hardy Garden* (New York: Macmillan, 1903), p. 67.

2 Martin Hoyles, *The Story of Gardening* (London: Journeyman Press, 1991), p. 194.

3 C. Paul Christianson, 'The London Gardener: A Tudor-Age Profile', *The London Gardener*, vol. 8 (2002), p. 23.

4 V.H. [Vera Higgins], 'Notable Women Gardeners', *Journal of the Royal Horticultural Society*, vol. 68, 1943, p. 52.

5 Bea Howe, *Lady with Green Fingers: The Life of Jane Loudon* (London: Country Life, 1961), p. 17.

6 Ibid., pp. 23–4.

7 John Abercrombie and Thomas Mawe, *Every Man His Own Gardener* (London: W. Griffin, 1767), p. 294.

8 *Octavia Hill's Red Cross Garden, Borough: A Historical Survey and Landscape Restoration Masterplan* (London: Bankside Open Spaces Trust & London Borough of Southwark Regeneration and Environment Department, n.d.), p. 1.

9 Edith L. Chamberlain and Fanny Douglas, *The Gentlewoman's Book of Gardening* (London: Henry & Co., 1892), p. 16.

10 Ibid., pp. 25–6.

11 Ibid., p. 26.

12 Ibid., pp. 26–7.

Swanley Misses

1 'Horticulture as a Profession for Ladies', *The Garden*, 7 September 1873, p. 208.

2 National Women's Library, *Lady's Pictorial* (1901).

3 Royal Botanic Gardens, Kew, *Kew Guild* (1894), p. 13.

4 Ibid.

5 Ibid.

6 Ibid., p. 69.

7 Archives of Girton College, Personal Papers, GCPP Procter 4/1/1.

8 Ibid.

9 *The Garden*, vol. 124 (1999), p. 203.

Hockey and Horticulture

1 Kay Sanecki, *A Short History of Studley College* ([Studley College Trust], 1990), p. 12.

2 Royal Horticultural Society, RHS Council Minutes, 16 June 1914.

3 Reading University, Archive of the Women's Farm and Garden Association, SR WFGA/F/1.

4 Frances Warwick, *Life's Ebb and Flow* (London: W. Morrow & Co., 1929), p. 304.

5 Reading University, Papers of Daisy, Countess of Warwick, WAR 5.8.5, *Birmingham Daily Mail*, 16 November 1910.

6 Sanecki, *Short History*, p. 18.

School for Lady Gardeners

1 Archives of Girton College (GC), Personal Papers, GCPP Procter 2/1.

2 Ibid., GCPP Procter 4/1/1.

3 Ibid.

4 Ibid., GCPP Procter 2/1.

5 From Frances Wolseley, *In A College Garden* (1916), quoted in Ursula Maddy, *Waterperry: A Dream Fulfilled* (Waterperry: Waterperry Gardens, 2001), pp. 14–15.

6 GC, GCPP Procter 4/1/1.

7 Letter, Viscountess Wolseley to Sir Henry Trueman, dated 13 February 1916, Ragged Lands, Glynde, Lewes, author's collection.

8 GC, GCPP Procter 4/1/1.

9 Brent Elliott, *The Royal Horticultural Society: A History, 1804–2004* (Chichester: Phillimore & Co., 2004), p. . 30925.

10 Maddy, *Waterperry*, p. 26.

11 Ibid., p. 31.

12 Oxfordshire Record Office (ORO), Waterperry prospectus (1937), quoted in *Oxford Mail*, 24 July 2007.

13 *The Garden*, vol. 124, March 1999, letters page.

14 Maddy, *Waterperry*, p. 80.

15 Ibid., p. 15.

16 ORO, ORO/06/1/C/4.

17 Ibid., ORO/06/1/C/3.

18 Ibid., ORO/06/1/X/4.

'Not Ladies in Any Sense of the Word'

1 Edith L. Chamberlain and Fanny Douglas, *The Gentlewoman's Book of Gardening* (London: Henry & Co., 1892), p. 208.

2 Ibid., p. 210.

3 Chelsea Physic Garden, Amherst Archive.

4 Cited in Kay Sanecki, 'The Ladies and the Gentlemen', *Hortus*, no. 32 (Winter 1994), p. 64.

5 Royal Botanic Gardens, Kew (RBGK), *Kew Guild*, 1, 1900, pp. 21–2.

6 RBGK, letters from J.D. Hooker.

7 RBGK, pK9 (331), Court Journal, 25 January 1896.

8 *Journal of Horticulture and Cottage Gardener*, 1896, p. 162.

9 RBGK, *Kew Guild*, 1897, pp. 23–4.

10 Ibid., 1898, pp. 11–13.

11 Ibid., 1897, pp. 9–10.

12 Ibid., 1898, pp. 11–13.

13 Ibid., 1900, p. 21.

14 Ibid., 1944, p. 403.

15 Ibid., 1908, p. 403.

Hardy Planters

1 Hextable Archive (HA), *The Horticultural College Record*, vol. 3, no. 5, 14 May 1903, pp. 3–4.

2 Reading University Archive of the Women's Farm and Garden Association, *Lady's Pictorial*, 2 November 1912.

3 National Women's Library (NWL), Papers of Margaret Smieton, letter to MS

from Secretary of the Central Bureau of the Employment of Women, 31 July 1918.

4 HA, *The Queen*, 23 January 1909, reprinted in *The Horticultural College Record*, vol. 9, I, no. 23 (April 1909), p. 3.

5 NWL, Mrs Ronald Wilkins, *The Training and Employment of Educated Women in Horticulture and Agriculture* (London: Women's Farm and Garden Association, 1915: rev. edn 1925), p. 7.

6 Howard Bailes, 'Procter, Chrystabel Prudence Goldsmith (1894–1982)', *Oxford Dictionary of National Biography*, Oxford University Press, 2004.

7 Archives of Girton College, Personal Papers, GCPP Procter 4/1/1.

8 Ibid.

9 Ibid.

10 Bailes, 'Procter'.

'We Must "GO TO IT"'

1 Royal Botanic Gardens, Kew (RBGK), *Kew Guild*, 1941, p. 61.

2 *Gardeners' Chronicle*, 23 December 1916, p. v.

3 *Journal of Horticulture*, 25 February 1915, p. 139.

4 RBGK, *Kew Guild*, 1945, p. 393.

5 *Illustrated London News*, 6 October 1917, pp. 388–9.

6 Maggie Andrews, *The Acceptable Face of Feminism: The Women's Institute as a Social Movement* (London: Lawrence & Wishart, 1997), p. 32.

7 RBGK, *Kew Guild*, 1945, p. 393.

8 Ibid., p. 394.

9 RBGK, *Kew Guild*, 1939–40, p. 854.

10 RBGK, 'Kewensia' pamphlet collection, 9 May 1942.

11 Ibid.

12 RBGK, *Kew Guild*, 1941, p. 57.

13 Ibid., p. 58.

14 Ibid., p. 60.

15 Ibid.

16 *Journal of the Royal Horticultural Society*, vol. 46, 1941, p. 4.

17 Imperial War Museum Sound Archive, ID No 20321: Viola Williams.

18 Archives of Girton College, Personal Papers, GCPP Procter 4/1/1.

19 Oxford Record Office, ORO/06/1/N3/1.

20 Ibid., ORO/06/1/N2/2.

21 Royal Archives, RA/PPTP/PERSO/1/B8/B (letter dated 7 September 1942); RA/PERSO/LTS/SOV/022/3.

The Nursery Slopes

1 *Gardens Illustrated*, 56 (2000).

2 Tessa Traeger and Patrick Kinmouth, *A Gardener's Labyrinth: Portraits of People, Plants and Places* (London: Booth-Clibborn Editions, 2003), p. 108.

3 Ibid.

4 Carola Cochrane, *Two Acres Unlimited: A Market Garden Success Story* (London: Crosby Lockwood & Son, 1954), p. 26.

5 Ibid., p. 99.

6 Ibid., p. 28.

7 Dawn MacLeod, *Down-to-Earth Women* (Edinburgh: Blackwood & Sons, 1982), p. 153.

8 Imperial War Museum Sound Archive, ID No 20321: Viola Williams.

Where Are the Women?

1 *Gardeners' Chronicle*, 25 May 1963, p. 373.

2 Ibid.

3 Ibid., 8 June 1963, p. 411.

4 Ibid., 29 June 1963, p. 463.

5 Ursula Buchan, *Garden People: The Photographs of Valerie Finnis* (London: Thames & Hudson, 2007), p. 13.

6 Ibid., p. 42.

7 Tessa Traeger and Patrick Kinmouth, *A Gardener's Labyrinth: Portraits of People, Plants and Places* (London: Booth-Clibborn Editions, 2003), p. 152.

8 Ibid.

New Shoots

1 Tessa Traeger and Patrick Kinmouth, *A Gardener's Labyrinth: Portraits of People, Plants and Places* (London: Booth-Clibborn Editions, 2003), p. 154.

2 Ibid., p. 155.

Notes

3 Correspondence with author, May 2009.

4 Ibid.

5 J.C. Loudon (ed. Mrs Loudon), *The Villa Gardener* (London: W.S. Orr & Co., 1850), p. 6.

INDEX

Index

Index

Index

Index

Index